China's Emerging Outsourcing Capabilities

Technology, Work and Globalization

The Technology, Work and Globalization series was developed to provide policy makers, workers, managers, academics and students with a deeper understanding of the complex interlinks and influences between technological developments, including information and communication technologies, work organizations and patterns of globalization. The mission of the series is to disseminate rich knowledge based on deep research about relevant issues surrounding the globalization of work that is spawned by technology.

China's Emerging Outsourcing Capabilities

The Services Challenge

Mary C. Lacity

Professor of Information Systems, University of Missouri, St Louis, USA

Leslie P. Willcocks

Professor of Information Systems, London School of Economics, London, UK

Yingqin Zheng

Research Associate, Information Systems and Innovation Group, Department of Management, London School of Economics

First published 2010 by
PALGRAVE MACMILLAN

Palgrave Macmillan in the UK is an imprint of Macmillan Publishers Limited, registered in England, company number 785998, of Houndmills, Basingstoke, Hampshire RG21 6XS.

Palgrave Macmillan in the US is a division of St Martin's Press LLC, 175 Fifth Avenue, New York, NY 10010.

Palgrave Macmillan is the global academic imprint of the above companies and has companies and representatives throughout the world.

Palgrave® and Macmillan® are registered trademarks in the United States, the United Kingdom, Europe and other countries.

ISBN-13: 978–0–230–23844–2 hardback

This book is printed on paper suitable for recycling and made from fully managed and sustained forest sources. Logging, pulping and manufacturing processes are expected to conform to the environmental regulations of the country of origin.

A catalogue record for this book is available from the British Library.

A catalog record for this book is available from the Library of Congress.

10   9   8   7   6   5   4   3   2   1
19   18   17   16   15   14   13   12   11   10

Printed and bound in Great Britain by
CPI Antony Rowe, Chippenham and Eastbourne

Contents

List of Tables and Figures

Tables

Figures

List of Appendices

Series Preface

We launched this series in 2006 to provide policy makers, workers, managers, academics and students with a deeper understanding of the complex interlinks and influences among technological developments, including in information and communication technologies (ICT), work, organizations and globalization. We have always felt that technology is all too often positioned as the welcome driver of globalization. The popular press neatly packages technology's influence on globalization with snappy sound bites, such as, "Any work that can be digitized will be globally sourced." Cover stories report Indians doing US tax returns, Moroccans developing software for the French, Filipinos answering UK customer service calls, and the Chinese doing everything for everybody. Most glossy cover stories assume that all globalization is progressive, seamless, intractable, and leads to unmitigated good. But what we are experiencing in the twenty-first century in terms of the interrelationships between technology, work and globalization is both profound and highly complex.

The mission of this series is to disseminate rich knowledge based on deep research about relevant issues surrounding the globalization of work that is spawned by technology. To us, substantial research on globalization considers multiple perspectives and levels of analyses. We seek to publish research based on in-depth study of developments in technology, work and globalization and their impacts on and relationships with individuals, organizations, industries and countries. We welcome perspectives from business, economics, sociology, public policy, cultural studies, law and other disciplines that contemplate both larger trends and micro-developments from Asian, African, Australia and Latin American, as well as North American and European viewpoints.

As of this writing, we have reached a critical milestone in the series in that we have ten books published or under contract. These ten books are introduced below.

1. *Global Sourcing of Business and IT Services* by Leslie P. Willcocks and Mary C. Lacity is the first book in the series. The book is based on over 1000 interviews with clients, suppliers and advisers and 15 years of study. The specific focus is on developments in outsourcing, offshoring and mixed sourcing practices from client and supplier perspectives in a globalizing world. We found many organizations struggling. We also found some organizations adeptly creating global sourcing networks that are agile, effective and cost-efficient. But they did so only after a tremendous amount of trial and error and close attention to details. All our participant organizations acted in a context of fast moving

technology, rapid development of supply-side offerings, and ever changing economic conditions.

2. *Knowledge Processes in Globally Distributed Contexts* by Julia Kotlarsky, Ilan Oshri and Paul C. van Fenema, examines the management of knowledge processes of global knowledge workers. Based on substantial case studies and interviews, the authors – along with their network of co-authors – provide frameworks, practices and tools that consider how to develop, coordinate and manage knowledge processes in order to create synergetic value in globally distributed contexts. Chapters address knowledge sharing, social ties, transactive memory, imperative learning, work division and many other social and organizational practices to ensure successful collaboration in globally distributed teams.

3. *Offshore Outsourcing of IT Work* by Mary C. Lacity and Joseph W. Rottman explores the practices for successfully outsourcing IT work from Western clients to offshore suppliers. Based on over 200 interviews with 26 Western clients and their offshore suppliers in India, China and Canada, the book details client-side roles of chief information officers, program management officers and project managers and identifies project characteristics that differentiated successful from unsuccessful projects. The authors examine ten engagement models for moving IT work offshore and describe proven practices to ensure that offshore outsourcing is successful for both client and supplier organizations.

4. *Exploring Virtuality within and Beyond Organizations* by Niki Panteli and Mike Chiasson argues that there has been a limited conceptualization of virtuality and its implications on the management of organizations. Based on illustrative cases, empirical studies and theorizing on virtuality, this book goes beyond the simple comparison between the virtual and the traditional to explore the different types, dimensions and perspectives of virtuality. Almost all organizations are virtual, but they differ theoretically and substantively in their virtuality. By exploring and understanding these differences, researchers and practitioners gain a deeper understanding of the past, present and future possibilities of virtuality. The collection is designed to be indicative of current thinking and approaches, and provides a rich basis for further research and reflection in this important area of management and information systems research and practice.

5. *ICT and Innovation in the Public Sector* by Francesco Contini and Giovan Francesco Lanzara examines the theoretical and practical issues of implementing innovative ICT solutions in the public sector. The book is based on a major research project sponsored and funded by the Italian government (Ministry of University and Research) and coordinated by Italy's National Research Council and the University of Bologna during the years 2002–2006. The authors, along with a number of co-authors, explore the complex interplay between

technology and institutions, drawing on multiple theoretical traditions such as institutional analysis, actor network theory, social systems theory, organization theory and transaction costs economics. Detailed case studies offer realistic and rich lessons. These cases studies include e-justice in Italy and Finland, e-bureaucracy in Austria, and Money Claim On-Line in England and Wales.

6. *Outsourcing Global Services: Knowledge, Innovation, and Social Capital* edited by Ilan Oshri, Julia Kotlarsky and Leslie P. Willcocks assembles the best work from the active participants in the *Information Systems Workshop on Global Sourcing* which began in 2007 in Val d'Isere, France. Because the quality of the contributions was exceptional, we invited the programme chairs to edit a book based on the best papers at the conference. The collection provides in-depth insights into the practices that lead to success in outsourcing global services. Written by internationally acclaimed academics, it covers best practices on IT outsourcing, business process outsourcing and netsourcing.

7. *Global Challenges for Identity Policies* by Edgar Whitley and Ian Hosein provides a perfect fit for the series in that the authors examine identity policies for modern societies in terms of the political, technical and managerial issues needed to prevent identity fraud and theft. The scale of the problem exceeds political boundaries and the authors cover national identity policies in Europe and the rest of the world. Much of the book provides in-depth discussion and analysis of the United Kingdom's National Identity Scheme. The authors provide recommendations for identity and technical policies.

8. *E-Governance for Development* by Shirin Madon examines the rapid proliferation of e-Governance projects aimed at introducing ICT to improve systems of governance and thereby to promote development. In this book, the author unpacks the theoretical concepts of development and governance in order to propose an alternative conceptual framework, which encourages a deeper understanding of macro- and micro-level political, social and administrative processes within which e-Governance projects are implemented. The book draws on more than 15 years of research in India during which time many changes have occurred in terms of the country's development ideology, governance reform strategy and ICT deployment.

9. *Bricolage, Care and Information Systems*, edited by Chrisanthi Avgerou, Giovan Francesco Lanzara and Leslie P. Willcocks, celebrates Claudio Ciborra's *Legacy in Information Systems Research*. Claudio Ciborra was one of the most innovative thinkers in the field of information systems. He was one of the first scholars who introduced institutional economics in the study of IS; he elaborated new concepts, such as 'the platform organization', 'formative contexts'; and he contributed to the development of a new perspective altogether through Heideggerian phenomenology. This book contains the most seminal work of

Claudio Ciborra and work of other authors who were inspired by his work and built upon it.

10. *China's Emerging Outsourcing Capabilities* edited by Mary C. Lacity, Leslie P. Willcocks and Yingqin Zheng, marks the tenth book in the series. The Chinese government has assigned a high priority to science and technology as its future growth sectors. China has a national plan to expand the information technology outsourcing (ITO) and business process outsourcing (BPO) sectors. Beyond the hopes of its leaders, is China ready to compete in the global ITO and BPO markets? Western companies are increasingly interested in extending their global network of ITO and BPO services beyond India and want to learn more about China's ITO and BPO capabilities. In this book, we accumulate the findings of the best research on China's ITO and BPO sector by the top scholars in the field of information systems.

In addition to the books already published and under contract, we encourage other researchers to submit proposals to the series, as we envision a protracted need for scholars to deeply and richly analyse and conceptualize the complex relationships among technology, work and globalization. Please follow the submissions guidelines on the Palgrave website (www.palgrave-usa.com/Info/Submissions.aspx). Stephen Rutt (email: s.rutt@palgrave.com) is the publishing director for the series.

Leslie P. Willcocks
Mary C. Lacity
July 2009

Acknowledgements

The editors, publishers and authors are grateful for permission to reproduce in full or in part versions of prior work that were initially published elsewhere.

Chapter 2, "Chinese Providers in IT Services Offshoring: It Takes 10 Years to Sharpen a Sword" by Erran Carmel, Guodong (Gordon) Gao and Ning (Annie) Zhang was initially published in *MIS Quarterly Executive*, 7 (4): 157–170.

Chapter 3, "China and the World" by Accenture and CCIIP was edited by John Hindle. This chapter is an abridged version of a research report jointly published by Accenture and the China Council of International Investment Promotion (CCIIP), originally released in December 2008. The full report can be accessed at: www.accenture.com/Global/Outsourcing/ChinaReport.htm.

Chapter 5, "Mediated Offshore Software Services Models in China: A Two Stage Study of Operational Capabilities Development" by Sirkka Jarvenpaa and Ji-Ye Mao is an expanded version of the manuscript that appeared in *Journal of Information Technology*, 23: 1–17.

Chapter 8, "The Role of Trust and Control in IS Offshoring from Vendors' Perspectives" by Ji-Ye Mao, Jae-Nam Lee and Chun-Ping Deng is a revised version of their work reprinted from *Information and Management*, 45/7, Ji-Ye Mao, Jae-Nam Lee and Chung-Ping Deng, Perspectives on Trust and Control in Offshore Information Systems Outsourcing, 482–492, Copyright (2008), with permission from Elsevier.

Chapter 9, "Drivers and Obstacles of Outsourcing Practices in China" by Kwok Hung Lau and Jianmei Zhang was originally published in the *International Journal of Physical Distribution & Logistics Management*, 36 (10): 776–792, with permission from Emerald Group Publishing.

Notes on Contributors

Niklas Åkerman is a doctoral candidate at the Baltic Business Research Center, Linnaeus School of Business and Economics, Sweden. His research interest is directed to International Business Marketing. His present research revolves around internationalization of SMEs. Niklas is also lecturing in International Business, at the master programme Growth Through Innovation and International Marketing at the Linnaeus School of Business and Economics, Sweden.

Erran Carmel is Professor of Information Technology and International Business Research Professor at Kogod School of Business, American University, Washington DC. His 1999 book *Global Software Teams* was the first on the new distributed nature of software work and is considered a landmark in the field. His second book *Offshoring Information Technology* (2005) was published by Cambridge University Press. He has written many articles about offshoring and the globalization of the software industry.

Robert Davison is an associate professor of Information Systems at the City University of Hong Kong. His current research focuses on Virtual Knowledge Management and Collaboration in Chinese SMEs. He has published over 100 articles in a variety of journals and conferences. Robert is the Editor of the *Electronic Journal of Information Systems in Developing Countries*, and an associate editor for the *Information Systems Journal, Information Technology & People* and *MIS Quarterly*. He has also edited special issues of the *IEEE Transactions on Engineering Management* (Cultural Issues and IT Management), the *Communications of the ACM* (Global Application of Collaborative Technologies), *Information Technology & People* (Virtual Work, Teams and Organisations) and the *Information Systems Journal* (Information Systems in China). For more details see: www.is.cityu.edu.hk/staff/isrobert.

Chun-Ping Deng is a lecturer in the School of Computer Science and Technology at Beijing Technology and Business University. He holds a PhD from Renmin University of China. His research has been published in international conference proceedings and several Chinese journals. His current research covers IS outsourcing, knowledge management and accounting information systems.

Guodong (Gordon) Gao is an assistant professor in the Decision, Operations and Information Technologies department at the R.H. Smith School, University of Maryland, College Park. His research interests include business value of IT, and certification and quality management in outsourcing and healthcare. His recent work has been published in *Manufacturing & Service Operations Management, Journal of Management Information Systems, Electronic Commerce Research and Applications*, and in the proceedings of multiple conferences like ICIS.

John Hindle is Senior Manager, Outsourcing Marketing, with Accenture, and Adjunct Professor of Human and Organizational Development at Vanderbilt University. His responsibilities at Accenture include managing research and thought leadership programmes, industry events, and relationships with analysts and sourcing advisers. He also serves as Vice-chairman of the HR Outsourcing Association (HROA), Co-chairman of HROA-Europe, and President-elect of the Vanderbilt University Alumni Association. John has an extensive international business background, with over 30 years' experience as a senior executive and adviser to companies in the USA and Europe. John received his MA degree from the University of Memphis and his PhD from Vanderbilt, where he also did his undergraduate work. He holds dual US and UK citizenship, and publishes widely in trade, practice and academic media.

Sirkka Jarvenpaa is the James Bayless/Rauscher Pierce Refsnes Chair in Business Administration at the McCombs School of Business, University of Texas at Austin where she is the director of the Center for Business, Technology, and Law. During 2008–2012, she also holds Finnish Distinguished Professorship at the Helsinki University of Technology. She is the co-editor-in-chief of the *Journal of Strategic Information Systems*. She is the senior editor of *Organization Science*. She has served as the editor-in-chief of the *Journal of Association for Information Systems* and as the senior editor of *Information Systems Research* and *MIS Quarterly*. She is a frequent contributor in academic and industry forums on inter-organizational innovation, virtual teams, virtual organizations and virtual communities.

Wendell Jones, a former corporate executive, is presently an outsourcing consultant, speaker, adviser and a management professor at the University of Southern Nevada. His former management positions include Senior Vice-President, NASD/NASDAQ; Vice-President, Compaq; GM, McDonnell Douglas Information Services Company; and Chair of the Computer Science Faculty at West Point. He has consulted to private and public-sector organizations worldwide, including the governments of China and Jordan. He enjoys a leading profile as an outsourcing practitioner and thought leader. As a corporate executive at McDonnell Douglas, he implemented and managed one of the largest outsourcing relationships, a $3 billion contract with IBM, and later pioneered offshore outsourcing for the securities industry. As an outsourcing service provider, he managed global delivery of outsourcing services for Digital Equipment Corporation and Compaq Computer Corporation. He was awarded the Outsourcing World Achievement by PricewaterhouseCoopers and was nominated to the Outsourcing Hall of Fame.

Kwok Hung (Charles) Lau is a senior lecturer of Logistics in the School of Management at the Royal Melbourne Institute of Technology University of Australia. He holds a graduate degree in geography, an MBA, an MSc in information systems, a master's degree in urban planning, and a PhD in geocomputation. He has research articles published in journals and conference proceedings such as *Environment and Planning* (Part B), *Supply Chain Management: an International Journal, International Journal of Physical Distribution and Logistics Management, International Journal of Information Systems and Supply Chain Management, Australasian Transport Reform Forum, International Conference on City Logistics,* and *Australian and New Zealand Marketing Academy Conference.* His areas of research interest include modelling and simulation in logistics, e-supply chain management, outsourcing, reverse logistics and green logistics.

Jae-Nam Lee is an associate professor in the Business School of Korea University in Seoul, Korea. He was formerly on the faculty of the Department of Information Systems at the City University of Hong Kong. He holds MS and PhD degrees in MIS from the Graduate School of Management of the Korea Advanced Institute of Science and Technology (KAIST) in Seoul. His research interests are IT outsourcing, knowledge management, e-commerce, and IT deployment and impacts on organizational performance. His published research articles appear in *MIS Quarterly, Information Systems Research, Journal of MIS, Journal of the AIS, Communications of the AIS, IEEE Transactions on Engineering Management, European Journal of Information Systems, Communications of the ACM, Information & Management,* and others. He has presented several papers at the ICIS, HICSS, ECIS, DSI and IRMA Conferences, and serves on the editorial boards of *MIS Quarterly, Information Systems Research, Journal of the AIS,* and *Information & Management.*

Ji-Ye Mao is a professor in the School of Business, Renmin University of China. Previously, he taught at the University of Waterloo in Canada (1995–2001) and the City University of Hong Kong. He received his PhD in MIS from the University of British Columbia (1995). His areas of research include user participation in the design and implementation of information systems, human computer interaction (HCI), and IT outsourcing management. His research has appeared in *Journal of MIS, Journal of AIS,* and leading HCI journals. He is on the editorial boards of several international journals such as the *Journal of Database Management,* and *Journal of AIS* (Association for Information Systems).

Maris G. Martinsons is a professor of Management with the City University of Hong Kong, director of the Pacific Rim Institute for the Studies of Management, and co-founder of the Far Eastern Latvian Cultural Association (TALKA). He helped to establish the worldwide Association of Information Systems and internationalize the (US) Academy of Management. Maris has extensive experience as a consultant and adviser, providing advice to organizational leaders on five continents while mentoring many young businesspeople, teachers and researchers. His publications on strategic management, organizational change and knowledge management/information systems have appeared in at least 10 languages and received over 1000 citations, according to Google Scholar.

Carol Xiaojuan Ou is a certified IS auditor and a Lecturer in the Department of Computing at the Hong Kong Polytechnic University, Hong Kong SAR. She is currently serving as a senior editor of *The Electronic Journal of Information Systems in Developing Countries*, and *The International Journal of E-Adoption*. Her studies have appeared in *Communications of the ACM, Journal of Information Technology Management, Journal of the Association for Information Systems, Commercial Research, Chinese Management Studies* and *China Marketing*, among others.

Laura Poppo, Professor and Fred Ball Faculty Fellow at the University of Kansas (lpoppo@ku.edu), received her PhD from The Wharton School of the University of Pennsylvania. Her research examines current theoretical perspectives and topics in strategic management and sociology, such a transaction cost economics, knowledge management, and social institutions (such as trust, relational governance and managerial networks) with recent interests in emerging economies. Researched phenomenon includes outsourcing, alliances, vertical integration, contracting, social networks, the multi-divisional corporation, information technology, and even baseball free agents. Her research has been published in numerous journals, including *Administrative Science Quarterly, Organizational Science, Strategic Management Journal, Journal of International Business Studies*, and *Journal of Management Studies*. Dr Poppo is also an associate editor of *Journal of Management* and serves on the editorial boards of *Organization Science, Strategic Management Journal, and International Journal of Strategic Change Management*. Dr Poppo's teaching interests include business-level and corporate-level strategy, and leadership, which she has taught to undergraduates, managers and executives and for which she has won teaching awards.

Joachim Timlon is an assistant professor at the Baltic Business Research Center, Linnaeus School of Business and Economics, Sweden, where he teaches and researches in the field of International Business Marketing and Logistics with a focus on expansion and growth in emerging country markets, such as Russia, China and Brazil, with emphasis on innovation and organizational learning processes. He teaches at the international Master Programme, Growth through

Innovation and International Marketing, Strategic Marketing, Strategy Business Plan implementation through Organizational Learning and International Business Marketing Strategies for Growth in New Emerging Country Markets.

Bo Yang is an assistant professor at the Department of Economic Information Management at Renmin University in Beijing, China. His research focuses on outsourcing, CIO and IT governance. He has been in the outsourcing research field for six years. He serves as an adviser to many government agencies in China and has visited almost 30 suppliers in China. He is the author of the book *IT Service Outsourcing: From the Dual Perspective of Clients and Suppliers* (in Chinese) published in 2009.

Jianmei (Jasmine) Zhang currently works for an information technology company in China and has been involved in international business for many years, focusing on the Chinese markets. She obtained her postgraduate degree in business at the Royal Melbourne Institute of Technology University in 2005 specializing in supply chain and logistics management. Her ongoing research interest is outsourcing practices in China. Her work has been published in the *International Journal of Physical Distribution and Logistics Management*.

Ning Zhang is a professor at the School of Information at Central University of Finance and Economics, China. She is also Vice-Dean of the school. Her current research focuses on software and information service outsourcing, operational model of mobile payments and government process management. Her textbook on information systems development and project management was published by China Higher Education Press and is used nationwide. Professor Zhang's research on information system topics has been published widely both in the proceedings of international conferences and in core Chinese journals.

Kevin Zheng Zhou is Associate Professor of Marketing and International Business at the School of Business, the University of Hong Kong. Dr Zhou received a BE (with honours) in Automatic Control and an MS in Economics and Management at Tsinghua University, and a PhD specializing in Marketing and Strategy from Virginia Polytechnic Institute and State University. Dr Zhou has published numerous papers in prestigious journals such as *Journal of Marketing, Strategic Management Journal, Journal of International Business Studies, Organization Science, Journal of the Academy of Marketing Science*, among others. He has presented his work at American Marketing Association, Academy of Management, Strategic Management Society, and Academy of International Business conferences. He has rich consulting experiences working with companies such as Federal Pharmaceutical, 3M, Riche Monde and TCH. He currently serves as the editorial board member of *Journal of the Academy of Marketing Science* and *Asia Pacific Journal of Management*.

Introduction

China's Emerging Outsourcing Capabilities

Mary C. Lacity, Leslie P. Willcocks and Yingqin Zheng

China has the world's third largest economy[1] after the United States and Japan, with a nominal gross domestic product (GDP) of US $4.4 trillion in 2008. China has had the fastest-growing economy among major nations for the past 25 years, with an average annual GDP growth rate above 10 per cent. While the country is known for its immense manufacturing base, in recent years, the Chinese government has assigned a high priority to science and technology as its future growth sectors. A slogan frequently used in the Chinese media is "From Made in China to China Service" (Rottman and Lou, 2008). The Chinese government is supporting this vision with the establishment of research and technology parks, favourable tax incentives, grants to help Chinese firms achieve certifications in CMMI and ISO 20000, investments in infrastructure, and promotion of IT outsourcing (ITO) and business process outsourcing (BPO) services.[2] Beyond the aspirations of its leaders, is China ready to compete in the global ITO and BPO markets? Many Western managers are interested in the answer to that question. Western companies are increasingly interested in extending their global network of ITO and BPO suppliers beyond Indian and near-shore providers and want to learn more about China's ITO and BPO capabilities.

Consulting firms (e.g. Accenture, ChinaSourcing, Everest Research Group and Gartner), industry associations (e.g. The China Software Industry Association and The International Association of Outsourcing Professionals), and Chinese ministries and councils (e.g. Ministry of Industry and Information Technology and China Council of International Investment Promotion) provide good information on the overall Chinese ITO and BPO markets and suppliers. These organizations size the Chinese ITO and BPO markets, create lists of top Chinese ITO and BPO suppliers, and offer in-depth analyses on specific Chinese firms. Estimates, lists and trends vary across these sources owing to differences in research methods, data collection and time of study. For example, there are large variations in the size of market estimates. Estimates range

1

from $273 million in 2007, reported by Gartner, to $2 billion in 2006, reported by Everest (Bahl et al., 2007). Estimates reported by Chinese sources report higher figures. For example, one estimate by Devott, a Chinese consulting firm, sized the Chinese outsourcing services market at $11 billion in 2006. Another Chinese White Paper sized the outsourcing market at $15.2 billion.[3] Lists of top 10 and top 50 Chinese ITO and BPO suppliers are ever changing owing to mergers and acquisitions and differences in research methods (see Chapter 2 for one such list). In addition, these organizations help track fast-changing economic, institutional, structural, political and legal factors, which significantly affect China's ITO and BPO business. For example, the global recession has decreased the rate of growth in ITO and BPO in 2009, particularly from overseas clients in the financial sector (Devott, 2008).

Beyond the general picture of China's emerging ITO/BPO capabilities, how do Western managers successfully engage Chinese ITO/BPO suppliers? Many management and international business scholars have studied China's culture and its affects on business partnerships with Western firms. These cultural attributes include guanxi, collectivism, Confucianism, and power distance (see, for example, Boisot and Child, 1996; Chen, 2001; Child and Mollering, 2003; Davison et al., 2005; Hofstede, 2001; Lovett et al., 1999; Park and Luo, 2001; Shin et al., 2007; Xin and Pearce 1996). Within the field of information systems, prior academic research has helped us understand how information and communication technologies (ICT) are implemented and used in Chinese firms and joint ventures (Bin et al., 2003; Burrows et al., 2005; He, 2004; Liang et al., 2004; Ma et al., 2003; Martinsons, 2004; Martinsons and Hempel, 1998; Martinsons and Westwood, 1997; Newman and Zhao, 2008; Quan et al., 2005; Westrup and Liu, 2008; Zhu and Wang, 2005).[4] In addition, some prior research has specifically addressed China's ITO and BPO markets (Carmel et al., 2008; Jarvenpaa and Mao 2008; Qu and Brocklehurst, 2003; Rottman and Lou, 2008; Zhang et al., 2008).

We invited top scholars and practitioners carrying out leading research on China's ITO and BPO sector to contribute chapters to this book. We organized the ten chapters into two sections. In Part I, four chapters address the entire Chinese ITO and BPO markets. These chapters analyse the strengths and weaknesses of China's ITO and BPO markets, categorize and analyse Chinese suppliers, project future trends in China's ITO and BPO capabilities, and prescribe lessons for Western managers seeking to engage Chinese suppliers. In Part II, six chapters contain studies of Chinese suppliers, or clients of Chinese suppliers, providing particular ITO or BPO services (see Table I.1). Two of these chapters focus on information technology services. Four chapters address specific BPO services: procurement, media relations, logistics, and research and development. The most difficult functional area to outsource is research and development (R&D) because of high task uncertainty and high asset specificity.

Table 1.1 Research by authors

Chapter	Research Method	Primary Research Data	Characteristics of Chinese Firms Studied	Research gathered from/about	Functional focus
1 (Zheng et al.)	Multi-method	30 supplier surveys; 30 supplier interviews	30 Chinese software service providers from Beijing, Shanghai, and Xi'an	Suppliers	IT services
2 (Carmel et al.)	Secondary Data	Several industry rankings of top Chinese software suppliers	39 Chinese software companies: 12 multinational ventures, 12 legacy firms, and 15 new generation firms	Suppliers	IT services
3 (Hindle et al.)	Multi-method	37 client surveys; 53 supplier surveys; 15 interviews	Chinese firms are analyzed by their target client markets: e.g., Domestic; US/Europe; Japan/Korea; and Undifferentiated	Clients and suppliers	IT and BPO services
4 (Jones)	Formal presentations and site visits	34 formal presentations by Chinese executives	20 Chinese software firms in Beijing and Shanghai	Suppliers	IT services
5 (Jarvenpaa and Mao)	Case Studies	21 interviews with Chinese managers and IT staff	Three small Chinese suppliers located in Beijing that use a mediated model of outsourcing.	Suppliers	IT services
6 (Poppo and Zhou)	Field interviews	361 structured interviews with Chinese managers responsible for managing suppliers	20.8% were state-owned, 27.7% were private, and 12.7% were listed stock companies 38.8% were foreign-owned firms or joint ventures.	Clients	Procurement

Table I.1 (Continued)

Chapter	Research Method	Primary Research Data	Characteristics of Chinese Firms Studied	Research gathered from/about	Functional focus
7 (Davison et al.)	Mixed method	77 interviews with Chinese employees at Eastwei; 75 surveys from Chinese employees at Eastwei; Author observation and participation	Eastwei, a Chinese company that provides media relations services and employs about 100 people; headquartered in Beijing with offices in Shanghai, Chengdu and Guangzhou.	Supplier	Media Relation Services
8 (Mao et al.)	Mixed method	Interviews with Chinese suppliers; Survey of 110 project managers in 9 Chinese firms	These 9 Chinese firms perform coding, unit testing, and detailed design primarily for Japanese ITO firms; Thus, the authors studied a mediated outsourcing model.	Suppliers	IT services
9 (Lau and Zhang)	Case studies	6 interviews with logistics managers from 6 Chinese firms	Two state-owned firms, two private-owned firms, and two foreign-owned firms; 5 were located in Beijing, 1 in Shanghai	Clients	Logistics
10 (Timlon and Åkerman)	Case study	9 interviews with Chinese and Danish managers and scientists	Danish pharmaceutical company, Novo Nordisk, with R&D centre in Beijing	Both headquarters & captive centre	R&D captive centre

For this reason, the client in Chapter 10 chose to build a captive R&D centre rather than to outsource directly to a Chinese firm.

Across the ten chapters, authors used field interviews, case studies, surveys, formal presentations, participant observation and secondary data to study both Chinese suppliers and their clients (see Table I.1). Four chapters are based on a combination of these methods. All told, this book reports on findings from 519 interviews, 305 surveys, 11 detailed case studies, and 34 formal presentations. We summarize specific findings from each chapter below.

In Chapter 1, Zheng, Willcocks and Yang provide an overview of China's emerging software services outsourcing (SSO) industry. Based on public data and preliminary research findings on Chinese suppliers, which include 30 surveys and 30 interviews, the authors discuss the rapid changes occurring in China and the surging competitiveness of China as a major global outsourcing player. They look at principal factors for the growth and presence of Chinese SSO suppliers in the global market, as well as challenges and opportunities that the industry currently faces. Constraints include the lack of national branding and of a strong trade association, fragmentation of the industry, as well as supplier capabilities, although it is suggested that the current economic crisis provides an opportunity for consolidation and scaling of the industry. The chapter also discusses China's domestic market and research and development capabilities, arguing that these two factors could provide the potential for China's SSO industry to move up the global value chain.

In Chapter 2, Carmel, Gao and Zhang used secondary sources to analyse the top 39 Chinese ITO suppliers. They categorized the Chinese suppliers into three types:

(1) multinational ventures that entered China as far back as the 1980s primarily to access Chinese labour to provide ITO services to the parent multinational;
(2) legacy ITO firms that primarily serviced the domestic IT Chinese market before offering services to companies outside China; and
(3) new generation ITO firms that are start-up ventures specifically targeted to offer ITO services to foreign customers.

In the sample, nine new generation ITO firms are Chinese-owned and six are foreign-owned. The authors also assessed the maturity of these 39 firms, as well as the pros and cons of each type from a Western client perspective. The major benefit of multinational ventures is that they understand Western practices; the major disadvantage is that they give priority to the multinational owner. The major benefits of legacy firms are strong technical competence, experience with large-scale projects, and low cost; the major disadvantages are bureaucratic mentality, difficulty in understanding Western practices, high set-up costs and language barriers. The major benefits of new generation firms are flexibility, responsiveness, Western-style management teams, and focus on outsourcing; the major disadvantages are variation in quality and susceptibility to industry restructuring.

Chapter 3 presents the findings from a joint research project by Accenture and the China Council of International Investment Promotion (CCIIP). John Hindle, Senior Manager of Outsourcing Marketing for Accenture, edited the report for inclusion in this book. The chapter is based on data collected from 37 client surveys, 53 Chinese supplier surveys and 15 in-depth interviews. The report is aimed at three audiences: potential clients that want to outsource to China, Chinese-owned and foreign-owned Chinese suppliers, and Chinese government officials. Overall, the researchers found that China's main advantages are the government's commitment to developing an excellent service sector, an educational system that is preparing a vast number of highly educated people, and a cost advantage that will last for the foreseeable future. China is currently trying to address some key challenges, including a stronger legal system, adoption of international standards and better protection of intellectual property. Progress is steady; for example, 38 Chinese companies had obtained CMMI level 5 by 2006.

In Chapter 4, Jones accumulates the lessons he learned from two sponsored trips to China comprising delegates of business executives from the United States and Europe. During his 20 days in China, the author visited 20 Chinese software firms and listened to 34 formal presentations from Chinese software executives. He also had many informal discussions with government officials and American executives doing business in China. The author, one of the internationally recognized leaders in large-scale outsourcing from both client and supplier sides, identified seven important lessons for Western managers seeking to engage Chinese suppliers. These lessons address Chinese business practices, how to evaluate Chinese suppliers, how to decide which functions to outsource, and how to manage people and change. Each lesson is accompanied by specific practices that Western managers should consider while engaging Chinese suppliers.

In Chapter 5, Jarvenpaa and Mao examine supplier capabilities in small Chinese IT suppliers that service Japanese clients indirectly and directly through a Japanese IT supplier. The authors call this a mediated offshore software services model. The large Japanese IT suppliers contract with the Japanese clients and thus are directly accountable for project outcomes. The large Japanese IT suppliers in turn subcontract to small Chinese providers for discrete tasks that may or may not require the Chinese supplier to work directly with the Japanese clients. Based on interviews in three Beijing IT suppliers, the authors questioned how these suppliers build three critical operational capabilities: human resources capabilities, process capabilities and client-specific capabilities. At first, suppliers focused on client-specific capabilities. Over time, suppliers later focused on process capability development. Human resources capabilities remained the most challenging capability in the mediated model, yet human resources capabilities were the main determinants of the other two capabilities (client-specific and process). This chapter contributes to our understanding of China by demonstrating how small and medium-sized Chinese suppliers that deploy the mediated model build operational capabilities over time.

In Chapter 6, Poppo and Zhou apply their extensive knowledge of outsourcing decisions made by Western clients to study outsourcing decision making in China. Poppo and Zhou trained research assistants in China to interview 361 Chinese managers about their outsourcing suppliers, asking questions about contractual and relational governance. They found the following similarities and differences between Western outsourcing clients and Chinese outsourcing clients:

- Consistent with studies of Western managers: Chinese managers craft custom contracts for infrequent exchanges.
- Inconsistent with studies of Western managers: Chinese managers rely more on social ties than contractual governance.
- Inconsistent with studies of Western managers: Chinese managers do not craft increasingly complex contracts in the face of increased asset specificity and higher environmental uncertainty.

Overall, the Chinese firms that were more likely to adopt Western style governance were small, privately-held Chinese firms that hire outsiders. Specifically:

- State-owned Chinese firms are more likely to rely on social ties than privately-held Chinese firms because state-owned Chinese firms can rely on close relationships with government officials (rather than relying on contracts) if they encounter difficulties with suppliers.
- Chinese firms stay in relationships longer with Chinese suppliers than with foreign suppliers.
- Chinese managers with longer job tenure keep the same suppliers longer than Chinese managers with shorter job tenure.

In Chapter 7, Davison, Martinsons and Ou used a multi-method approach to study how leadership styles and guanxi-facilitated knowledge networks affect teamwork quality and organizational agility within a Chinese professional services firm called Eastwei. The authors spent two years studying this firm. They used multiple methods such as interviews, surveys and observation to amass data from 80 per cent of the 100 employees. The authors found that transformational leadership (leaders who empower subordinates) and guanxi-facilitated knowledge sharing (in-group sharing through interpersonal contact) significantly increased organizational agility in terms of speed and responsiveness. The authors found that transformational leadership and transactional leadership (exchange of rewards for subordinate compliance) were both significantly related to teamwork quality, but guanxi-facilitated knowledge sharing was not. Why not? The authors' observations helped them interpret this finding. The authors observed an excessive amount of instant messaging by employees. Some employees had over 500 contacts in their IM contact lists. Increased knowledge sharing among in-group dyads was not necessarily focused on work, and thus may not directly affect teamwork quality. However, such vast networks of in-group relationships most certainly help scan the environment and disseminate knowledge across teams, and thus explain how guanxi-facilitated knowledge networks improve organizational agility.

In Chapter 8, Mao, Lee and Deng conducted interviews and administered a survey to 110 project managers in nine Chinese ITO firms. The authors began their research with interviews in Chinese firms to first ascertain if there were any unique characteristics in Japanese–Chinese outsourcing. They found that the Chinese suppliers were part of the mediated model, in which ITO services are provided to Japanese ITO suppliers, not directly to Japanese clients. They also determined that these Chinese suppliers were mostly small and relied heavily on the Japanese ITO company for the majority of their revenues. Thus, in this context, there are power asymmetries that favour the Japanese ITO suppliers. From these interviews, the authors designed a survey to test whether the Japanese ITO's willingness to share information, to communicate effectively, and to adapt schedule, work procedures and process standards with the Chinese supplier built trust. Indeed, the authors found significant positive relationships between information sharing, communication and inter-firm adaptation with the building of trust. Moreover, they also found that trust was significantly and positively related to project quality, but trust was negatively related to cost controls. The authors write, "It appears that a high level of trust in a client is associated with higher quality standards and level of effort, which can increase cost." This is consistent with previous research in which product quality increases production costs, but will later save on maintenance/support costs.

In Chapter 9, Lau and Zhang studied the drivers and obstacles of outsourcing logistics in six Chinese firms. These firms outsourced various logistics services, including transportation, warehousing, freight settlement, customers, inspection, insurance and IT support. Overall, all the client interviewees claim to be satisfied with their Chinese service provider's performance. However, none of the people interviewed said that they achieved the desired benefits from outsourcing logistics services! One of the obstacles is the lack of a national infrastructure: there is little integration of transportation networks, IT, ware-housing and distribution facilities in China. Local regulations and protection have made it difficult for third-party logistics suppliers in China to meet client needs. All six client firms subsequently reported a loss of control over logis-tics, including unreliable pick-up and delivery times and high rates of loss or damaged goods. The authors also compared the drivers of outsourcing in their Chinese firms with the drivers of outsourcing reported in Western-studied firms. The common drivers include cost reduction and strategic factors, such as the desire to accelerate re-engineering and to focus on core competencies. In addition, the Chinese firms in this study cited the desire to facilitate market penetration as an outsourcing driver.

The authors next compared the obstacles and problems of outsourcing encountered by their Chinese firms with the obstacles and problems of out-sourcing reported in Western-studied firms. In the latter, the two most fre-quently cited problems were loss of control and loss of critical skills. In the Chinese firms, the most frequently cited problems were loss of control, lack of capable service providers, poor infrastructure (IT and transportation), and local protection regulations. The authors note that the Chinese government is committed to solving these problems and has invested in logistics infrastruc-ture, relaxed regulations and promoted economic reform. China is beginning to see the consolidation of firms, leading to the emergence of national logistics chains.

In Chapter 10, Timlon and Åkerman study the barriers and enablers when transferring R&D practices from Denmark to China. Using a case study method, they interviewed Danish and Chinese scientists and managers involved in the establishment of a Danish pharmaceutical company's R&D centre in Beijing. The Danish company – Novo Nordisk – primarily entered China to expand their global R&D network by collaborating with partners in China. At first, Timlon and Åkerman argue, the differences in cognitive structures between the Danish and Chinese scientists and managers created barriers to optimal performance. The Danish scientists have non-authoritarian relationships with Danish managers, and are therefore free to challenge assumptions, try new things, and self-organize job tasks. Danish scientists solve R&D problems in parallel, testing many solutions at once. In contrast, Chinese scientists have authoritarian relationships with managers, follow rules, and do not question practices. Chinese scientists solved R&D problems in sequential order. From the Danish company's perspective, the challenge was to motivate Chinese sci-entists and managers to behave more like the Danes in terms of questioning authority and initiating innovative solutions to R&D problems. Several prac-tices facilitated this process. Danish managers understood the importance of building social relationships with their Chinese counterparts and, thus, several trips were scheduled for this purpose. The Danish company offered free weekly

English lessons for Chinese employees and free Chinese courses for Danish expatriates. To help institutionalize a culture of innovation, the Danish company implemented mandatory idea proposals. The Danish employees learned never to criticize a Chinese employee in public; and any feedback was given quietly one to one. Most importantly, the Danish company had to constantly affirm that "mistakes" are part of the process of innovation. The outcome was that the Chinese scientists and managers increased their willingness to take risks and to initiate their own innovative solutions to R&D problems.

Overall, then, the in-depth studies we have brought together in this one volume provide multiple perspectives on, highly useful, and carefully researched insights into the burgeoning Chinese outsourcing services industry – at country, regional and firm levels. As all the chapters make clear, we are observing an evolving phenomenon. Chapter after chapter details the already established strengths of China and the massive opportunity before it. At the same time, the research shows that there is still a great deal of work to be done if China is to punch its weight and create a large-scale, sustainable outsourcing services industry that is competitive on price, quality and breadth of services, both globally and domestically. The authors of Chapter 2 quote aptly an old Chinese saying, derived from the ancient sword masters who took a long time to hone their skills and temper their weapons in preparation for a major battle: "It takes ten years to sharpen a sword." This captures the state of preparation and emergence of the Chinese outsourcing and offshoring industry revealed in this book. To date, the growth of the industry has been slow and deliberate. In terms of maturity, the industry was, as of late 2009, still at Stage One (initial growth), although we concur with Erran Carmel, Guodong Gao and Ning Zhang, that Stage 2 (shake-out/consolidation) may well be not far off (see Chapter 2).

At the same time, China's development will not be merely a matter of getting its internal act together. It will inevitably occur in a dynamic global context. Here, between 2008 and probably early 2011, an economic recession affects buyers and sellers of services worldwide. This means suppliers will need to be sharper than ever in cost control, standardization, financial planning and innovation, both for themselves and for their clients. ITO and BPO service companies will need to exploit global delivery resources to achieve low costs, scalability and flexibility. Suppliers will also need to be inventive with how they add value in contracts. This could be by acting as managing sub-outsourcing contracts, helping to introduce innovation, or offering some financial terms that are attractive. All this impacts on the pace and character of Chinese emergence, Chinese industry structure, and the strategies, business models and requisite capabilities of its service firms.

In practice, in the present climate, there is likely to be a mix of global demand and supply pressures that will inevitably shape client and supplier offshoring strategies in China as well as elsewhere. Large Indian players will be moving up the value chain, bestshoring, acquiring and moving into new sectors. Large suppliers will be offering 'multi-tower' – that is integrated – services across not just IT but also across some previously separated BPO areas such as procurement, accounting, finance, HR and R&D. At the same time, many clients will pursue multi-sourcing, developing a portfolio of suppliers, with some bound in as strategic allies, and others treated more as commodity service providers. Meanwhile, there are improving services from over 120 ambitious centres in different countries around the world. At the same time, world economic and business pressures will exert downward pressures on costs, but also higher expectations on innovation from suppliers. The central leitmotif of the global outsourcing industry will be the unending search for new sources of skill and better labour models at more attractive prices.

China's emerging outsourcing capabilities will necessarily need to respond to, and help to shape, these dynamic global pressures. In the nineteenth century, military strategist Helmuth von Moltke suggested that plans rarely survive the first engagement with the enemy. It remains a compelling message for a country looking to become a major player in what has become a highly dynamic global outsourcing industry. Maybe you can spend too much time sharpening a sword. Actually, we find, China's sharpening sword already needs to see action.

Notes

1. However, China ranks 89th in GDP purchasing power parity (PPP) per capita due to China's population of 1.3 billion people, according to the World Bank.
2. "Policy support" issued on 27 March 2009 by China Ministry of Commerce and Ministry of Finance, translated by Aihua Yan, PhD student in Information Systems at the University of Missouri-St Louis.
3. www.chinabusinesssolutions.com/dbimg/white_paper_on_chinas_software_and_information_service_outsourcing.pdf.
4. Within China, there are thousands of papers written in Chinese by Chinese scholars about the implementation of information technologies in China (Davison et al. 2008). Few of these papers, however, address managerial issues or offshore outsourcing of IT or business processes.

References

Bahl, S., Arora, J. and Gupta, A. (2007), "What's happening in China," The Everest Group, ERI.2007,2.W.0172.

Bin, Q., Chen, S. and Sun, S. (2003), "Cultural differences in e-commerce: A comparison between the United States and China," *Journal of Global Information Management*, 11 (2), 48–55.

Boisot, M. and Child, J. (1996), "From fiefs to clans and network capitalism: Explaining China's emerging economy," *Administrative Science Quarterly*, 41, 600–628.

Burrows, G., Drummond, D. and Martinsons, M. (2005), "Knowledge management in China," *Communications of the ACM*, 48, 73076.

Carmel, E., Gao, G. and Zhang, N. (2008), "Chinese providers in IT services offshoring: It takes 10 years to sharpen a sword," *MIS Quarterly Executive*, 7 (4), 157–170.

Chen, M. J. (2001), *Inside Chinese Business: A Guide for Managers Worldwide*. Boston, MA: Harvard Business School Press.

Child, J. and Mollering G. (2003), "Contextual confidence and active trust development in the Chinese business context," *Organization Science*, 14 (1): 69–80.

Davison, R., Vogel, D. and Harris, R. (2005), "The e-transformation of Western China," *Communications of the ACM*, 48, 62–66.

Davison, R., Kien, S. S. and Ying, D. X. (2008), "Introduction to the special issue on information systems in China," *Information Systems Journal*, 18, 325–330.

Devott (2008), *ChinaSourcing – Top 50 Service Outsourcing Providers in China 2008*, available from www.chinasourcing.com, accessed August 2009.

Jarvenpaa, S. and Mao, J. (2008), "Operational capabilities development in mediated offshore software service models," *Journal of Information Technology*, 23 (1), 3–17.

He, X. (2004), "The ERP challenge in China: A resource-based perspective," *Information Systems Journal*, 14, 153–167.

Hofstede, G. (2001), *Culture's Consequences: Comparing Values, Behaviors, Institutions, and Organizations across Nations*, Sage, London, 2nd edition.

Liang, H., Xue, Y., Boulton, W. and Bryd, T. (2004), "Why Western Vendors don't Dominate China's ERP Market," *Communications of the ACM*, 47 (7), 69–72.

Lovett, S., Simmons, L. and Kali, R. (1999), "Guanxi versus the Market: Ethics and Efficiency," *Journal of International Business Studies*, 30, 231–247.

Ma, J., Buhalis, D. and Song, H. (2003), "ICTs and internet adoption in China's tourism industry," *International Journal of Information Management*, 23, 451–467.

Martinsons, M. (2004), "ERP in China: One package, two profiles," *Communications of the ACM*, 47, 65–68.

Martinsons, M. and Hempel, P. (1998), "Chinese business process re-engineering," *International Journal of Information Management*, 18, 393–407.

Martinsons, M., and Westwood, R. (1997), "Management information systems in the Chinese business culture," *Information and Management*, 32, 215–228.

Newman, M. and Zhao, Y. (2008), "The process of enterprise resource planning implementation and business process re-engineering: Tales from two Chinese small and medium-sized enterprises," *Information Systems Journal*, 18 (4), 405–426.

Park, S. H., and Y. Luo (2001), "Guanxi and organizational dynamics: Organizational networking in Chinese firms," *Strategic Management Journal*, 22, 455–477.

Qu, Z. and Brocklehurst, M. (2003), "What will it take for China to become a competitive force in offshore outsourcing?" *Journal of Information Technology*, 18 (1), 53–67.

Quan, J., Hu, Q. and Wang, X. (2005), "IT is not for everyone in China," *Communications of the ACM*, 48, 69–72.

Rottman, J. and Lou, H. (2008), "Can China compete with India in the global ITO/BPO market?" in *Offshore Outsourcing of IT Work*, Lacity, M., and J. Rottman (eds), Palgrave, Houndmills, 180–208.

Shin, S., Ishman, M. and Sanders, G. (2007), "An Empirical Investigation of Socio-Cultural Factors of Information Sharing in China," *Information and Management*, 44, 165–174.

Westrup, C. and Liu, W. (2008), "Both global and local: ICTs and joint ventures in China," *Information Systems Journal*, 18 (4), 427–443.

Xin, K. and Pearce, J. (1996), "Guanxi: Connections as substitutes for formal institutional support," *Academy of Management Journal*, 39, 1641–1658.

Zhang, M., Sarker, S. and Sarker, S. (2008), "Unpacking the effect of IT capability on the performance of export-focused SMEs: A report from China," *Information Systems Journal*, 18 (4), 357–380.

Zhu, J. and Wang, E. (2005), "Diffusion, use, and effect of the Internet in China," *Communications of the ACM*, 48 (4), 49–53.

Part I

Perspectives on China's Emerging Outsourcing Capabilities

1
China's Emerging Software Services Outsourcing Industry

Yingqin Zheng, Leslie Willcocks and Bo Yang

Introduction

China's outsourcing capabilities started to emerge from the late 1990s (see also Chapters 2 and 3). Only in the last five to six years has the software services outsourcing (SSO) industry picked up momentum, as part of a larger global trend (Willcocks and Lacity, 2009). The India–Pakistan crisis in 2003 was a turning point for China's outsourcing industry. According to IDC, in 2007, the size of China's offshore outsourcing market reached USD 1.97 billion, a 42.4 per cent growth from 2006. It is estimated that the offshore market will grow to USD 8.95 billion by 2012 (IDC, 2008).

This chapter provides an overview of China's emerging software services outsourcing industry. Software Services Outsourcing (SSO) is a term commonly used in China, generally referring to Information Technology Outsourcing and IT-enabled Business Process Outsourcing. Based on pilot projects in China and secondary data, we present a preliminary analysis of the key characteristics of the SSO industry, and the challenges and opportunities it faces. Our study is based on publicly available data from government agencies and industrial reports,[1] complemented by a survey with over 30 Beijing-based SSO companies conducted in 2007–2008, as well as 30 semi-structured interviews with SSO companies in Beijing, Shanghai and Xi'an conducted in 2008–2009. These findings constitute part of an ongoing study on China's software services industry, and this chapter reports early stage findings. The study is not meant to be a comprehensive and exhaustive introduction to China's software services industry (see Chapters 2, 3 and 4 for greater detail), but to present a snapshot and perspective to highlight key aspects of the phenomenon. Given that limited research has been done with regard to China's emerging capabilities in ITO and BPO, especially from a supplier's perspective, we hope that an overview of the industry will help put those studies in context.

Development of the SSO industry: principal factors

In the last 30 years China has achieved remarkable economic development by serving as the world's factory, leveraging the abundant supply of skilled labour to provide low value-adding service. However, the economic success has come at a high cost – aggressive consumption of resources, rapid environmental deterioration, and a structural imbalance in the economy. The problem of low sustainability and over-reliance on export-oriented manufacturing is further exacerbated in the current economic crisis, manifested by, for example, the large-scale closedown of manufacturing factories in coastal areas. There is an imminent need for China to adjust its industrial structure and strengthen the development of service-based industries, such as software services outsourcing. Advocates of SSO argue that it is a green industry and consumes little natural resources, in addition to generating employment opportunities that help absorb some of the over-supplied educated workforce produced by Chinese higher education institutes every year.

While China has made considerable progress in information technology and software production with some governmental support, it seems that the government was still trying, even in 2009, to have a clear vision and strategy for a software services outsourcing industry. As a result, we see government policies coming out aimed at supporting SSO development on the one hand, and inconsistency, confusion in policies and regulations, as well as inefficient internal industrial competition on the other. In this section, we draw upon the Oval Model of Principal Success Factors for a National Software Export Industry (Carmel and Tjia, 2005: 210; Heeks and Nicholson, 2004) to provide a contextual understanding to the development of the Chinese SSO industry. This oval model suggests that the principal success factors are: government vision and strategy; technology infrastructure; capital; quality of life; human capital; wages and costs; the industry; and the linkages to external markets. We look at these factors in closer detail.

Government vision and strategy

China was a latecomer in promoting the software industry, compared to India and Brazil (Veloso et al., 2003). In June 2000, the State Council published the document *Policies on Encouraging the Development of Software and Integrated Circuit Industries*. In the following years, the Chinese government showed increasing awareness of the importance of a service-based industry, as indicated by its plan to transit *From Made in China to China Services* (Ji, 2008). In 2006, the Ministry of Commerce launched the 1000-100-10 project, which sought to establish 1000 internationally accredited outsourcing providers nationwide, to attract 100 leading multinational firms to transfer a substantial proportion of their outsourcing services needs to China, and to build 10 globally competitive outsourcing bases in China. The plan set the target of increasing the export revenue of software and information technology services to over $10 billion by 2008 (see Chapter 2).

In 2007, the State Council issued the *Guidelines for Speeding up the Development of the Service Industry ([2007] No. 7)*, encouraging the strategic development of a service sector for the purpose of reconfiguring the positioning of China's foreign trade, with an emphasis on offshore service outsourcing as a point of growth in service exportation. The guideline details policies to support services outsourcing enterprises with international standard certifications, and designates a number of cities as outsourcing development bases.

However, none of these policies were designed directly for software services outsourcing. SSO suppliers find themselves still being evaluated in the same way as a software production company (e.g. on ownership of copyright), which excludes them from receiving certain governmental support. A manager from a government agency that promotes the SSO industry in Beijing commented to us:

> The central government has never been clear what software service is. There has always been a tendency to see software as a tangible product rather than service ... as a result, the central policies often do not directly apply for SSO suppliers. You would also find it impossible to find consistent statistics about the SSO industry because there hasn't been a consensus about what is SSO and what is not.

In January 2009, the State Council issued the *Official Reply of the State Council on Promoting the Development of the Service Outsourcing Industry ([2009] No. 9)* (State Council, 2009), which attempts to elevate the industrial development of service outsourcing to a national level. The document formally announced the establishment of 20 Service Outsourcing Base Cities, including not only internationally renowned cities like Beijing, Shanghai and Shenzhen, but also coastal cities like Dalian, Suzhou, Nanjing, as well as major cities in western China such as Xi'an, Chengdu and Chongqing. Figure 1.1 shows the location of most of these cities on a map of China. These cities enjoy more preferential and much wider range of taxation policies and subsidies than before. For example, selected service outsourcing enterprises can enjoy 15 per cent reduction in income tax; and selected offshore service providers will be exempt from business tax. They also enjoy substantial subsidies to facilitate staff training, exhibitions and marketing activities, and accreditation.

Despite clear financial incentives and subsidies, many companies believe that the government could have done more, for example, to establish a trade association like the NASSCOM in India, which provides strong support, leadership and promotion for the industry, and serves as an interface and key channel connecting Chinese suppliers and offshore clients. A senior manager in a big

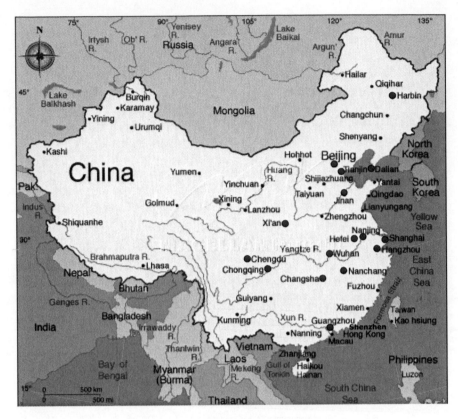

Figure 1.1   Location of software service base cities in China
Source: The graph is created on the basis of a map of China at www.newchinatravelguide.com/
map.html.

ITO supplier made the following comment, and her view was echoed by other
leading SSO firms:

> What we need is an integrated image, an effective country branding which
> conveys the message that China is ready for outsourcing...Our biggest
> challenge is not service delivery; that is not a problem at all. The biggest
> challenge is for opportunities to come to China, people who really under-
> stand what China can do...It seems to me that the central government
> hasn't quite made up their mind what to do. If only they took out the same
> determination for the Beijing Olympics, all problems can be resolved.

Infrastructure, capital and quality of life

China's fast economic development has been supported by the government's
heavy investment in infrastructure, especially in housing, telecommunications

Table 1.1 Telecom infrastructure in China

Parameter	2001	2006	2007	2011
Telephone main lines (m)	168.4	396.0	439.6	549.6
Telephone main lines (per 100 population)	13.2	30.1	33.2	40.7
Mobile subscribers (m)	145.2	444.5	493.4	616.9
Mobile subscribers (per 100 population)	11.4	33.8	37.3	45.7
Internet users (m)	33.7	127.7	143.0	198.1
Internet users (per 100 population)	2.6	9.7	10.8	14.7
Broadband subscriber lines (m)	0.7	62.5	81.4	136.7
Broadband subscriber lines (per 100 population)	0.1	4.8	6.2	10.1
Total IT spending (US$ m)	22,162	34,722	39,126	57,441

Source: Equaterra (2008).

Table 1.2 Infrastructure and competitiveness of some of the outsourcing base cities

Software outsourcing Base Cities	International & domestic air Routes	Infrastructure Index[1]	Living environment Index[2]	Software revenue (RMB billion)	Software personnel (thousand)	Number of World Top 500 Enterprises
Beijing	152	0.965	0.809	126.3	228	201(inc. 46 independent research institutes)
Shanghai	152	1	0.755	80.18	204	178
Shenzhen	110	0.623	1	100	100	145
Wuhan	124	0.627	0.612	12.5	30	70
Dalian	84	0.65	0.701	21.5	60	38
Xi'an	119	0.623	0.58	13.88	42	24
Nanjing	45	0.659	0.632	36.2	70	75
Hangzhou	45	0.765	0.737	30	43	53
Jinan	46	0.53	0.581	16	60	15
Tianjin	43	0.646	0.621	15.2	30	127
Chengdu	31	0.553	0.693	31	100	32

[1] The index of infrastructure sets Shanghai has the highest benchmark at the value of 1 and shows the indicator for other cities compared to Shanghai.
[2] The index of living environment sets Shenzhen has the highest benchmark at the value of 1 and shows the indicator for other cities compared to Shenzhen.
Data source: CASS 2007 and BSIPC 2008.

and transportation. Most of the major cities have developed a relatively high level of infrastructure. Tables 1.1 and 1.2 provide some indices about the infrastructural conditions of some of the service outsourcing base cities. China has extensive networks of airlines, railways and highways. Beijing and Shanghai have direct flight connections with most major cities in the world, and there are two to four flights between Beijing and Shanghai every hour. Xi'an, Shenzhen, Dalian and Wuhan are all domestic hubs of transportation. China's telecom infrastructure is well developed – comparable to developed countries in major and coastal cities – and provides reliable support for Chinese suppliers to communicate easily with their offshore partners via direct international phone lines and video conferencing. In terms of living conditions, Shenzhen is considered to be the most liveable city in China, followed by Beijing and Shanghai. These cities host large communities of foreign expatriates stationed there on a long-term basis, who find the quality of life similar to economically advanced countries in many aspects.

A marketing director of a BPO company in Xi'an told us that the Beijing Olympics had enabled foreigners to have a better understanding of China:

> Clients sometimes asked us stupid questions before they came to China, such as "Do you have mobile phones?". Then they visited China and found out that mobile technology is even more advanced in China than in the US.

All the SSO suppliers we visited have teams that work with clients on a distributed basis regularly, using technologies like email, virtual meetings, direct phone calls and video conferencing.

In terms of access to capital, the government's initiative in early 2009 was to provide Renminbi (RMB) 5 billion credit through the China Development Bank to support the infrastructural development of service outsourcing base cities and the expansion of successful suppliers (Hou and Xu, 2006). Other channels to raise capital include venture capital, listing on offshore and domestic stock exchanges, merger and acquisition (M&A), private funding and angel investment. Activities of capital acquisition are mostly concentrated in Beijing, Shanghai and Shenzhen. For example, according to a government report (BSIPC, 2008), in 2007, Beijing saw 83 cases of capital raising in the IT industry (telecom, internet, software, etc.), involving capital amounting to an estimated USD 2 billion. Eleven companies successfully went public, raising USD 0.81 billion. Moreover, there were 52 venture capital cases, 17 M&A, two private funding cases and one angel capital. Most of the cases involved fast-growing companies rather than start-ups. The software services outsourcing sector raised USD 65 million in 2007. In comparison, a much lower level of capital raising activity took place in 2008 under the credit crunch (BSIPC, 2009).

Human capital and linkages

The literacy rate in China is above 90 per cent, and about 57–59 per cent of the population are in the age group of 20–59 years (D&B, 2008). China has significantly expanded enrolment in higher education in recent years and produces a large number of college and university graduates each year. According to data from Ministry of Education, there were 23.7 million students in higher education in 2006, including 1.1 million doctoral and masters students. In 2007, nearly 5 million college and university graduates entered the job market, 265,500 of whom from IT-related subjects.

Nevertheless, college graduates can rarely be put directly on the job, thus a strong emphasis is placed on training. Local governments and software parks usually provide subsidies and organize training programmes for new recruits in SSO firms. Most of the firms we visited also had their own training programmes covering aspects like language, cultural awareness, technical skills and managerial skills.

Wage levels differ among the SSO base cities. Beijing and Shanghai, being most international and accessible, have the highest costs in human resources, operation and living. Thus, there has been a trend for outsourcing providers to move to second- or third-tier cities such as Xi'an and Chengdu, although most major offshore suppliers still locate their headquarters in Beijing or Shanghai. Nevertheless, for some the leading firms that have established long-term relationship with clients, cost is no longer a major concern. A senior manager from a big Beijing-based supplier said: "Our clients are not just after low costs. What is more important is to establish trust relationship with them and deliver the service they need."

An increasing number of high-level managers in Chinese suppliers have an overseas background. They are either overseas returnees, or still hold foreign residency. A significant number have work experience from multinational enterprises in China. Despite a large pool of IT personnel in China, the SSO sector has found it difficult to attract high-level talent. This is also related to the image of the SSO industry as one that is low-end and labour intensive. A senior manager in a Japanese subsidiary commented:

> Many students from top universities consider outsourcing as a low-end job. They would much prefer working for big IT companies than in an outsourcing firm, where they have to do as they are told, and not having the freedom to be creative and innovative. Since top universities graduates usually don't stick around for long, we actually prefer to recruit students from second tier universities.

This of course to a certain extent reflects the nature of IT service provided by Chinese vendors, especially those focusing on Japanese clients. Almost all the SSO firms that responded to the survey consider the shortage of human capital, especially in terms of high-level technical and managerial skills, as the biggest barrier for organizational development. The situation may improve over time when the outsourcing industries gradually move towards providing high-end services and will be able to attract more talent. The increasing number of returnees from Western countries is expected to give a boost to China's human capital. The government has taken some active measures to promote the provision of human capital for the service outsourcing industry. The Beijing municipal government issued a policy in 2001 to allow 80 per cent tax rebate for high-level managers and senior technical experts with an annual salary of over 100,000 yuan in the software industry. Over 12,000 software personnel benefited from the policy in 2007 (CASS, 2007). Following earlier policies to attract talents into software outsourcing, in April 2009, a new government initiative set the target to train and supply 1.2 million service outsourcing personnel, to generate 1 million extra employment opportunities for college graduates, and to enlarge the offshore outsourcing business to the scale of USD 30 billion.

Characteristics of the SSO industry

It is important to distinguish software services outsourcing from the IT and software industry as a whole. Unlike in India, China's SSO industry has developed on the basis of a well-established IT and software industry mainly driven by the domestic market (Veloso et al., 2003). By the end of 2007, China's software industry accounted for 8.74 per cent of the global software market, generating a total revenue of RMB 583.4 billion (about USD 83 billion), of which only 12.5 per cent came from software exportation, while offshore SSO accounted for merely 20 per cent of the export revenue (MII and CSIS, 2008). The revenue arose from five main areas: software products (32 per cent), embedded software (21 per cent), integrated circuits design (3 per cent), system integration (20 per cent), and software services (24 per cent). This is in contrast with India where software export, consisting of mainly offshore ITO and BPO, took up 65 per cent of its total software revenue (D&B, 2008).

China has produced some IT and software giants with strong global presence. Some of them are even comparable to the leading firms in India in terms of size and revenue (Qu and Brocklehurst, 2003), but few of them focus on software service outsourcing. Most of the SSO firms are new generation companies emerging after year 2000, or in the late 1990s (see Chapter 2 for a classification of firms). They are much smaller in terms of size and revenue in comparison to the big IT and software production companies (Kshetri, 2005).

Industrial structure

China's software service outsourcing industry is highly fragmented. By the end of 2008, there were about four thousand SSO firms in China, employing more than 330,000 people (Devott, 2009). A high proportion of them are small companies with 50–100 employees, which survive on small subcontracts. Over half are private enterprises, 5 per cent state owned, 30 per cent foreign companies, and some 12 per cent of them joint ventures (CSIP et al., 2008).

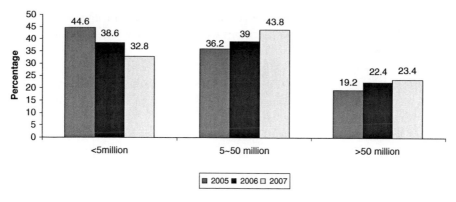

Figure 1.2 Composition of firms in terms of sales revenue (RMB) (CSIP et al., 2008)

Owing to the high level of competition in the industry, many small firms resort to a cost-cutting strategy to attract clients. Similarly, severe competition exists among the outsourcing base cities, which also compete with each other by offering more preferential policies and tax rates. Not surprisingly, we found many calls for a more consolidated and stratified industrial structure.

Figure 1.2 shows that the number of small firms with sales revenue under RMB 5 million has been decreasing in the last few years, while the percentage of those above the line has been on the rise. This indicates a general trend of growing firm size and revenue in the industry. There have been some M&A initiated by leading firms in the industry over the last few years. In the current (2009) crisis, it is anticipated that more M&A will take place. Indeed, in the first half of 2009, we saw signs of a new wave of consolidation initiated by leading SSO firms (SinaFinance, 2009). Senior management in companies we interviewed repeatedly pointed out to us that the government should provide more support for leading firms to scale up, for example:

Chinese outsourcing firms are not comparable to Indian ones in terms of size. For the industry to develop faster, the government should focus on facilitating the largest and best performing firms to grow even bigger and stronger. Merger and acquisition is very important for the development of an industry, which requires the government to play a key role.

A senior manager from a leading ITO firm believed that we will see a breakthrough in Beijing's outsourcing industry during 2010–12:

We have been exploring the possibilities of forming alliances with other firms since 2004. The economic crisis has provided a good opportunity. It is my personal view that the scaling of top firms and the scaling of the industry

will intensify over the next three years. More companies of over 10,000 people will emerge, and the gap between the dozen of leading firms and other
companies will widen.

Offshore service delivery capabilities

The SSO industry has experienced significant development in terms of market
share and organizational capabilities. This has occurred in several directions,
for example, shifting from focusing on the domestic market to expanding in
the offshore market, from serving clients in one country to several countries,
and from mainly providing ITO to gradually developing BPO capabilities.

Figure 1.3 shows the composition of China's SSO market (see also Chapter 3).
Japan and Korea have been the dominant offshore markets for China over
the last decade. According to a governmental report, in 2007, Japan was the
source of 45 per cent of China's total SSO income, although the growth rate
has been slowing down in the last few years (CSIP et al., 2008). This is mainly
due to cultural and language connections, as the northeast of China was once
under Japanese occupation. The proportion of the European-American market
has also been increasing rapidly, for example 60 per cent higher in 2008 than
in 2006 (ibid.). As Japan had been severely affected by the financial crisis from
2008, many Japan-focused suppliers began to realize that total reliance on Japan
might not be sustainable, hence a higher level of interest and effort in exploring
the European and American markets.

The service provided to offshore clients has been dominantly ITO, whereas
BPO still seems to be in its early stages (see also Chapter 3). Even though more
than 30 per cent of the suppliers provide BPO services, only about 10 per cent

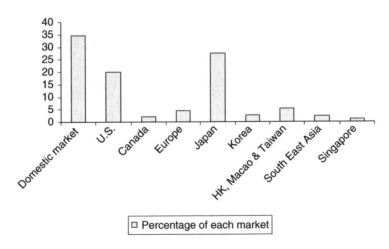

Figure 1.3   Composition of total software outsourcing revenue
Data source: CSIP et al., 2008.

consider it as their core business. Among the ITO firms, two out of three specialize in software development. Other services range from software testing, systems integration, application implementations, to IT consulting and IT training. Clients are distributed across a number of sectors, mainly in finance, telecommunication and manufacturing. BPO services cover areas of accounting and finance, human resources, client relationship management, research and development, and sales and marketing, among which sales and marketing service outsourcing is the most prevalent. For both ITO and BPO suppliers, offshore services account for about half of their revenue (although a large proportion arise from subcontracts), and about one third of the suppliers focus solely on offshore services.

We provide only one perspective here, and the reader is also referred to later chapters in Section 1 of this book. Our small and selective sample of SSO firms does, however, suggest the following types of access to offshore markets:

- local Chinese firms obtaining contracts from offshore clients directly;
- local Chinese firms purchasing an overseas company in order to enter the target market;
- subsidiary of foreign firms, only serving parent company and clients of parent company;
- joint ventures, getting offshore contracts from the foreign partner company– the Chinese firm may, after building up some capabilities, set up offshore subsidiaries to obtain contracts directly.

The number of firms with CMM/CMMI accreditation increased from 2 in 2000 to 904 by the end of 2008, among which 40 passed grade five, 25 passed grade four and 526 passed grade three (BSIPC, 2009). Chinese suppliers also realize that accreditation is only the first step towards gaining trust from clients (see Chapter 8). What is more important and challenging is to deliver satisfactory service to clients. Research by Feeny, Lacity and Willcocks (2006) shows that clients look for suppliers who can respond to the customer's changing needs (i.e. have a delivery competency); can radically improve service both in terms of quality as well as cost (i.e. have a transformation competency); and are willing and able to align its business model to the values, goals and needs of the customer (i.e. have a relational competency). Countries that have suppliers who are able to do this are in a better position to attract more complex, knowledge intensive and strategic activities. Where are Chinese suppliers at the moment, and how will they develop? It is very clear that very few Chinese suppliers indeed could claim that being such a full service firm is anything but an aspiration. Most outsourcing suppliers are focused on lower-level delivery work not requiring such a mix of capabilities, and some have chosen specific niches in ITO (rather less often in BPO), rather than being full service operations. In particular, transformation competence is the most lacking at this stage.

It is, therefore, important to assess the level of different types of capabilities of the Chinese suppliers (see Chapter 8). Presented here is a survey conducted in 2008 on over 30 Beijing-based suppliers, investigating the suppliers' capabilities mainly in terms of their delivery and relational competencies (see Yang, 2009 for more details). More specifically they were broken down to the following capabilities: technological capability, service delivery, project and process management, domain expertise, human resources, marketing and contracting and relationship management (see Table 1.3). Figure 1.4 shows the average capability level of the firms studied on a scale of 0–5.

Table 1.3   Evaluating Chinese suppliers' capabilities

Technological capability	*Availability and exploitation of technology; technological skills and methods; learning of new techniques*
Human resources capability	*Talent pool; recruitment and incentives; training and staff development; team work*
Project and process management	*Process improvement; project management, quality assurance*
Marketing and contracting capability	*Reputation management; market exploration; planning and contracting;*
Delivery capability	*Service delivery procedure, value of service*
Relationship management	*Cultural difference management; intellectual property protection; information security; trust*
Domain expertise	*Professional knowledge and experience*

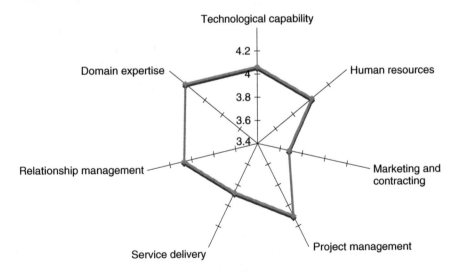

Figure 1.4   Evaluating Chinese suppliers' capabilities

The suppliers were found to be most confident in their domain expertise and project and process management capabilities. Marketing and contracting capability was found to be the weakest. Service delivery (procedure and value) and human resources constituted major challenges, while technological capabilities and relationship management were considered roughly satisfactory. For the dozen of leading SSO firms at the top of the pyramid, several of whom we visited, the challenge no longer lies with delivery capabilities, but with expanding their client base in offshore markets. "National branding and marketing channels are the most important", said one of our interviewees from a top Chinese ITO firm. "What we need is to let people know that we can deliver very well."

The domestic market: challenges and opportunities

The enormous potential domestic market is what distinguishes China's service outsourcing industry from India, where offshore outsourcing was the key driver (see also Chapters 2 and 3 for a more detailed analysis). Following the government policy to "informationalize" the country in pursuit of an information society in the early 1990s, the central government actively promoted and invested in initiatives to promote IT adoption and diffusion across all sectors, such as e-health, e-commerce, e-education, e-government, e-transportation, and so on. Thousands of ITO suppliers have emerged and grown from leveraging business opportunities in the domestic market.

Outsourcing in financial services emerged after 2000, and one of the earliest and most prominent examples is China Development Bank (www.cioage.com, 2009). Starting from an ITO contract with Hewlett-Packard in 2003, China Development Bank (CDB) has contracted over 60 IT outsourcing arrangements and the number is still growing. At the end of 2008, there were over 330 onsite outsourcing personnel regularly based at the CDB Beijing headquarters. Most of the outsourcing contracts held by CDB last 1–5 years and are renewable. CDB claimed that outsourcing had cut their overall IT costs by 30 per cent, and allowed them to focus more on core business. On the other hand, CDB is still on the learning curve in terms of managing suppliers and leveraging business value from supplier performance. Over-reliance on suppliers and loss of control over key IT functionalities had become major concerns. As indicated by a senior IT manager at CDB, one of the key challenges for them is to formulate a clear strategy on retained capabilities vis-à-vis outsourced functionalities, and to strengthen in-house ability for facilitating communication between business units and IT services (Willcocks et al., 2006).

While ITO companies have clearly benefited from government investment in IT infrastructure and IT-enabled public services, it has proved difficult for

BPO suppliers to achieve a similar degree of success in the domestic market. For example, CompuPacific in Xi'an, one of the biggest BPO suppliers, which gained a global reputation from a report by *The Economist* (2006), mainly specializes in low-end services such as capturing information from documents to deliver organized, accessible data for critical business processes. Despite some successes in offshore markets such as the USA, they have encountered serious obstacles in the domestic market. After all, few organizations, whether public or private, have established stable business processes, and the frequent changes of government policies create major difficulties. A senior manager gave an example from the medical services:

> In North America they talk about coding a lot – drug coding, hospital coding – there is none here. [Although] we have the capability to build the coding ourselves, six months later the drug regulations might have changed, and all our investment would be wasted.

The lack of information standardization affects insurance and financial institutes, which in turn impacts on BPO service providers:

> The banks told us to wait. We could get in very fast, we have the people, infrastructure, and we can tell them that you give the service to us, we link the portals, VPN launch, boom, next day, service. But they said it is not ready, even the forms are not standardized. So the banks themselves are far from being ready. But they are doing a lot of IT outsourcing, their platforms are being built by big IT outsourcing companies, and their maintenance.

In addition to factors relating to business culture and historical legacy, the lack of experience and capabilities of domestic clients to manage outsourcing arrangements also constrains collaborations. Many SSO suppliers find themselves providing free consulting service for domestic clients because the clients are often unclear what technology and service they require. A business analyst from InfoSys' Shanghai subsidiary comments:

> Domestic clients often lack a structured approach, and a lot more time is needed to communicate with them. They would say 'Why do you do things this way? We have been doing it that way for decades.' We have to make extensive explanation in order to achieve some mutual understanding with them.

Domestic clients thus tend to change requirements frequently, haggle on costs, and have little experience in managing outsourcing arrangements. Moreover, owing to local complexities of politics and *guanxi*, building and managing relationships with domestic clients is very different from collaborating with offshore clients (see Chapter 6). Chinese suppliers often comment that offshore clients, especially European and American clients, are much more straightforward and easy to do business with.

Multinational enterprises (MNCs) also play a key role in China's SSO industry. While India's outsourcing industry took off by providing "bodyshopping" to offshore clients during the period of Y2K crisis (D&B, 2008), many Chinese companies started by providing outsourcing service to multinational companies in China. The enormous Chinese market attracted many MNCs to invest in China and set up subsidiaries, which require local IT support (see Chapter 3). MNCs are one of the most important channels for Chinese suppliers to reach out to global clients. Meanwhile, Chinese suppliers sometimes serve as strategic partners for foreign enterprises to enter the Chinese market. Moreover, experience and capabilities accumulated by working for MNCs and offshore clients enable suppliers to position themselves as providers of consulting and business solutions for domestic clients, although not all of the knowledge and expertise are directly transferable (Chua and Pan, 2008; Oshri et al., 2007). Research has shown that local firms' collaboration with MNCs provides them with vital technological and organizational training, which the local firms use strategically to develop their market networks and innovative capacity in the home market (Zhou and Xin, 2003).

One of the most invested areas from MNCs in China is research and development (R&D). China has attracted a lot of global R&D activities over the years (see Chapters 3 and 10). In 2007, there were already more than a thousand R&D centres established by multinational enterprises in China (Xie, 2008). For example, the Zhongguancun Software Park in Beijing has been an incubator for hi-tech start-ups and IT companies, and is considered China's Silicon Valley (Chen, 2008). It concentrates scores of universities, including top institutes such as Beijing University, Qinghua University and Chinese Academy of Science, and hundreds of research labs and institutes. Since the 1990s, it has attracted a number of MNCs to set up R&D labs in the area. Microsoft Research Asia, the largest computing research institute outside the USA, was established in Beijing in 1998, and has over 1500 researchers.

China thus seeks not just to remain as the world's factory, but also to become a hub for IT innovations, which positions it as a potential innovation outsourcing supplier. Offshore outsourcing has increasingly been considered as an opportunity for innovation. As argued by Powell et al. (1996), the locus of innovation can often be found in inter-organizational networks of learning rather than within individual firms. Nowadays, open source software has provided unprecedented low-cost opportunities for IT professionals and companies to acquire up-to-date technologies and IT solutions, enabling them to innovate and customize IT solutions to fulfil different client needs. The internationally renowned Red Flag Linux developed by a Chinese company with government support is a good example for developing countries to leverage innovative opportunities arising from open sourcing.

Discussion and implications

From an external or client's perspective, it is useful to consider China's present and future attractiveness as an offshoring and outsourcing location. Willcocks, Griffiths and Kotlarsky (2009) have proposed six factors to assess location attractiveness: cost, availability of skills, environment, quality of infrastructure, risk profile and market potential. A quick overview would suggest that cost is certainly an attractive factor, though this is eroding faster in the major cities of Beijing and Shanghai and is leading to increased development of work in other more provincial areas and cities. The skills pool is impressive in terms of numbers but has weaknesses in terms of management experience, outsourcing-specific skills, languages for non-Asian markets, and the fragmented nature of the supplier base (see, in particular, Chapter 3). Environment and quality of infrastructure tend to be very supportive in most areas.

China's major cities are far less affected by natural disasters and terrorist attacks (EquaTerra, 2008). The issue usually pointed to on risk profile is intellectual property risk, though the government has been strengthening the protection of patents and privacy in recent years (Chan, 2005). Eltshinger (2007) suggests seven potential risk "wildcards" for China going forward, although he sees the risks of them becoming major issues as mostly low. These risks include changes in regulation, English and foreign language communications, the ageing of China's population, greening of environment policies, and other countries' protectionism measures. However, he does rate the risks as somewhat higher for currency and trading fluctuations, and rural and poverty-linked social unrest.

China's market potential is considerable, but at the moment (as detailed in Chapter 3), and the overall software service and ITO/BPO revenue figures suggest, China has not yet set itself up sufficiently to deliver on this. We suggest that the domestic outsourcing market is also of huge potential. It is clear that state-owned enterprises as well as government agencies will continue the trend to outsource non-core functions and processes. It would be interesting to observe whether, and how, software services outsourcing deliver business value and performance for domestic clients. Collaborating with offshore clients will allow Chinese outsourcing suppliers to deepen their domain expertise, accumulate experience and understanding of business processes, and improve their capabilities to provide high-end, more value-added service, which hopefully would move them up the value ladder in the future. Figure 1.5 suggests that

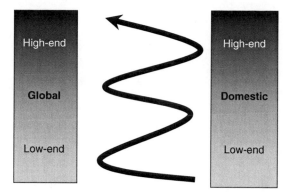

Figure 1.5 Climbing the value chain by straddling both markets

a strategic model designed to leverage both offshore and domestic markets may open the path for Chinese SSO suppliers to gradually move up the value chain. Indeed, we have found evidence in our preliminary research that suppliers are often able to provide consulting service and business solutions to Chinese enterprises or government agencies by learning from collaborations with offshore clients.

Finally, in view of China's transitional economy and its pursuit of the information society, we also need to pay attention to the potential social benefits brought by software services outsourcing. One such benefit is the huge potential for knowledge transfer and sharing (Mowery et al., 1996; Inkpen, 2000), especially in terms of business processes and technological exploitation. For example, offshore clients raise different technological challenges from those of domestic clients, owing to different technological platforms and infrastructures, as well as business requirements. Undertaking such tasks provide incentives for learning and innovation. Moreover, the needs of offshore clients often reflect different institutional arrangements, business standards, and corporate structures and practices. The accumulation of such knowledge and the IT solutions that encapsulate them will become resources to be drawn upon by domestic clients. In other words, Chinese software service providers have a role as "translators" of knowledge and innovation.

Knowledge transfer among outsourcing alliances has always been challenging (Imsland and Sahay, 2005; Chua and Pan, 2008), and few Chinese suppliers have a sophisticated understanding of knowledge management (Chapter 7). Despite these challenges, it is clear that developed countries have increasingly turned to emerging economies for R&D capabilities (Chapter 10). What is yet to be explored is China's potential to provide knowledge and innovation outsourcing to the world (Bardhan, 2006; Yang, 2009). Future research is needed in this area.

Conclusion

To summarize, China's SSO industry is facing huge challenges as well as opportunities. Although Chinese SSO suppliers are far from catching up with their Indian competitors, our study shows that Chinese suppliers have started to compete against Indians at the level of US$10–20 million deals. It is possible that the financial crisis will help consolidate the SSO industry and enable China to become a real global player in IT and business process outsourcing.

The Chinese government needs to provide even clearer guidance and support for the development of the SSO industry. Country branding and promotion is needed for China to be recognized as a global outsourcing destination. As SSO is a knowledge-intensive industry distinct from manufacturing, which in China is labour intensive, suppliers are calling for clearly formulated policies and market regulations specific to the industry. Meanwhile, the 20 outsourcing base cities need to develop a strategy to craft out their own niche and identities in the market, and avoid inefficient regional competition within the industry.

Note

1. Note that data from various government and commercial agencies in China are often inaccurate and inconsistent. While we have tried to verify wherever possible, please read them as a rough indicators, and compare with data provided by later chapters in this book.

References

Bardhan, Ashok Deo (2006), "Managing globalization of R&D: Organizing for offshoring innovation," *Human Systems Management*, 25(2): 103–114.

BSIPC (2008), *Blue Book of Beijing Software Industry Development 2008*, Beijing Software Industry Productivity Centre, Beijing.

BSIPC (2009), *Blue Book of Beijing Software Industry Development 2009*, Beijing Software Industry Productivity Centre, Beijing.

Carmel, E. and Tjia, P. (2005), *Offshoring Information Technology: Sourcing and Outsourcing to a Global Workforce*, Cambridge, Cambridge University Press.

CASS (2007), *Blue Book of City Competitiveness 2007*, Chinese Academy of Social Science, Beijing.

Chan, Savio S. (2005), "IT outsourcing in China: How China's five emerging drivers are changing the technology landscape and IT industry," The Outsourcing Institute, www.outsourcing.com/ (accessed 1 February 2009).

Chen, Yun-Chung (2008), "Why do multinational corporations locate their advanced R&D centres in Beijing?" *Journal of Development Studies*, 44(5): 622–644.

Chua, A. L. and Pan, S. L. (2008), "Knowledge transfer and organizational learning in IS offshore sourcing," *Omega*, 36: 267–281.

www.cioage.com (2009), "China Development Bank Sets Example for Outsourcing in Financial Services." www.szedu.com.cn/zixun_8/71000.shtml (accessed 29 April 2009).

CSIP et al. (2008), *Research Report on China's Software & Information Service Outsourcing Enterprises in 2008*, The Ministry of Information Industry Software and Integrated Circuit Promotion Center (CSIP), Chinese Alliance of the Software and Information Service Outsourcing Industry, and BearingPoint Management Consulting (Shanghai) Ltd, Shanghai.

Devott Ltd. (2009), *Chinasourcing – Top 50 Service Outsourcing Providers in China 2008 White Paper*. www.chnsourcing.com/top50/2008/ (accessed 3 June 2009).

D&B (2008), *India's top ITeS and BPO companies 2008*, Dun & Bradstreet Information Services India.

Eltshinger, C. (2007), *Source Code China: The New Global Hub of IT Outsourcing*, Wiley, New Jersey.

EquaTerra (2008), *China: The Sleeping Dragon* (3062EU), EquaTerra, London.

Feeny, D., Lacity, M. and Willcocks, L. (2006), "Assessing 12 supplier capabilities," in Willcocks, L. and Lacity, M. (eds), *Global Sourcing of Business and IT Services*, Palgrave, London.

Heeks, R. and Nicholson, B. (2004), "Software Export Success Factors and Strategies in 'Follower' Nations," *Competition and Change*, 8: 267–303.

Hou, J. and Xu, Z. (2006), *China Development Bank Opens the Path for Software Services Outsourcing with 5 Billion Credit 21st Century Economic Report*. http://news.csdn.net/n/20061216/99494.html (accessed at 12 April 2009).

Imsland, Vegar and Sahay, Sundeep (2005), "Negotiating knowledge: The case of a Russian-Norwegian software outsourcing project," *Scandinavian Journal of Information Systems*, 17(1): 101–130.

IDC (2008), *Analysis and Forecasting of China's Offshore Software Outsourcing Market* (in Chinese), International Data Group, New York.

Inkpen, A. C. (2000), "Learning through joint ventures: A framework of knowledge acquisition," *Journal of Management Studies*, 37(7): 1019–1045.

Ji, Qi, (2008), From "Made in China" to "Chinese Services". www.chinareviewnews.com/doc/1007/8/5/9/100785963.html?coluid=50&kindid=1078&docid=100785963 (assessed 2 February 2009).

Kshetri, Nir (2005), *Structural Shifts in the Chinese Software Industry*," IEEE Software, July/August: 86–93.

Li, Y., Liu, Y., Li, M. and Wu, H. (2008), "Transformational offshore outsourcing: Empirical evidence from alliances in China," *Journal of Operations Management*, 26: 257–274.

MII (2000), *Policies on Encouraging the Development of Software and Integrated Circuit Industries*, Ministry of Information Industry and China Software Industry Association, Beijing.

MII and CSIS (2008), *The Annual Report of the China Software Industry*, Ministry of Information Industry and China Software Industry Association, Shanghai.

Mowery, D. C., Oxley, J. E. and Silverman, B. S. (1996), "Strategic alliances and interfirm knowledge transfer," *Strategic Management Journal*, 17: 77–91.

Oshri, I., Kotlarsky, J. and Willcocks, L. (2007), "Managing dispersed expertise in IT offshore outsourcing: Lessons from Tata Consultancy Services," *MIS Quarterly Executive*, 6(2): 53–65.

Powell, W., Koput, K. and Smith-Doer, L. (1996), "Interorganizational Collaboration and the Locus of Innovation: Networks of Learning in Biotechnology," *Administrative Science Quarterly*, 41(1): 116–145.

Qu, Z. and Brocklehurst, M. (2003), "What will it take for China to become a competitive force in offshore outsourcing? An analysis of the role of transaction costs in supplier selection," *Journal of Information Technology*, 18: 53–67.

SinaFinance (2009), *New Waves of Software Outsourcing M&A Emerge*. http://chinasourcing.mofcom.gov.cn/dq/content2.jsp?id=38216 (accessed 30 May 2009).

State Council of People's Republic of China (2009), *Official Reply of the State Council on Promoting the Development of the Service Outsourcing Industry* ([2009] No. 9). www.szbti.gov.cn/bulletin_temp/b20090310003.html (accessed 1 June 2009).

The Economist (2006), "Outsourcing to China: Watch out, India," 4 May: 69–70.

Veloso, F., Botelho, A. J. J., Tschang, T. and Amsden, A. (2003), *Slicing the Knowledge-Based Economy in Brazil, China and India: A Tale of 3 Software Industries*, Report published by Massachusetts Institute of Technology.

Willcocks, L., Griffiths, C. and Kotlarsky, J. (2009), *Beyond BRIC – Offshoring in Non-BRIC Countries – Egypt a New Growth Market*, London School of Economics, London.

Willcocks, Leslie, Feeny, David and Olson, Nancy (2006), "Implementing core IS capabilities: Feeny – Willcocks IT governance and management framework revisited," *European Management Journal*, 24(1): 28–37.

Willcocks, L. and Lacity, M. (2009), *The Practice of Outsourcing: From Information Systems to BPO and Offshoring*, Palgrave, London.

Xie, Weiqun (2008), People's Daily: From "Made in China" to "Created in China". http://news.xinhuanet.com/politics/2008-07/11/content_8526529.htm (accessed 26 April 2009).

Yang, B. (2009), *IT Service Outsourcing: Based on the Perspectives of Clients and Suppliers (in Chinese)*, Publishing House of Electronics Industry, Beijing.

Zhou, Yu and Xin, Tong (2003), "An innovative region in China: Interaction between multinational corporations and local firms in a high-tech cluster in Beijing," *Economic Geography*, 79(2): 129–152.

2
The Maturing Chinese Offshore IT Services Industry: It Takes Ten Years to Sharpen a Sword

Erran Carmel, Guodong Gao and Ning Zhang

Introduction

American and European IT managers are increasingly considering whether to outsource IT services to China-based companies. While these Western IT managers are familiar with the large Indian companies that provide offshore IT services, they are not familiar with their Chinese counterparts. This chapter complements the analyses of the Chinese offshore IT services industry provided by Chapters, 1, 3 and 4, with a focus here on the large, dominant players. We examined the Top 39 firms in detail, categorizing them into three types – multinational ventures, legacy and new generation. Each of these is described and illustrated by examples of firms.

The subtitle of this chapter is an old Chinese saying, derived from the ancient sword masters who took a long time to hone their skills and temper their weapons in preparation for a major battle. We believe this saying describes aptly the evolution of the Chinese offshoring industry. To date, the growth of the industry has been slow and deliberate, in preparation for making a major impact on the market for offshore IT services. In terms of maturity, the industry was, in 2008, still at Stage 1 (initial growth), although stage 2 (shake-out/ consolidation) may well be not far off. We describe the implications of our analysis for potential customers of Chinese offshore providers. In choosing a Chinese provider, business will need to make trade-offs determined by the attributes of the three types of provider.

The emergence of China's offshore IT services industry

China's emergence as an economic superpower has led to predictions that the country's offshore IT services industry will soon compete with India's. After all, many leading corporations in North America and Europe now contract with Chinese providers for at least some of their IT services. Yet China's offshore IT services industry has received far less attention than its Indian counterpart. IT managers in the West need a deeper understanding of China's industry to enable them to successfully include China-based providers in their companies' offshore sourcing strategies.

As Chapter 1 argued, China's offshore IT services industry cannot be understood without putting it in the context of the Chinese economy and its software industry. Since its economic reform in 1978, the Chinese economy has grown by an average of 9.5 per cent per year (real gross domestic product [GDP] growth rate).[1] From 1978 to 2006, the country's GDP increased by a factor of more than 12, compared to only 2.25 times for the USA.[2] This sustained economic growth has led to an increase in China's domestic demand for IT, and its software industry has flourished as well. During the 1990s, the software industry grew at an annual rate of over 30 per cent – three times the growth rate of China's GDP (CMII, 2001). China's overall software industry is now twice the size of India's in dollar value.

But China's software industry has been domestically focused, and its offshore IT services industry has been lacklustre compared to India's. Although China and India's offshore industries both emerged in the late 1980s, China's total software exports (including offshore) in 2006 were only about a quarter of India's: $6 billion compared to India's $24 billion (see Figure 2.1). While most of India's software industry revenue is accounted for by exports, China's software exports are small. In 2004, only about 10 per cent of the 720,000 employees in China's software industry were engaged in software exports (CMII, 2004). Moreover, the majority of China's software exports were embedded software.

It is important to recognize the strong influence of government in order to gain an understanding of the Chinese offshore IT services industry. The Chinese government is a major customer of the country's software companies, which are awarded highly profitable government contracts – like the "twelve golden projects" that comprise the first phase of e-government in China.[3]

In 2000, the Chinese government recognized the importance of offshore IT services and began to issue targeted policies to foster their growth. In 2006, for example, the government established a plan called "From Made in China to China Service", which set out China's intention to concentrate on, and increase its presence in, the global IT services market. The plan also set a goal to increase exports in software and related information services to more than $10 billion by 2010.[4]

With favourable policies in place and strong global demand, China's offshore IT services industry began to grow rapidly. According to a 2007 report from CCID Group,[5] this industry generated revenues of $1.43 billion in 2006 (part

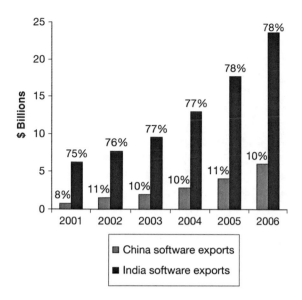

Figure 2.1 Software industry exports, China vs. India, 2001–2006

Note: Numbers on bars show the percentage of total domestic software production that was exported.
Sources: Adapted from China Software Industry Association, and National Association of Software and Service Companies [India].[6]

of the $6.06 billion total software exports in that year) and grew at an annual rate of 55.4 per cent.

Since 2000, Chinese IT services firms have made a strategic shift in the international markets on which they concentrate. Japan and South Korea used to be their main export markets, but in recent years the focus has shifted more to European and North American markets. For example, the share of China's total software exports accounted for by Japan dropped from 66.3 per cent in 2003 to 58.1 per cent in 2006, while the share of revenue from European and North American markets has increased.

Three periods of growth

We divide the evolution of China's offshore IT services industry into three periods: nascent, transition and current.

The nascent period: pre-1995

Before the advent of the public Internet, there was relatively little global trade in IT services. Even the "3 Is" of software – India, Israel and Ireland – had very small industries. But there was a tiny amount of offshore software development in China, with Japanese firms contracting with Chinese providers. The geographic proximity of the two countries, and their cultural similarities, meant that Japanese firms helped to lay the foundations of China's offshore IT services industry. In the late 1980s and early 1990s, Japanese multinationals like Omron, NEC and Fujitsu set up joint ventures, mainly with higher education institutes or local government. During this period, China-based firms providing offshore software services mainly engaged in low-end software development. Japanese multinationals commonly divided large projects into small pieces and then offshored some of these to Chinese providers. This tradition lingers today and distinguishes the type of offshore services provided to Japanese firms from the work done for other Western firms.

The transition period: 1995–1999

Several events happened in 1995/96, all of which spurred the growth of China's offshore IT services industry:

- The Internet began to grow rapidly.
- In early 1996, China's Ministry of Science and Technology started to boost software parks under the "National Torch Program", which helped domestic start-up companies. (By the end of 2006 there were 33 software parks across the country.)
- High levels of competition and decreasing profits in the domestic software market caused domestic IT firms (such as Neusoft) to diversify into the newly emerging offshore market.
- The booming Internet economy attracted foreign investors to China, leading to foreign start-ups.
- Chinese indigenous start-ups, like SinoCom, focusing on providing offshore IT services began to appear.

The current period: post 2000

The major milestone that signalled the start of this period was when the Chinese government formally recognized the importance of the IT services sector. In June 2000, the China State Council issued the *18th File Policy on the Encouragement of Software and Integrated Circuit Industry*. This policy was the first step taken by the Chinese government to launch the national campaign to support and promote the entire IT services industry. The policy provided inducements such as venture capital programmes, tax-free zones and tax benefits.

The government followed with several other significant actions:

- In 2002, the China State Council issued the *47th File Policy on the Encouragement of Software Industry (2002–2005)*.

- In June 2004, the Ministry of Science and Technology launched the "China Offshore Software Engineering Program" to encourage more software exports.
- In September 2006, nine ministries – including the Ministry of Commerce and the Ministry of Science and Technology – jointly issued "Advice on increasing software and information technology service export."
- In 2006, the government set up five outsourcing zones distributed in cities across China, with numerous finance and tax benefits. This was followed by the second batch of six cities in 2007, including Beijing. Local governments soon followed this lead. Regional policies were implemented and designed to cultivate competitiveness within major cities and attract foreign investment.
- In 2006, the Ministry of Commerce set up the "1000-100-10 Project" to nurture 1,000 outsourcing companies, to attract 100 major foreign companies to use offshore services in China, and to establish 10 outsourcing parks.

All these actions have helped spur the development of China's offshore IT services industry. Since 2000, more firms have entered the industry and existing companies have grown in one of three ways:

- Through a stock market initial public offering (IPO): e.g., in 2003 Chinasoft International became a public company quoted on the Hong Kong Stock Exchange.
- Strategic investment: e.g., Neusoft received $US 40 million investment from Intel in 2006, and Inspur received $US 25 million from Microsoft.
- Mergers and acquisitions: e.g., iSoftStone Technologies has acquired several companies since 2005; its size, measured by number of employees, jumped from less than 100 in 2002 to over 4,000 in 2007.

The market focus of China's offshore IT services industry has expanded from Japan to the USA and Europe. Until 2000, the industry was characterized by low-end coding work and localization. Since 2000, Chinese firms have moved into higher-level activities like system design and providing whole solutions. Accumulated experience, more trust from clients and larger size have all contributed to this trend.

Three types of Chinese offshore IT services firms

When assessing the state of a country's offshore IT services industry, the most important firms to examine are the largest companies (Chapters 1 and 3 provide

AsiaInfo Holdings, Inc.	**NEC** Advanced Software Technology
Bleum Inc.	(Beijing)
Changxiang Computer Co. Ltd.	**Neusoft** Group Ltd.
Chinasoft International Co. Ltd.	**Newtouch** Software Co. Ltd.
Datang Software Technologies Co.	**Objectiva** Software Solutions (Beijing)
Ltd.	Inc.
Double-Bridge Technologies Inc.	**PFU** Shanghai Co. Ltd.
Freeborders Co. Ltd.	**Powerise** Group
Fujitsu Nanda Software Technology Co.	**Prosoft** Technology Co. Ltd.
Ltd.	**Safe** Software Co. Ltd.
HiSoft Technology International Ltd.	**SinoCom** Computer System (Beijing)
Hi-Think Computer Technology	Co. Ltd.
Co. Ltd.	**Sorun** Beijing Co. Ltd.
Hundsun Electronics Co. Ltd.	**Summit** software Co. Ltd.
Insigma Technology Co. Ltd.	**SunJapan** Information Systems
Inspur Group Ltd.	Co. Ltd.
Intasect Communications (Chengdu)	**Tata** Information Technology (Shanghai)
Co. Ltd.	Co.
iSoftStone Technologies Ltd.	**Totyu** Soft Co. Ltd.
I.T. United Corporation	**U-soft** Co. Ltd.
Jianfeng Computer Systems Co. Ltd.	**Venus** Software Corporation Ltd.
(Beijing)	**Wicresoft** Co. Ltd.
JT-Hyron Software Co. Ltd.	**Yinhai** Software Limited Liability Co.
Kingdee International Software Group	(Sichuan)
Company Limited	**Yuandong** Digital Co. Ltd.
Megainfo Tech Co. Ltd.	

Figure 2.2   The top 39 Chinese offshore IT services firms

analyses of other, smaller players). In the USA, these are companies like IBM, Accenture and, now, HP. In India they are companies like TCS and Infosys. We have identified the Top 39 Chinese offshore IT services firms[7] that set the tone of the industry (see Figure 2.2).

Most of these 39 firms are concentrated in the north and east of the country (see the map in Figure 2.3). Specifically, 22 (56 per cent) have their headquarters in Beijing or Shanghai.

Southern manufacturing hubs, such as those in and around Shenzhen, play a lesser role in the software industry. This geographic distribution results from the concentration of the scientific elite in the northern and eastern cities. The top universities continue to be in Beijing and Shanghai, and the software industry has therefore emerged in and around these cities. In particular, there is a high concentration of software companies in Beijing's Z-Park (Zhongguancun Science Park) and in Pudong in Shanghai.

We have classified the Top 39 firms based on several attributes: strategy at origin, customer focus, management style, capacity, strengths and growth path. Three types of firms emerged from this classification, which we label:

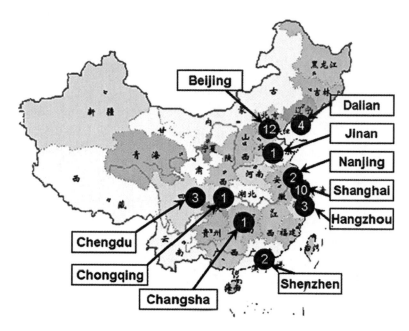

Figure 2.3   Geographic distribution of the Top 39 Chinese firms
Source: The authors.

1. *Multinational ventures*, which are initiated by a multinational company (though may be owned jointly by the Chinese government or institutes). They typically focus on serving the parent multinational. Most of these firms serve Japanese multinationals. Twelve of the Top 39 fall into this category.
2. *Legacy firms* are large and well-established Chinese IT firms, now typically with over 1,000 employees, which have served the domestic market and later also turned to serving multinationals in China or foreign markets, or both. Twelve of the Top 39 are legacy firms.
3. *New generation firms* are start-ups focusing on non-Chinese clients from their inception. Fifteen of the Top 39 fall into this category.

Figure 2.4 shows which of Top 39 firms fall into each type. It also indicates the size of each firm in terms of number of employees and shows which of the three evolutionary periods a firm first started to serve non-Chinese clients.

Multinational ventures
Major multinationals began to enter China as far back as the 1980s. Some came to penetrate the domestic market; others wanted to exploit China's labour

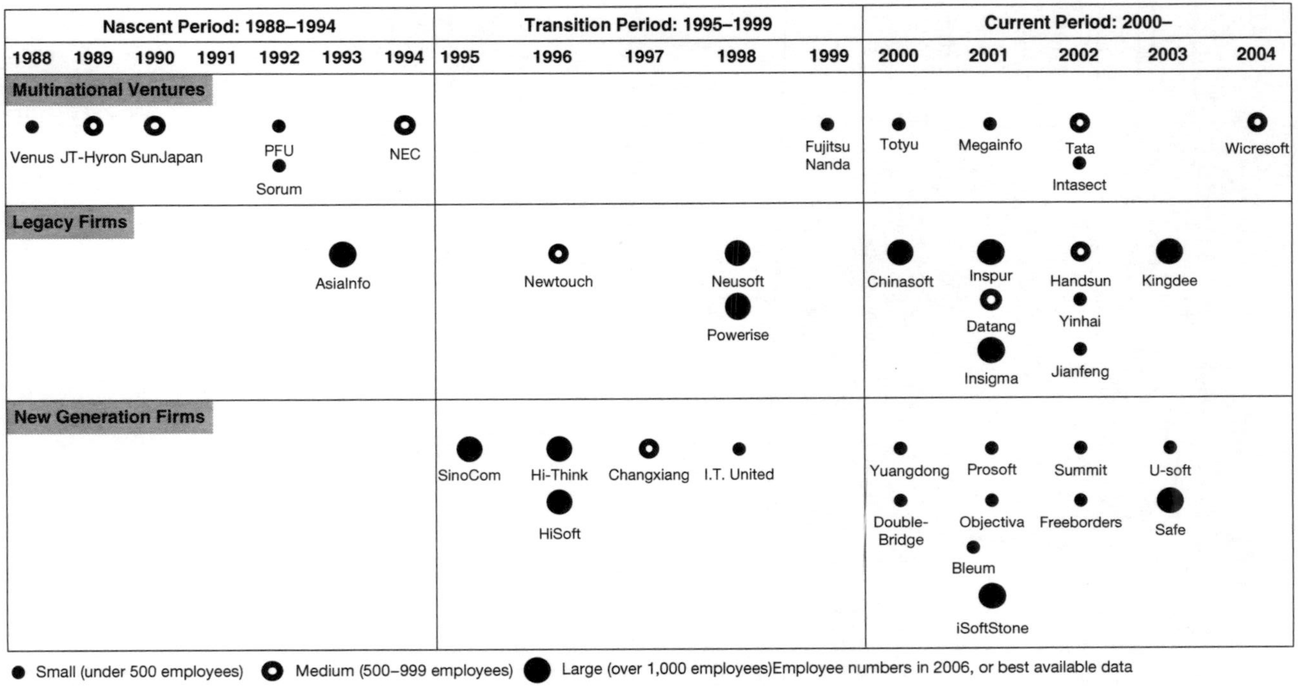

	Nascent Period: 1988–1994							Transition Period: 1995–1999					Current Period: 2000–				
	1988	1989	1990	1991	1992	1993	1994	1995	1996	1997	1998	1999	2000	2001	2002	2003	2004
Multinational Ventures	Venus	JT-Hyron	SunJapan		PFU / Sorum		NEC					Fujitsu Nanda	Totyu	Megainfo	Tata / Intasect		Wicresoft
Legacy Firms						AsiaInfo			Newtouch		Neusoft / Powerise		Chinasoft	Inspur / Datang / Insigma	Handsun / Yinhai / Jianfeng	Kingdee	
New Generation Firms								SinoCom	Hi-Think / HiSoft	Changxiang	I.T. United		Yuangdong / Double-Bridge	Prosoft / Objectiva / Bleum / iSoftStone	Summit / Freeborders	U-soft / Safe	

● Small (under 500 employees)   ◉ Medium (500–999 employees)   ● Large (over 1,000 employees)   Employee numbers in 2006, or best available data

Figure 2.4 Timeline of Top 39 Chinese firms by type, company size and year Non-Chinese clients first served

One of the earliest multinational venture firms is JT-Hyron, which was founded in 1989 as a joint venture between Omron Corporation, a large Japanese firm, and Shanghai Jiaotong University. Its initial business was to provide Unix technical support for a department in Omron. Later, the business expanded to Unix-based databases and information management systems in different industries like banking, security, insurance and mobile communications. Besides serving Omron, JT-Hyron also acquired business from other large companies in Japan, including NEC, NTT, Hitachi and Nomura Securities. In 2000, the firm became a domestic Chinese company when the university bought most of Omron's shares.

Another example of a multinational venture is NEC Advanced Software Technology (Beijing) Co., founded in 1994 by NEC and the China Academy of Science. Its major business is developing software for NEC for the education, communications and finance sectors. For its first 10 years, this company focused purely on exports. It was only in late 2004 that NEC began to enter the domestic Chinese market.

Figure 2.5   Examples of multinational ventures

cost advantage, mainly to provide services to the parent multinational or the parent's customers back home. These businesses were thus the first to serve non-Chinese clients.

In the 1980s and early 1990s, Chinese government regulation did not allow foreign investors to own more than 49 per cent of a Chinese firm. The multinationals therefore created joint ventures with Chinese government or university institutes. The Chinese partner also helped to provide access to high-quality and low-cost labour. Examples of multinational ventures are described in Figure 2.5.

Ten out of the 12 top firms classified as multinational ventures were established by Japanese multinationals. However, since 2000, non-Japanese multinationals have begun to enter the market. For example, in 2002, Tata (from India) set up a facility in Shanghai. And in 2003, Microsoft established a joint venture company in Shanghai called Wicresoft to provide call centre services to Windows customers in both China and North America.

Being associated with a multinational gives these offshore services firms great benefits during their initial period because the founding multinational guarantees business for the new firm. But there are also downsides. Future business expansion of the offshore services firm might be stifled because the multinational set up the company mainly to serve itself. In spite of their relatively long history of providing offshore IT services, most of these firms are still small, with most still having fewer than 1,000 employees (see Figure 2.4 above).

When firms in this category began to mature, their ownership tended to be adjusted to better fit the growth of the company. For example, JT-Hyron became a Chinese domestic firm in 2000 when Shanghai Jiaotong University bought most of the foreign partner's shares. Observers felt that the company had accumulated sufficient experience and faced a booming offshoring market where quick decision making is critical, making the joint venture arrangement inefficient. There are also reverse cases – when the multinational buys out the joint venture, especially since the recent relaxation of regulation on foreign ownership. For example, in 2006, NEC converted its joint venture with China Academy of Science into a wholly owned foreign company to better fit its strategy in China.

Legacy firms

Legacy firms are relatively large and well-established Chinese IT services firms that have served the domestic market and then, at a later stage, turned to serving multinationals in China or overseas.

Although China has a strong and fast-growing domestic IT industry, competition in the domestic market has intensified since the late 1990s. Some firms started to expand their business to provide offshore IT services because such services are more profitable. Examples of legacy firms are given in Figure 2.6.

Legacy firms are relatively large and well established, and their scale and experience provide them with advantages in the offshore IT services business. They are also more likely to obtain support from local governments in China, which were often their customers in the past. As a result, once these firms enter the offshoring market, they can scale up much faster than other types. For example, Neusoft's revenue from offshore IT software and services jumped from $US 33 million in 2004 to $62.7 million in 2005 and to $101 million in 2006, when it had over 4,000 employees working in offshoring.

Similarly, since 2004, Inspur's revenue from offshore IT services has grown at over 200 per cent annually, and it has established subsidiaries in both Japan

Neusoft is one of China's largest legacy firms. Historically, its major business was system integration and healthcare information systems. From 1998, Neusoft entered the offshoring business by serving Japanese clients in automobile audio and image recognition. In recent years, Neusoft's profit margin from traditional domestic business lines, like system integration, has been less than 15 per cent, compared to 30 per cent for its offshore services. By 2002, Neusoft's domestic business accounted for 70 per cent of its revenue, but only 5 per cent of its profit. Because of the high profitability of its offshoring business, Neusoft focused its strategy on offshoring and put this area under the direct supervision of the CEO.

Another legacy firm is Inspur, one of the biggest Chinese electronics companies with annual revenue over $1.5 billion in 2005. Inspur started in 1964 as a manufacturer of computer peripherals and electronic tubes, which makes it one of the oldest electronics companies in China. Inspur's major domestic business includes high-end servers, ERP software and industry solutions. In 2001, Inspur established an overseas unit and made offshore IT services its core business.

Figure 2.6   Examples of legacy firms

and the USA. Inspur was not listed in the Top 20 Chinese offshore IT services companies in 2004, but had jumped to fourth in 2005.

Since legacy firms are new to the offshore business, they lack expertise and international recognition. One way to overcome these deficiencies is to partner with multinationals. For example, Inspur formed an alliance with Microsoft and received a $25 million strategic investment from that company in 2005. This helped Inspur gain offshore contracts from the North America market. Another way for these big domestic firms to expand into the offshore market is to use some of their abundant financial resources to acquire existing foreign firms to gain a foothold in the market. For example, in 2006, Inspur acquired Shinwa, a Japanese company, so it could enter the Japanese market.

New generation firms

In the second half of the 1990s, a new type of offshore IT services firm began to emerge in China. Unlike multinational ventures and legacy firms, these new generation firms did not have a captive client base. Rather, they were established to target the offshore market. Like the new generation of hi-tech firms emerging in other nations around the world in the 1990s' technology boom, these Chinese offshore IT services companies were "born global". They bypassed the traditional incremental transition route to internationalization – first domestic, then foreign.

There are marked differences between new generation firms and the other two types described above. Unlike legacy firms, most new generation companies are start-ups. They also differ from multinational ventures in that they aim at the general offshoring market rather than limiting themselves to serving a specific multinational. Finally, unlike the other two types, new generation firms are more likely to be oriented to providing services to US clients.

New generation firms can be further divided into two subcategories, depending on the nationality of the founders: Chinese-owned (nine out of the 15 in the Top 39 list) and foreign-owned (six firms). The nine Chinese-owned companies in this group[8] are growing very quickly: four of them have over 1,000 employees, which is remarkable considering their relatively young age.

Figure 2.7 provides brief descriptions of two new generation firms

The assumption might be that a Chinese-founded company has disadvantages in accessing foreign clients compared to a foreign-owned firm, but in practice this is not so. First, most Chinese founders of new generation firms have either an overseas education or multinational work experience. Second, these firms quickly bring in professional managers who have broad overseas connections. Third, they enhance their access to overseas markets by either making strategic foreign investments or acquiring small foreign companies, as HiSoft has done (see Figure 2.7).

I.T. United is a typical foreign-owned New Generation firm. It was founded by a group of former EDS employees who, in 1998, were engaged in helping General Motors build up its information systems in China and saw the opportunity of providing low-cost IT services by leveraging the huge Chinese IT labour pool. The firm was founded in Beijing and set up development centres in Beijing, Shanghai and Xi'an selling to both the US and European markets.

HiSoft is an example of a Chinese-owned new generation firm. It was founded in 1996 by seven entrepreneurs who had previously worked for many years for a Japanese multi-national. In 10 years, the company grew to over 2,300 employees and ranked as the third-largest Chinese software export company in 2006. HiSoft has expanded its business from low-end coding and testing to providing industry solutions for large companies in Japan and North America. HiSoft is also the first company in mainland China to achieve Level 5 CMM (Capability Maturity Model) certification. In 2006, the company received $30 million investment funding from international investors, including Intel. In 2007, HiSoft acquired Envisage Solution, a US IT solution provider, so it could gain access to the US market.

Figure 2.7   Examples of new generation firms

Maturity of the Chinese Offshore IT services industry

Klepper and Graddy (1990) have proposed a generic three-stage industry maturity model (see Figure 2.8). In Stage 1 (initial growth), the number of firms is growing; Stage 2 is characterized as the shake-out period, where the number of firms is decreasing; and Stage 3 is when the number of firms stabilizes.

The Chinese offshore IT services industry is at Stage 1 maturity

Four characteristics indicate that the Chinese offshore IT services industry is still in Stage 1 (initial growth) of Klepper's model. First, there have been many new entrants in recent years. About 60 per cent of the top offshore IT services firms (23 out of 39) entered the market during 2000 or later (see timeline

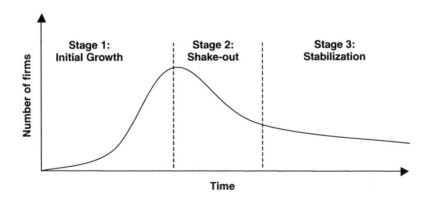

Figure 2.8   Klepper's generic industry maturity model

in Figure 2.4). Most of these more recent entrants into offshoring are either legacy firms or new generation firms set up by "Sea Turtles" (a Chinese term for Chinese people returning from overseas).

Second, the majority of the today's top Chinese technology firms – Digital China, Eusoft, Founder, Huawei, Putain, Zhongxin and so on – do not participate in the offshore IT services industry. Instead, they currently focus either on hardware equipment or on the domestic market. This would be analogous to American companies like IBM and HP, which started life as hardware firms, choosing not to participate in the global IT services market. The lack of involvement of the largest technology firms may indicate that the offshore IT services industry is still a long way from Stage 3 (stabilization).

Third, the concentration ratio is very small – that is, industry fragmentation is still fairly high. The industry mainly comprises relatively small players in many categories, which is a typical indicator of an early stage of maturity (de Filippo et al., 2005). Unlike Indian offshore IT services providers, there are no dominant players in the Chinese industry. The top 10 Chinese firms in 2005 accounted for less than 20 per cent of the total revenue for offshore IT services. However, there are signs that this may be quickly changing: the top three companies – Neusoft, HiSoft and Hi-Think – accounted for 15 per cent of total revenue in 2006. Another concentration measure is employee size; and the average size of Chinese offshore IT services providers is still small. Figure 2.4 depicts the number of employees for each of the Top 39 firms. Twenty-seven are small- or medium-sized firms with fewer than 1,000 employees. Of the 12 large firms, only Neusoft and Inspur had more than 10,000 employees in 2006, although this is for the entire company. In both cases, revenue from providing offshore services is a small part of the total business.

Fourth, the rankings of the players are still changing rapidly. This is also a characteristic of early maturity; in more mature industries there are few significant changes in the relative rankings of industry leaders.

The shake-out may be on the horizon

However, there are indicators suggesting that the Chinese offshore IT services industry may be near the peak of Stage 1 and will soon be entering Stage 2 as consolidation begins (see Chapter 3). Clearly, one driver of consolidation is that Chinese offshore IT services firms need to grow so they can provide full services to large global firms and can successfully market their services in multiple locations.

From about 2005, merger and acquisition (M&A) activity in the industry has picked up. Three of the Top 10 companies in the China Import and Export Software Network (CIESN)[9] 2004 ranking disappeared when they were acquired by other companies – Chinasoft Resource was acquired by Chinasoft, Ensemble International was acquired by HiSoft, and Beijing Innovation Software became part of Insigma. Additionally, Prosoft was acquired by VanceInfo in 2006, and iSoftStone merged with Shanghai Jiefeng in 2008.

Investment capital is also spurring M&A activity. For example, HiSoft received $30 million investment from Granite Global Ventures, which enabled it to acquire two other offshore providers in Beijing. And Neusoft received $40 million investment from Intel in 2006, which helped it to scale up its offshoring business.

Another indicator of the growing maturity of China's offshore IT services industry is that top firms are being acquired by foreign companies. Objectiva Software Solutions was acquired in 2004 by Document Sciences Corporation, which was subsequently taken over in 2008 by EMC, an American technology conglomerate. And in 2007, IT United was acquired by Softtek, Mexico's largest IT services firm.

Implications for potential customers of offshore IT services

As the subtitle of this chapter indicates, the sword of the Chinese offshore IT services industry is beginning to sharpen. Offshoring IT services to Chinese providers will become increasingly viable, and businesses will need to decide which type of provider to engage with and how to make outsourcing a success. The three types are distinctive in terms of their origins, ownership structure, expertise, management style and culture. Potential pros and cons of offshoring to each type are summarized in Figure 2.9.

Multinational ventures

One advantage of offshoring to multinational ventures is their modern management practices, which they have assimilated from their parent multinationals (Millington et al., 2006). Employee rotation in both directions is typical: expatriate managers are assigned from the parent multinational and newly hired employees are sent to the multinational for training.

On the other hand, because these firms mainly serve the parent multinational, their expertise tends to be more specialized, for example, Fujitsu Nanda. As the China-based R&D centre of the Japan Fujitsu Software Department, this organization is focused on Fujitsu's large servers.

Contract negotiations with multinational ventures may take longer because of the need to involve the parent multinational. For example, one reason for JT-Hyron changing its ownership structure was the long decision process, which had to involve the headquarters of its multinational partner.

Legacy firms

Legacy firms tend to be larger than firms in the other two types, and their years of experience in the domestic market provide them with technical competence.

	Ownership	Pros	Cons
Multinational venture	Generally, either a state-owned enterprise or an international joint venture.	Understands Western practices.	• Specialized. • Gives priority to multinational owner.
Legacy	Generally, either a state-owned enterprise or a private Chinese enterprise.	• Strong technical competence. • Experience with large-scale projects. • Low cost.	• Bureaucratic mentality. • Less likely to understand Western business practices. • High set-up costs. • Language barrier.
New generation	Generally, either a private Chinese enterprise or a wholly owned foreign enterprise.	• Most flexible and responsive type. • Western-style management team. • Outsourcing-focused.	• Quality variation across vendors. • Most susceptible to industry restructuring.

Figure 2.9 Potential pros and cons of contracting with each type of Chinese offshore IT services provider[10]

These firms also have the capability to develop large-scale projects. They may also be eager to gain a foothold in the offshore IT services market and therefore more willing to negotiate on price.

On the other hand, there can be some "hidden" costs in offshoring to legacy firms. First, the big legacy firms, especially those that are state-owned, are used to doing business with domestic clients, and their culture is thus typically Chinese – based on the "iron rice bowl"[11] and "Guanxi".[12] As a consequence, they may be less able to meet the standards of responsiveness and accuracy demanded by foreign clients (Saxenian and Quan, 2005; Su, 2008). Their bureaucratic mentality also limits lower-level employee involvement in quality management. To adhere to the specifications of foreign clients legacy firms may therefore need to restructure their service processes, and clients may need to closely monitor their work.

Additionally, the costs of setting up an offshore project with legacy firms may be higher because of their more limited experience with outsourcing, which means that standard business routines may not yet be well established. Higher set-up costs suggest that legacy firms are most suitable for long-term and large-scale projects. Another advantage of legacy firms, compared to multinational ventures and new generation firms, is that they are likely to remain dominant since they have experienced workforces that will enable them to quickly grow their offshoring businesses. An example is Inspur, which entered the offshoring market relatively late, but then moved quickly into the CIESN rankings.

New generation firms

New generation firms are mostly private Chinese firms or wholly owned foreign enterprises set up either by Sea Turtles or by foreigners. There is less of a language barrier with these firms and, culturally, they have been built from the ground up using Western management practices. This suggests that using new generation firms to provide offshore IT services may involve lower coordination costs. A distinguishing characteristic of these firms is their agility and entrepreneurial spirit. They are more willing to make big changes in their production processes, so may be more willing to customize their services to better meet the demands of their customers. The founder usually has a great influence on staffing matters, and decisions can be made very quickly.

On the other hand, given their relatively short history, new generation firms may lack experience in delivering big projects (see Chapter 5). They are also more likely to be subject to industry restructuring, so potential customers should consider the stability of the firm and its staff. Nearly all of the M&A activity in the Chinese offshore IT services industry to date has involved new generation firms – Prosoft, IT United, iSoftStone and others.

Comparison between Chinese and Indian offshore IT service industries

Many US and European IT professionals are familiar with the evolution of the Indian offshore IT services industry and recognize its largest players. But, as this analysis of China's industry shows, the Indian and Chinese industries have evolved in quite different ways (see also Popkin and Iyengar, 2007).

If we exclude Satyam as a result of its 2009 problems, the Indian offshore IT services industry is dominated by four companies – TCS, Infosys, Wipro and HCL. Although they all emerged in the 1970s and 1980s, most of them had no overseas clients until after 1990. During their early years of working with foreign clients, all these companies were primarily "body shops" (providing human resources but with little managerial value added). Wipro and HCL began as computer hardware companies and then evolved into IT services. TCS and Wipro evolved from their parent conglomerates, the former being one of India's largest.

Unlike the Top 39 Chinese providers, all of India's Top 4 (and also Satyam) would be classified as legacy firms. The difference here, though, is that during the 1990s each of them shifted their focus from the domestic market to an aggressive export-oriented strategy. One should also remember that when Indian offshore providers were emerging in the 1980s, the global software industry was too young and immature for there to be a new generation classification.

In summary, the Chinese industry is evolving quite differently from the Indian industry (which evolved quite differently from the Israeli software industry, which in turn evolved differently from the Irish software industry).[13] Each of these major national software industries took different trajectories in their early and middle stages, and now seem quite distinct.

Conclusion

In conclusion, our analysis of the Chinese offshore IT services industry shows that it is growing rapidly but is still at an early stage of maturity. The industry is still fragmented, and is still heavily influenced by foreign firms. However, there are indications that the industry will soon move into the shake-out stage of maturity. With consolidation just around the corner, the sword of the Chinese offshore IT services industry will soon be sharp enough to become a major force in the global market.

Appendix 2   The methodology for creating the Top 30 list

We used several industry rankings to generate the list of 39 firms included in our analysis. We began with the Top 20 offshore Chinese IT services companies listed by CIESN for 2004 and 2005 (published in late 2005 and late 2006). CIESN is regarded as the authority on ranking Chinese IT services firms. The combination of the two years' rankings produced 31 firms, although three firms merged with others in 2006. We augmented the CIESN lists with emerging offshoring firms from *Global Services* magazine's "Offshore 100 list" for 2005 and 2006. There were 12 Chinese firms in those lists, only two of which – Neusoft and Kingdee – were also listed by CIESN. We also added the China division of Tata Consultancy Services to our list, to represent the trend for Indian IT services firms to expand into China (as of late 2009, 14 large Indian firms had IT services operations in the country). Tata is not only the largest, but also the earliest to enter the Chinese market. Once we had created the Top 39 list, we collected information on each firm's history since its founding. We paid special attention to how a firm's offshoring business originated, its major clients and industry focus. We also collected data on the number of employees, location and major financing events.

We excluded major Western firms such as Microsoft, IBM, Oracle and SAP, which were establishing a presence in China in 2005/6 because they were serving mainly domestic clients and were therefore not providing offshore IT services. In any further investigation of the Chinese offshore IT services industry, we would recommend including these organizations' cross-border operations.

Notes

1. 2007 China Statistical Yearbook.
2. According to www.bea.gov/national/xls/gdplev.xls, U.S. GDP was $5.01 trillion in 1978 and $11.3 trillion in 2006 (measured in year 2000 dollar values).
3. *Recommendations on the Construction of E-Government in China*, State Council Document No. 17, 2002.
4. "Advice on increasing software and information technology service export," issued by nine Chinese ministries including the Ministry of Commerce and the Ministry of Science and Technology, September 2006.
5. Beijing-based CCID is a large-scale information service enterprise funded entirely by the China Center for Information Industry Development.
6. Data for India is published by fiscal year, which creates problems in international comparisons. For example, data for fiscal 2005 is shown as 2005 in Figure 1.1. Because there has been consistent growth, the impact on Figure 1.1 is to underrepresent the size of Indian software exports.
7. Appendix 2 describes the research methodology, including the way in which this Top 39 list was constructed.
8. Changxiang, HiSoft, Hi-Think, Prosoft, Safe, SinoCom, Summit, U-soft and Yuandong.
9. See Appendix 1.
10. This discussion is extended from Millington, A., Eberhardt, M. and Wilkinson, B. (2006) "Supplier performance and selection in China," *International Journal of Operations and Production Management*, 26 (2): 185–201. This article divides Chinese supplier companies – of all kinds – into four types based on ownership: State Owned Enterprises (SOEs), Private Chinese Enterprises (PCEs), International Joint Ventures (IJVs) and Wholly Owned Foreign Enterprises (WOFEs).
11. A Chinese term used to refer to an occupation with guaranteed job security, as well as steady income and benefits.
12. Guanxi describes the basic dynamic in personalized networks of influence, and is a central concept in Chinese society.
13. Arora, A. and Gambardella, A. (2005) *From Underdogs to Tigers: The Rise and Growth of the Software Industry in Brazil, China, India, Ireland and Israel*, Oxford University Press.

References

CMII China Ministry of Information Industry (2001), *The Tenth Five-year Development Plan of Information Industry*, China Ministry of Information Industry, Beijing.

CMII China Ministry of Information Industry (2004), *White Paper on China Software and Information Service Industry Development in 2004*, China Ministry of Information Industry, Beijing.

De Filippo, G., Hou, J. and Ip, C. (2005), "Can China compete in IT services?" *The McKinsey Quarterly*, No. 1.

Klepper, S. and Graddy, E. (1990), "The evolution of new industries and the determinants of market structure," *RAND Journal of Economics*, 21(1): 27–44.

Millington, A., Eberhardt, M. and Wilkinson, B. (2006), "Supplier performance and selection in China," *International Journal of Operations and Production Management*, 26 (2): 185–201.

Popkin, J. and Iyengar, P. (2007), *IT and the East: How China and India are Altering the Future of Technology and Innovation*, Harvard Business School Press, Boston.

Saxenian, A. and Quan, X. (2005), "Government and Guanxi: The Chinese software industry in transition," in Commander, S. (ed.) *The Software Industry in Emerging Markets*, Edward Elgar Publishing, London.

Su, N. (2008), "Internationalization strategies of IT vendors from emerging economies: The case of China," *International Conference of Information Systems (ICIS)*, December.

Related studies

China's offshore IT services industry has received far less attention than its Indian counterpart. However, the following recent studies provide some insights into the Chinese industry:

- Qu, Z. H. and Brocklehurst, M. "What will it take for China to become a competitive force in offshore outsourcing? An analysis of the role of transaction costs in supplier selection," *Journal of Information Technology*, Vol. 18, 2003, pp. 53–67.
  Suggests that the transaction costs of offshoring to China are much higher than to India.
- Xue Tschang, F. and Xue, L. "The Chinese Software Industry," in *From Underdogs to Tigers: The Rise and Growth of the Software Industry in Brazil, China, India, Ireland and Israel*, edited by Arora, A. and Gambardella, A., Oxford University Press, 2005.
  Provides an overview of the Chinese software industry, but not specific to the offshoring sector.
- De Filippo, G., Hou, J. and Ip, C. "Can China compete in IT services?" *The McKinsey Quarterly*, 2005, No. 1.
  This McKinsey report found that Chinese firms are too small for large-scale projects.
- Saxenian, A. and Quan, X. "Government and Guanxi: The Chinese Software Industry in Transition," in *The Software Industry In Emerging Markets*, edited by Commander, S., Edward Elgar Publishing, 2005.
  Highlights that Chinese software firms have had to rely on guanxi—relationships with the government.
- Popkin, J. and Iyengar, P. *IT And the East: How China And India Are Altering the Future of Technology And Innovation*, Harvard Business School Press, 2007.

Examines the impact of the emergence of China and India on high-tech outsourcing and the competitiveness of Western companies.

- Jarvenpaa, S. and Mao, J. "Capabilities Building in Chinese Software Services Firms," *Proceedings of the First Global Sourcing Workshop,* Val d'Isere France, March 2007. Examines the development of internal capabilities in indigenous Chinese vendors.

3
China, Services Outsourcing and the World

Joint research by Accenture and the China Council of International Investment Promotion (CCIIP) edited by John Hindle

Introduction[*]

Since the early 1990s, China's performance as an industrial power has been remarkable. The country has had phenomenal success in developing an export economy that takes advantage of its supply of cheap and abundant labour. "Made in China" labels appear on retail shelves from Argentina to Australia and from Brazil to the United Kingdom, on everything from pencils and shoes to televisions and mobile phones. Its industrial companies have made striking inroads in markets as demanding as machine tools and high quality steel. In mineral and fossil fuel extraction, Chinese companies have become global heavyweights. And with strong capital resources behind them, companies such as Nanjing Automobile, Huawei and computer maker Lenovo have been assertively acquiring foreign corporations and operating units (BBC News, 23 July 2005; Huawei, 2006).

Yet, as shown in Chapters 1 and 2, there is a notable weakness in the country's economic system: China lacks a mature services sector. It is an imbalance that must be addressed before the nation can develop long-term economic stability. China's success in the global services arena will not be so clearly linked to low cost and large scale as it has been in the nation's manufacturing sector. Nor will the country have the head start that it enjoyed over its rivals when entering the manufacturing sector. From Eastern Europe across the Middle East to Southeast Asia, many developing countries have young service sectors of their own.

Rising international demand in the global services marketplace is spurring on these nations. It is expected that spending on global offshore outsourcing in 2011 will be triple 2005 levels. Growth rates in the Asia Pacific region are

---

[*] *Editor's note: This chapter is an abridged version of a research report jointly published by Accenture and the China Council of International Investment Promotion (CCIIP), originally released in December 2008. The full report can be accessed at:* www.accenture.com/Global/Outsourcing/ChinaReport.htm.

impressive already: The compound annual growth rate of outsourcing spending between 2005 and 2011 is about 30 per cent in this region compared with 21 per cent in the United States (IDC, 2007).

Contributing to other developing nations' viability as outsourcing centres are their competitively priced niche skills and their cultural alignment with clients in neighbouring countries. Developed countries have also taken note, with widely circulated studies showing that every new global service position results in the creation of up to 12 additional jobs in supporting industries. Consequently, governments in developed nations have added emphasis and resources to policies and programmes that support domestic service providers and their efforts to be more competitive on the global stage.

China's government leaders are well aware of the nation's economic imbalance. That is why the Ministry of Commerce, in cooperation with other government agencies, launched the 1000-100-10 Project in 2006 (see Chapters 1 and 2). In tandem with this project, the China Council of International Investment Promotion (CCIIP) formed a partnership with leading global management consulting, technology services and outsourcing company Accenture to sponsor a wide-ranging research programme. This research programme was designed to provide a deeper understanding of the scope and scale of China's embryonic outsourcing industry and to spotlight the opportunities and competition the industry faces (see Appendix for further details of the survey, interview research approach and research base).

This chapter first gives an overview of the programme's key research findings. We then assess China's position in the global services marketplace; assess in detail the Chinese service provider landscape by product offering and by industry presence; analyse the client base for Chinese outsourcing services and notable additional phenomena in the Chinese marketplace; and, finally, offer three global trends to watch in the context of their further development in China.

Overview of key research findings

China's challenges

The research identified several significant barriers that China must address before it can be considered an outsourcing leader. Yet encouraging signs were appearing already by 2009. Among the clients that now use China-based providers, outsourcing is helping them to become high-performance businesses by enabling them to cut costs, downsize their operations and improve their business processes. Many survey respondents reported high degrees of satisfaction with their Chinese service providers. At the same time, it seems that Chinese providers are rapidly learning which factors are most critical to the success of outsourcing engagements. Through the research, it became apparent that China's BPO and ITO sectors, as of 2009, faced the following significant challenges:

- The outsourcing sectors in China are still in the early stages of development. Clients are concerned about issues of trustworthiness and confidentiality, the expertise of China's service providers and the value they think they may gain from outsourcing.
- Only a third of survey respondents are currently (2009) outsourcing services in China or are planning to do so. Among those who are now outsourcing, the key drivers of high performance are cost, service quality, intellectual property rights protection, workforce skills and industry expertise, along with a high degree of comfort and familiarity with the use of outsourcing as an effective business practice.
- Among Chinese clients responding to the survey, half admit to having limited or no understanding of outsourcing – meaning that there is a big opportunity for education. The clear implication is that China's goal of developing a successful outsourcing industry is heavily dependent on how quickly Chinese clients grasp the importance of outsourcing and its potential to enable high performance.
- China is still predominantly providing BPO services to clients outside the country; Chinese organizations are not yet using such services. Most local outsourcing consumption tends to be of ITO and processing services. However, locally owned Chinese companies are reluctant to fully embrace the ITO services offered in their own country.
- The talent crunch affecting many sectors of China's economy is even more prominent in the emerging outsourcing sector.

China's potential as an outsourcing leader

In contrast to China's challenges, our research uncovered myriad advantages in China's mission to become a centre of outsourcing activity. Respondents widely agreed that price currently ranks as the nation's premier advantage, even though nearly a third of those surveyed expect this differential to be eroded over the next few years as China's cost structure grows more burdensome. China's status as a global manufacturing centre also offers unique advantages when providing offshore R&D services. And the nation benefits from its long time investment in education for all.

The research also shows that China's outsourcing providers have a potent competitive advantage, thanks to China's proximity (both geographical and cultural) to Japan and Korea. Indeed, many Chinese service providers are targeting Japan and Korea for future growth.

In addition, respondents expressed great confidence that the country's outsourcing providers will quickly improve in key areas such as talent acquisition and development, service quality, reputation and branding and intellectual property rights protection. Benefiting from almost 30 years of economic reform, China has built a solid foundation for the opportunities ahead. The nation's transportation, telecommunications and network infrastructures have grown rapidly and improved consistently, some achieving the quality seen in developed countries. High-speed Internet access is standard in all of China's largest metropolitan areas, backed by an uninterrupted dual power supply. Approximately 150 airports now connect most of the primary and secondary cities. Also, in developed regions such as the Pearl River Delta, the Yangtze River Delta and the BoHai Bay area, industrial clusters form a firm foundation for the transfer of service and outsourcing skills.

Critical next steps for China

Our research confirms that China views its burgeoning outsourcing industry as a crucial component of the nation's future economic growth and has committed the government at all levels to providing strong political and economic support for outsourcing development. Yet government officials and business leaders alike are realistic about what it will take to achieve success. They are constantly aware that India is China's most formidable competitor in providing global outsourcing resources. They know that, to be a serious contender in this market, Chinese providers must continue to improve the fluency of their business English and the strength of their management skills. These leaders know that new service providers must fully grasp the contract, legal and sourcing frameworks of Western multinational corporations (MNCs). Although due diligence and security measures can limit many sources of risk exposure for its customers, China must continue to strengthen its legal system, improve intellectual property rights protection, and encourage companies to obtain international standards certification if they are to lure reluctant global consumers and establish China as a serious global outsourcing player.

China's positioning in the global ITO and BPO landscape

Scope of outsourcing

Although almost any business service can now be outsourced, the areas of greatest activity in China are information technology outsourcing (ITO) and business process outsourcing (BPO). We focus on these areas, but with some discussion also devoted to the trend toward knowledge process outsourcing (KPO) as a high-end outsourcing offering and an ancillary service to BPO, as well as to contract research organizations, a type of outsourcing with more established roots in China. Just as the outsourcing marketplace changes dynamically, so does the scope of the term "services outsourcing". ITO, for example, is defined differently by many different vendors and clients. In general terms, ITO refers to the outsourcing of IT processes in order to deliver IT-related products and services such as custom developed software applications, and management or maintenance of IT assets such as data servers.

Similarly, BPO is subject to many different interpretations. Gartner, the market research firm, defines BPO as "the delegation of one or more IT-intensive business processes to an external provider that, in turn, owns, administrates and manages the selected processes based on defined and measurable performance metrics", including enterprise services such as finance and accounting, human resources, supply management, demand management and operations. On the other hand, many companies use the term BPO to refer to certain types of business processes provided and managed by specialist service providers. The business processes tend to be operations-oriented rather than strategic; they are typically higher volume and lower-margin processes in terms of profitability and rarely involve a business's differentiating core activities.

The forces driving the emergence of the multi-polar world – the rapid growth of emerging economies, closer economic integration across geographies, and unparalleled advances in information and communications technologies – are transforming the global outsourcing landscape. In a world that now sources services from multiple locations, China has aggressive plans to ensure that a significant portion of global outsourcing spending will flow to its coffers. The following two sections draw on Gartner research data to present the current and future ITO and BPO spending landscapes.

Analysis of the global outsourcing market for ITO

Despite instability in the global markets during 2009, the data suggests that the value and scale of bulk outsourcing contracts will continue to grow steadily. Gartner recently forecast that total revenue for ITO spending, including discrete IT services, will rise to $829 billion in 2012 compared to $592 billion in 2007, while total IT outsourcing revenue will reach $378 billion in 2012 compared to $261 billion in 2007 (Gartner, "Forecast", 2008).

As Figure 3.1 shows, despite the relatively small size of China's current market, it will most likely demonstrate the most dramatic compound annual growth rate from 2007 to 2012. By contrast, the US and Japan, which boasted larger market shares in 2007, will probably experience less ebullient growth, with Japan moving at the slowest rate. However, the overall focus of the global ITO market will remain in Western Europe, the USA and Japan, owing to the considerable size of these countries' spending base, which accounts for nearly 83.2 per cent of the global total in 2007 and is forecast to hover at 79.5 per cent in 2012.

As for the Asia Pacific region, the Gartner data predicts that demand, particularly from Japan, Korea, Australia/New Zealand, Singapore and Hong Kong, will experience remarkable growth, tripling in 2011 from 2006 levels owing largely

Region	Service	2007		2012		CAGR 2007–2012 (%)
		Market size ($millions)	Market share (%)	Market size ($millions)	Market share (%)	
Western Europe	IT outsourcing	94,234	36.1	133,750	35.4	7.3
	Discrete IT services	122,739	37.0	159,167	35.3	5.3
	IT spending	216,973	36.6	292,917	35.3	6.2
US	IT outsourcing	92,266	35.4	126,295	33.4	6.5
	Discrete IT services	107,991	32.6	143,661	31.8	5.9
	IT spending	200,258	33.8	269,957	32.5	6.2
Japan	IT outsourcing	32,571	12.5	43,569	11.5	6.0
	Discrete IT services	42,680	12.9	52,574	11.7	4.3
	IT spending	75,252	12.7	96,143	11.6	5.0
Asia Pacific	IT outsourcing	15,592	6.0	24,468	6.5	9.4
	Discrete IT services	26,217	7.9	40,181	8.9	8.9
	IT spending	41,809	7.1	64,648	7.8	9.1
Latin America	IT outsourcing	10,047	3.9	23,355	6.2	18.4
	Discrete IT services	11,386	3.4	21,281	4.7	13.3
	IT spending	21,433	3.6	44,636	5.4	15.8
Others	IT outsourcing	16,037	6.2	26,807	7.1	10.8
	Discrete IT services	20,416	6.2	34,296	7.6	10.9
	IT spending	36,453	6.2	61,104	7.4	10.9
Total	IT outsourcing	260,747	100.0	378,244	100.0	7.7
	Discrete IT services	331,429	100.0	451,160	100.0	6.4
	IT spending	592,176	100.0	829,405	100.0	7.0
China	IT outsourcing	1,073	0.4	2,904	0.8	22.0
	Discrete IT services	4,845	1.5	10,083	2.2	15.8
		5,918	1.0	12,987	1.6	17.0

Figure 3.1   Forecasted ITO spending is on the rise
Source: Gartner, Forecast, Outsourcing, Worldwide, 2007–2012.

to cost and competitive pressures in the financial and high-tech industries. European countries are finally increasing their focus on developing offshore and nearshore capabilities, and spending on outsourcing has risen, especially in France and Germany.

Gartner also forecasts that discrete outsourcing contracts, such as application development services, will continue to constitute the bulk of outsourcing spending in the near future. Analysts expect custom application development to see the strongest growth, with significant growth from outsourcing of systems upgrades and rebuilds as well.

On the IT outsourcing spending front, discrete IT services still account for the largest portion of the market, followed by data centre, network and enterprise application (Gartner, "Forecast", 2008). Application development, network and desktop outsourcing, and systems integration work will continue to constitute the bulk of IT service imports in the Asia Pacific region. The largest markets, which necessarily hold the greatest potential, are hosted application management (AM) in Australia; network, desktop and application outsourcing in India; network and desktop outsourcing in China; and Information Systems (IS) outsourcing in India, China and Malaysia.

Most offshore contracts still centre on discrete application development and maintenance. Yet within the global ITO market, Accenture and CCIIP have found that the trend is for clients to purchase higher-value-added, integrated, outsourced services in order to reduce the costs of their routine services. These more sophisticated, strategic services are increasingly driving outsourcing decisions. The demand for integrating ITO and BPO services is growing as clients seek to reduce the complexity of their processes, strengthen the governance functions of outsourced contracts, and feed strategic growth opportunities. Technological developments that facilitate remote project management have made the integration of ITO and BPO not only possible but profitable.

Gartner's findings also suggest that many small and medium enterprises first engage in offshore ITO as a means to grow their businesses and compete with the resources of larger companies.

The global outsourcing market for BPO

On the BPO front, Gartner reports that global spending reached $156 billion in 2007 and is expected to reach $239 billion by 2012, with a compound annual growth rate of 9.0 per cent (Gartner, Outsourcing Worldwide, 2008). In terms of total BPO spending, Gartner believes the USA will hold on to its position as the largest market in the world for the purchase of business outsourcing services for the next five years, with a market size of $92 billion (59.1 per cent of the total) in 2007 and $138 billion (57.7 per cent of the total) in 2012.

The data indicates that demand management will be the fastest growing BPO outsourcing category in the US market; within that category, customer selection and customer acquisition services will grow strongly. Other fast-growing categories will be enterprise services, such as human resources and payment processing, and supply management, which includes procurement. Enterprise services will continue to be the largest part of the outsourcing market with 41.8 per cent market share in 2012 compared to 42.4 per cent in 2007. Worldwide, the trend is more or less the same: the only significant difference will be in operations services, such as healthcare operations, which are the third fastest-growing BPO category globally (Gartner, "Forecast", 2008).

According to Gartner, Japan will comprise the next largest global market for the purchase of business outsourcing services but show the lowest five-year compound annual growth rate among the leading markets, at 5.7 per cent. The Asia Pacific region as a whole (excluding Japan) will show a five-year compound annual growth rate of 12 per cent from 2007 to 2012, followed by 15.5 per cent for Latin America, 13.2 per cent for the Middle East and Africa, and 12.7 per cent for Eastern Europe.

Although China's share of the BPO spending market remains small, it is growing steadily and rapidly, spurred by the nation's strong economic growth. Gartner anticipates that BPO spending in China will jump dramatically in the next five years, from $273 million in 2007 to $721 million by 2012, with a five-year compound annual growth rate of 21.4 per cent. For now, though, most of China's outsourcing business is nearshore, with only a fraction in offshore outsourcing.

The BPO industry has kept pace with the increasing sophistication of clients in multinational and multifunctional engagements. Cost is still a major driver for companies looking to outsource non-core business procedures, but clients may uncover even greater savings by using outsourcing to create economies of scale across conglomerates. As a result, in parallel to the ITO market, BPO providers are evolving beyond simple and isolated tactical processes toward strategic, cross-functional, and higher-value-added services. Thus, new models of service delivery, such as bundled outsourcing (see below), are born out of necessity.

By 2012, the USA will still be the world's largest client for outsourced services; it will account for about one-third of worldwide demand for ITO services and more than half of overall BPO demand (Gartner Group, 2008). A significant part of that spending will flow to China; some market-watchers expect China's outsourcing revenue to show average annual growth of 25 per cent.

In general, the outsourcing market in China is still at an embryonic stage and has not yet developed a robust field of outsourcing providers (see also Chapters 1 and 2). China remains predominantly an exporter, rather than a consumer, of BPO services; most of the nation's domestic outsourcing consumption tends to involve IT outsourcing and processing services. Even when consuming ITO, however, Chinese corporate clients show only limited acceptance of broad suites of ITO services, preferring to pick and choose discrete services. Contract values remain small. We now look in more detail at the Chinese service provider landscape.

The Chinese service provider landscape

An increasing number of China's local service providers are obtaining international certifications and qualifications, narrowing the gap with foreign rivals and allowing them to compete seriously for significant offshore contracts. These certifications have made an impact on the numbers. By 2006, of the approximately 80 Chinese software companies with more than 1,000 employees, 35 boasted annual sales greater than 1 billion RMB compared to only 12 in 2002.

By the end of 2006, 38 software companies had obtained Capability Maturity Model Level 5 CMM5 (including Capability Maturity Model Integration Level 5 CMMI®5), the highest level certification. Twenty-three had won CMM4 (including CMMI®4) certification, and more than 200 had obtained CMM3 (including CMMI®3) certification. In addition, 2,136 Chinese companies ranked as qualified system integrators. The results of our survey showed that more than 60 per cent of Chinese local providers had obtained CMMI®3 and about 44 had won ISO27001 – a clear indication that more and more local providers have noticed the importance of international certifications and improved their delivery capabilities.

Leading global BPO and ITO vendors that establish joint ventures or plant branches in China are also hastening the maturing of China's BPO and ITO capacity. In 2006, two of the 20 organizations worldwide that published their Level 4 achievements were in China, as were 16 per cent of those announcing CMMI® Level 5 certification (Eltschinger, 2007).

China's outsourcing sector is consolidating rapidly. Numerous mergers and acquisitions (M&A) occurred in 2006 and 2007. This M&A surge is a predictable outcome of the rapid growth of China's outsourcing sector. In turn, that growth has been accelerated since late 2007 because of injections of venture capital – from local financiers such as Legend Capital as well as large, non-Chinese sources of capital such as Citigroup. Many service providers, such as CDG and VanceInfo, have experienced more than two rounds of financing already.

Providers are starting to offer more types of outsourcing services. More and more of China's ITO service providers have been expanding into BPO services, and vice versa. Within the ITO category, there is a strong focus on application outsourcing. With BPO, the push is on customer relationship services. As a result, in both cases, the services provided by China's vendors remain narrowly focused. Given the burgeoning demand for the services these providers currently offer, and the management attention they require, local providers will find it challenging to move up the value chain, expand their services, and compete with those firms offering more profitable services such as R&D and full-suite services (see Figures 3.2 and 3.3).

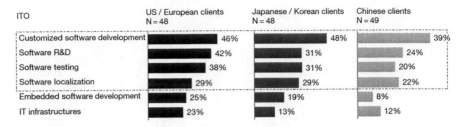

Figure 3.2   Market breakdown by outsourcing type, ITO

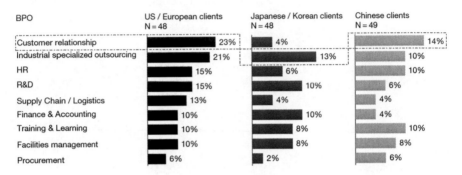

Figure 3.3   Market breakdown by outsourcing type, BPO

Most local service providers started as traditional software companies or systems integrators. Then they entered the ITO market, and now some have begun offering BPO services. Our survey results reveal that the wave of home-grown ITO outsourcing activity in China precedes that of BPO activity. Many of the current BPO service providers started out as traditional software companies or systems integrators and entered the outsourcing sector as opportunities opened up in the market. The new players, such as CDG and ICSS, which began as systems integrators, now have gained rich industry experience that they can leverage to offer services in specialized industries. However, a truly deep understanding of specialized business processes will separate the long-term survivors from their less capable rivals.

Indian service providers are China's biggest competition (see below). More than half of the local Chinese outsourcing provider respondents cited Indian service providers as their most formidable global competitors. Next on the list of rivals come the China-based MNC outsourcing providers. Recently, many top Indian outsourcing vendors have set up offices and established joint ventures in China, stoking local providers' competitive sense. However, many opportunities remain for Chinese providers to vie successfully against the Indian players. Despite their achievements in other markets, many Indian providers have faced cultural challenges in China, leaving an advantage for Chinese providers to exploit. In addition, both Chinese and Indian firms must keep a watchful eye on burgeoning competition from outsourcing providers originating from Mexico, Russia and Eastern Europe.

Both Chinese providers and MNC providers view quality of services as important. Respondents to our survey were asked to list the factors that are critical, important and neutral to their business development efforts and their future success, as gauged by both MNC providers and Chinese providers. Critical factors include: quality of service; security and intellectual property protection; and the ability to quickly understand the clients' specific needs. Important factors were: price; a skilled workforce that can meet demand; having good communication channels with client; industry experience; and reputation. Neutral factors listed were: good understanding of our business culture; foreign language ability of workforce; low talent attrition; scale of service provider; and geographic proximity.

Neither group appears to have a clear competitive advantage in the area of quality of service. Survey respondents ranked MNCs as offering superior service to clients but stated that China's providers have the upper hand on price. Survey respondents ranked the two groups equally on critical factors such as the ability to quickly understand clients' needs and having a skilled workforce.

China's outsourcing providers worry most about talent and cite three major barriers to their development: lack of suitable talent with specialized technology backgrounds (e.g., knowledge of SAP), lack of a strong brand and lack of capital, in that order (see Figure 3.4). Their lack of strong brand recognition globally is also a matter of concern for many Chinese outsourcing providers. While the Chinese government has pushed to promote the image of the Chinese outsourcing industry in general, the effort has been undercut to some extent by the individual promotional campaigns of specific Chinese cities – a factor that respondents to our Accenture-CCIP survey believe wastes public resources.

Attracting and retaining talent remains a top issue. Outsourcing providers we surveyed feel hampered by the competition for talent in their ability to scale their operations in outsourcing hubs, particularly Dalian, Beijing and Shanghai. However, these Tier One cities remain the hubs for outsourcing activity because of their proximity to clients, superior industry infrastructure and stronger talent bases, among other reasons.

In a related concern, providers told us they struggle with talent management, particularly when it comes to their employees' acquisition of foreign language skills – and especially business English. Providers also grapple with the soaring costs of retaining top talent. The retention pressure may experience some relief from recent efforts by China's Ministry of Commerce, such as allowances to companies for their staff training or recruitment expenditures. However,

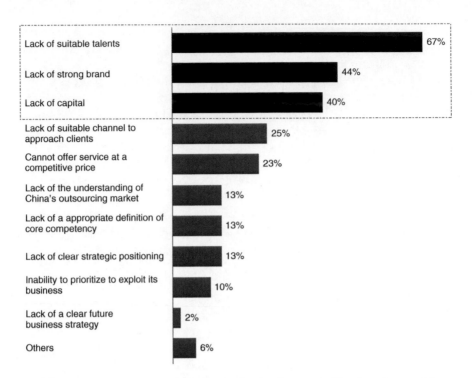

Figure 3.4   Barriers that currently constrain the development of local service providers

turnover rates are still not at the high levels faced by most Indian outsourcing providers in their local market.

In general, attracting and retaining management talent is becoming more critical as the local outsourcing providers grow rapidly and they have to compete for relatively limited qualified human resources compared to the expanding speed with other players, including other service providers in the market and other organizations which also need staff with similar skills. Some companies have already recruited senior executives from large MNCs. A significant group of service providers surveyed are considering shifting delivery locations to inland and western areas of China to reduce employment costs. The research survey indicates that 55 per cent of respondents are considering making this shift in order to reduce the costs of retaining talent.

There are three major reasons for this trend. First, as some multinational clients relocate to China's Tier Two cities (Chengdu, Xi'an, Tianjin, Hangzhou, Wuxi, Wuhan, Nanjing, and others defined by the Chinese government), they create demand for high-quality, fast-response services nearby. Second, providers can use their local environments to improve margins quickly, since labour costs, facilities and taxes are generally lower in China's inland provinces. And third, the governments of Tier Two cities are more likely to offer incentives to attract

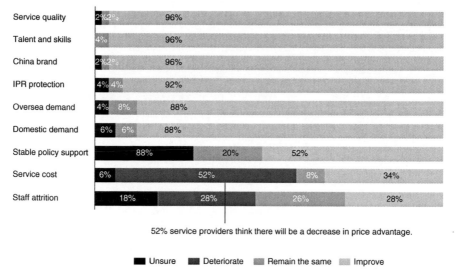

52% service providers think there will be a decrease in price advantage.

■ Unsure ■ Deteriorate ▓ Remain the same ▒ Improve

Figure 3.5 Respondents' views on the future of China's price advantage (N = 51)

investment from MNCs and local outsourcing vendors. However, the management teams of outsourcing providers must compare carefully the considerable costs of relocation against the benefits. Such costs may weigh heavily on smaller firms and may be feasible only for the larger service providers.

Quality and reputation will climb, but China's pricing advantage will probably not endure. According to the survey data, outsourcing providers believe that, within the next five years, China in general and the outsourcing sector in particular will have made noteworthy strides in quality of service, quality of talent, reputation and intellectual property rights protection. Yet more than half of respondents think the gains will probably be at the expense of Chinese providers' pricing advantage (see Figure 3.5).

Analysis of service provider landscape by product offering

Information technology outsourcing

From a technical standpoint, China's software companies have yet to match the sophisticated, high-value offerings of their global competitors because they lack the necessary skills and experience. Like those rivals, they too will have to experience the three key stages of maturity: localization and globalization; testing and application development; and software R&D. They can expect their profit margins to improve with each step of maturity.

For now, though, thousands of types of software products need to be localized, and a rich opportunity awaits China's outsourcing providers. Although the margin at this stage is not especially impressive, many global service providers, including leading Indian vendors, are targeting China's huge localization market. If outsourcing providers can match their business models to the appropriate cost structures and skills mixes, they could enjoy promising growth in the market for localization services for some time to come.

At the same time, local outsourcing providers have a golden opportunity in the IT upgrades demanded by the many levels of government in China. Many agencies are investing in relatively straightforward upgrades to their existing management information systems and concurrently evaluating and implementing new systems. These less ambitious projects typically span system development and systems integration as well as maintenance services.

Although this basic-level ITO holds many attractions for China's outsourcing providers, it should not prevent them from striving to deliver higher-value services. However, as a rule these providers still have much skill and experience to gain, and attracting and retaining talent for these more complex services may prove doubly difficult. Planning for growth into these high value markets is vital for the future of China's outsourcing industry.

Business process outsourcing

As earlier chapters also confirmed, China's BPO market remains in its earliest stages, and the country stands largely as a BPO exporter rather than a large consumer of domestic BPO activities. The major local BPO consumers are MNCs in China, and the secondary consumers are financial services companies.

According to survey respondents, one reason for the lack of BPO growth from in-country consumers is that most local enterprises still struggle in deciding which services to outsource and which to retain in-house. Respondents also point to the limited number of qualified and powerful local BPO service providers in China as a hindrance to the industry's growth. However, BPO in China holds plenty of promise. Buoyed by the nation's overall economic growth, the sector will receive a boost as the Chinese government promotes the nation's IT sector and its telecom industry, and as reforms and restructuring begin to sharpen the competitiveness of China's financial industry. A brief overview of the status of China's BPO market follows.

> *Finance and accounting*: Accounting firms dominate this segment of BPO in China. Clients mainly outsource repetitive, easily automated back-office functions, such as ledger entries, data entries, financial record management, and so on. In the financial services industry, much of the BPO demand is to outsource finance and accounting services.
>
> *Human resources (HR)*: Recruiting, staffing and HR service centres lead the way. Staffing will drive the major growth, as a shortage of workers with the right skills at the right cost in the right places becomes more acute. More

and more local companies are turning to headhunting companies to find senior managers with strong leadership and management skills.

Training and education: Outside the MNCs' China offices, this survey found little spending on training and education in BPO. However, as soft skills increase in importance in the workplace, training and education will necessarily become more complex and costly. As a result, we expect to see a healthy market for speciality providers of these learning BPO services.

Procurement: This segment remains quite small. Although other global markets make strategic use of this area, in China, the BPO procurement providers focus on less complex tasks such the outsourcing of transactional, repetitive and administrative activities related to purchasing, sourcing and procurement spend management. As such, procurement offers a potential area for BPO growth in China.

Client relationship management: Call centres tend to dominate this segment and there is a further discussion of call centres below. The players include pure call centre outsourcing providers such as China Center for Information Industry Development (CCID), companies' own call centres (such as Lenovo's), and local telecom carriers like China Telecom. Consumers look increasingly to call centre certification when choosing a provider, though cost efficiency, process efficiency, service quality and security remain critical criteria as well.

R&D: Survey respondents mainly brought up research and development services in reference to contract research organizations, which is discussed below.

Supply chain/logistics: The fast development of third-party logistics services is a significant BPO trend. However, this is still a very small business in China, which is in the early stage of the BPO industry and needs more education and popularization.

Industry-specific outsourcing: These kinds of outsourcing services can help clients attain high performance through both cost savings and process efficiency enhancements – at least as long as China remains a relatively low-cost place to do business. In financial services, for example, the scope of outsourcing opportunities has grown from relatively simple account data entry work to all but the very core banking processes. Credit card processing serves as a prime example in this sector. Often, service contracts will package several outsourcing processes. For example, a card processing service deal may include account origination services, credit checks, business statistics and bill printing.

Huge opportunities await in the banking sector in China, thanks to significant domestic demand. In particular, China's own banks face challenges in managing enormous growth in demand for credit cards, fostering an increasing need for these outsourcing services. The sections below provide more detailed views of two highly interesting facets of BPO in China: call centre and contract research services.

Call centre services

The call centre industry fits into three groups: in-house call centres, outsourcing call centres and ASP (application service providers). The term "outsourcing call centre" usually refers to the complete turnkey service, from client service and sales and marketing to equipment lease and operations management, while "ASP" refers to the providers that lease others' equipment and technology. With more than ten years of rapid development, outsourcing has now become the mainstay of the entire call centre industry worldwide. Japanese and South Korean companies are increasingly transferring the implementation and management of their call centres to China and enormous potential demand lies in China's domestic market.

Since the late 1990s, the outsourcing market of China's call centres has been cultivated by the local providers who gradually accumulated operating experience, trained staff and climbed the learning curve. Years later, along with some providers updating their equipment, they began to build their brands, and started to see profits against steady revenues. In recent years, second-generation call centres have begun to emerge, the market started to mature, and in the economically developed cities, market competition became fierce. And since 2007, this industry has been accelerated by demand from the 2008 Olympic Games, the 2010 World Expo, and a proliferating array of conferences and trade fairs. At the same time, falling equipment costs have encouraged many enterprises to start building their own call centres.

Several factors will exert a drag on the rapid development of the call centre industry in China. First, a sense of what constitutes best-practice service remains hazy within the industry. Limited operational management expertise exists within call centres. And high staff turnover and a lack of talent continue to plague providers.

Contract research

China is already well known as a "world factory" in the pharmaceutical industry. According to the data from China Chamber of Commerce of Medicines & Health Products Importers & Exporters, its companies produce more than 300 billion tablets a year and over 70 billion capsules. In 2005, China's exports of pharmaceutical raw materials totalled US$7.9 billion, accounting for a quarter of the global market, while the number already increased to $US 10.6 billion in 2006. Much of that volume was shipped to multinational clients. But now, China hopes to become an even stronger competitor in the contract research organization industry.

Contract research organizations (CRO) first appeared in the USA some years ago and companies such as Quintiles, Covance and MDS Pharma have held the top three spots in the field for a long time. Asia Pacific companies became involved in the CRO business because of the continent's cost advantages. Japan boasts a well-developed industry (where the largest provider is EPS, founded by China native Yan Hao) with a significant presence in both Singapore and India.

China joined the CRO sector relatively recently. In 1998, China's State Food and Drug Administration (SFDA) set up a series of new laws and regulations governing drugs, especially the "Clinical Trials of Drug Quality Control", which directly galvanized the development of the CRO market. The SFDA classifies CRO service providers into four main organizational types: universities and not-for-profit public research institutions managed along academic lines; foreign-owned CROs, founded mainly by multinational contract research organizations or with foreign capital; local CRO companies such as Excel and NewSummit Biopharma; and joint ventures such as KendleWits and EPS.

Some, such as WuXi PharmaTech, are focused on pre-clinical research during the research and development of new drugs, mainly involving work on related chemicals, such as preclinical pharmacology and toxicology tests. Others, like KendleWits, specialize in clinical trials. And others are engaged in advisory services for R&D on new drugs, such as new drug approval.

The CRO business deals in large numbers. The future of isolated CROs looks uncertain; many small players are struggling for want of funding and talent. One solution for these smaller firms would be to raise funds through overseas listings on public markets – a move that would help China build a healthy core CRO industry. In early 2005, Shanghai established a base of biomedical outsourcing services as well as the Pudong biomedical research and development outsourcing centre. At a Chinese medicine development summit meeting in July 2006, 22 organizations, including the Beijing Pharmaceutical Group and Zhongguancun Life Sciences, teamed up to form the Zhongguancun CRO Union. Currently, there are more than 300 large and small CRO companies in China, presenting an array of choices for foreign customers.

The challenge for China's CRO industry is its youth. Local vendors still lack extensive experience, and other nations provide significant competition. Very active contract research organizations from India and the USA are eager to establish firm footholds in new markets before China's CRO sector matures. India is especially well positioned to compete, with more than 220 universities and extensive use of English-speaking researchers. India's CROs have also benefited from the country's well developed software industry. Good database management and rigorous R&D process management have strengthened their advantages. And India has a strong cost incentive: clinical trials there cost about three-fifths of what they cost in the USA.

Indian contract research organizations also attract orders from multinational pharmaceuticals based on their quality and efficiency. India has 61 manufacturers authorized by the US Food and Drug Administration (FDA), the largest number outside the USA. For the foreseeable future, Indian contract research organizations will be the most formidable competitors for their counterparts in China.

Of course, the Chinese contract research organizations offer cost advantages as well. Clinical trials in China cost about one-third of the price tag in the USA. However, the best market opportunities for China's contract research organizations will be won by those that quickly can achieve good laboratory practice standards (GLPS) and good clinical practice (GCP). With China's integration into the global clinical trials system, an increasing number of valuable projects will move to China. Contract research organizations that cannot provide sufficient database capacity and sound management of clinical trial processes will gradually lose out.

Analysis of service provider landscape by industry

According to Gartner, the financial services and communications industries together accounted for nearly half of all IT spending in China in 2007 (see Figure 3.6). The manufacturing sector also served as a major client. Our survey of Chinese IT outsourcing providers paints a similar picture of the spread of

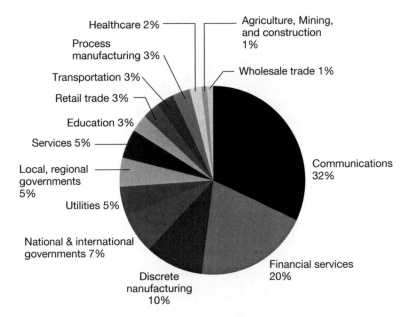

Figure 3.6   IT services spending in China segmented by industry
Source: Gartner MarketView Database, IT Services Market Metrics, 2008.

client spending by industry. Financial services rates highly worldwide, with the media and entertainment industries in the USA and Europe spending significantly, and the communications industry and government sector in China spending notably.

BPO in the financial services sector possesses some unique characteristics compared to other industries. Barriers to entry are high, and potential providers will face daunting requirements for fast, reliable and secure information infrastructure as well as a demand for top-notch talent. Financial institutions tend to be sensitive to outsourcing pricing. And client relationships develop largely in stages: first, software development and services; then data centre management, and eventually, in some cases, internet banking.

China's BPO outsourcing providers offer several advantages to financial services clients. First, the Chinese government offers strong levels of support: In May 2006, the government founded the Research Center of Financial Outsourcing Services – the Chinese outsourcing industry's first base for financial information services – in Shanghai Bank Card Industry Park. China UnionPay, Bank of Communications, Industrial Bank, Shanghai Futures Exchange, and other financial institutions already have moved their credit information centres and settlement centres to this new industry park. China also presents financial firms with a sound business environment. This is particularly crucial in the area of financial services BPO, which usually requires significant time to implement, test and fine-tune processes.

However, some obvious obstacles stand in China's path, such as a limited system of credit, the high costs of cheque processing, the risks of unreliable data, and the need to develop sound oversight mechanisms. While progress is being made on all of those fronts, China still must travel some way down the road of progress before it can boast truly world-class financial services outsourcing capabilities.

Clients for China's outsourcing services

As of 2009, most consumers of outsourcing work in China were MNCs. However, China's state-owned enterprises (SOE) were starting to embrace outsourcing as well.

Our research uncovered several interesting insights with regard to outsourcing clients in China. First, potential clients lack a clear understanding about outsourcing, which indicates opportunities to raise awareness and provide education in the market. Second, these prospective clients express substantial distrust of the relatively immature outsourcing market in China. Only a third of those surveyed currently are outsourcing or planning to do so in the next three years – a strong indication of the reservations these clients feel about local outsourcing providers' value, expertise and control of confidential information.

Among those companies already outsourcing, the survey results indicate that key criteria for choosing providers include service quality, intellectual property rights protection, skilled workforce and industry expertise. Existing outsourcing clients believe that outsourcing helps them to cut costs and improve processes; and most are satisfied with their service providers. The most critical factor in the success of an outsourcing project is the compliance of the service provider with the service level agreement (SLA).

Chinese clients surveyed also agree with providers that China has a particular advantage in outsourcing over Japan and Korea – culturally and geographically as well as in terms of cost. Further, they agree that China will rapidly improve in terms of talent, quality of service and reputation for reliable outsourcing services that deliver high performance.

China's outsourcing providers' client base

So where do China's international outsourcing clients come from? The Accenture-CCIIP research indicates that about 44 per cent of current (2009) outsourcing revenue comes from the USA and Europe, with 34 per cent from Japan and Korea, and roughly 20 per cent from Chinese clients.

The research shows that China's outsourcing providers, generally speaking, have not yet selected one target market as their priority for the next five years. The Japanese market will grow at a steady rate, while the European and North American markets will continue to be the main outsourcing segments. China's domestic market also holds significant promise for local outsourcing providers. Figure 3.7 gives an overall market outlook breakdown by client groups, based on the responses from local outsourcing providers.

Markets	Market Size	Market Share	Potential	Profitable	Risk[14]	Competition
US	Largest	Small	Big but need substantial effort to develop the market	High	High	Intense
Japan	Large	Large	Middle as the growth of the total market size due to system upgrading of many Japanese companies	Middle	Low	Moderate
Domestic	Small	Middle	Great but need relatively long period promotion of outsourcing concept	Middle	Low	Moderate
EU	Middle	Small	Hard to say as the market is strongly influenced by government policy	Highest	High	Intense
Korea	Small	Middle	Good	Middle	Middle	Moderate

Figure 3.7   Outsourcing outlook by market

China's outsourcing market: notable phenomena

In our work we noted a number of further interesting developments, namely: MNC use of shared service and R&D centres; the widespread use of sub-contracting; the expansion into designated parks and cities; and the talent situation together with the training policy response. We now examine these in more detail.

Multinational corporations' shared service centres

MNCs are establishing shared service centres in China to support their global or regional business operations. In a shared service environment, common supporting functions are consolidated rather than spread across an enterprise. Implementing a shared service model requires changes in business processes, infrastructure and even corporate culture. Yet the model brings big benefits: organizations gain a better understanding of their entire business operation, enabling them to analyse, change and optimize the services they provide to internal clients. Additionally, companies that leverage shared services can real-ize increased flexibility in instituting business changes, more manageable costs and greater control. Large corporations often implement the shared service concept as a last step when readying themselves for outsourcing. Accordingly, China has witnessed an increase in MNCs establishing regional shared service centres in tandem with the growth of its outsourcing industry.

Multinational corporations' research and development centres

In recent years, foreign enterprises have established and expanded their R&D centres in China. According to the Ministry of Commerce, there are currently more than 800 R&D centres in China founded by multinational enterprises from North America, Europe, Japan, South Korea, Taiwan and others. These centres focus on several manufacturing industries, including electronics and communication, transportation, and pharmaceuticals and chemicals.

The R&D centres are concentrated in big cities – such as Beijing, Shanghai, Shenzhen and Tianjin – although the Western cities like Chongqing, Xi'an and Chengdu are drawing new R&D centres, owing to their lower costs. Increas-ingly, firms are founding R&D centres as sole proprietorship enterprises. Only a few centres have been founded as joint ventures, including those for Lenovo and Intel, and Motorola and HuaWei.

China has become a vibrant region for R&D centres for several reasons, including the vast potential of the Chinese market, improvements in the investment environment, and the lower cost of R&D talent. Currently, R&D centres in China mainly engage in technical support and applied research to develop products that are adapted to the Chinese market. However, owing to the Chinese government's efforts to encourage independent innovation, the

R&D centres of MNCs are starting to track emerging new technologies and autonomous local standards. As they cultivate increased technical power and accumulate research and development experience, more MNCs will most likely upgrade their R&D institutions into global research centres.

The use of subcontracting in outsourcing

Subcontracting in outsourcing – typically referring to the transfer of work from MNC service providers to China's local providers – is a notable trend. MNCs that typically subcontract in China include IBM, Capgemini, CSC, HP, Bearing-Point, Fujitsu, NEC and NTT. Key findings from the survey of service providers appear below.

- Half of the providers surveyed are using subcontracting as a means to access talent and skills.
- The primary reason for providers to subcontract is to focus on their core outsourcing business, followed by making use of other suppliers' specialized skills.
- For the service providers interviewed in this survey, the three main criteria in selecting a subcontractor are service quality, workforce skill and IT security.
- Respondents acknowledged that, while subcontracting improves efficiency and costs, its major drawback is lack of quality control.
- As a result, subcontracting could have a negative impact on outsourcing, because quality is the key criterion for clients.

Designated industry parks and cities

In line with the 1000-100-10 Project, the Ministry of Commerce – in conjunction with the Ministry of Information Industry, the Ministry of Science and Technology, and the Ministry of Education – has named a group of major metropolitan areas as designated outsourcing cities. The cities were chosen based on their capacity to undertake offshore outsourcing. Similarly, the Ministry of Commerce has named a group of state-level showcase areas – including national economic and technical development zones, high-tech parks and software parks – that it hopes will play a pivotal role in promoting the outsourcing business of the designated outsourcing cities and surrounding areas.

To date, 14 designated cities and four state-level showcase areas have been chosen. Dalian, Chengdu, Shanghai, Xian, Shenzhen, Beijing, Tianjin, Nanjing, Hangzhou, Jinan, Wuhan, Hefei, Guangzhou and Changsha comprise the cities, and the showcase areas are Suzhou Industry Park, Wuxi huan-taihu Protection Zone, Daqing Outsourcing Industry Park and Nanchang High-tech Development Zone.

The designated cities and state-level showcase areas will enjoy support from China's central government in the form of macroeconomic policies, investment and coordination. In addition, special purpose funds will be earmarked for the construction of public information platforms, the development of HR, the improvement of infrastructure and the investment environment. Most of the designated cities have also issued local policies to promote the outsourcing industry.

Industry parks are an important enabler for the outsourcing industry. Our survey results identified four factors cited by more than 50 per cent of respondents who have moved to an industry park as benefits they sought when choosing their location. Respondents listed, in order of importance: favourable policies, available talent supply, support from local government and reduced operating costs. For service providers that have not moved into industry parks, high migration costs seem to be the main factor keeping them away.

The designated cities and industry parks are making significant efforts in support of China's outsourcing industry. From an infrastructure and technology perspective, many have reached the level of developed countries. However, several requirements that are essential to the outsourcing industry, such as intellectual property rights protection and business convenience, have not yet been sufficiently addressed.

In addition, this study determined that the management body of the cities and parks must shed its current role in the mould of a real estate developer, in which it merely aims to offer sound infrastructure and lower costs. Instead, it must focus on improving the cities' and parks' ability to meet the needs of the outsourcing industry – offering everything from financial support to laws to protect intellectual property rights.

Another challenge is the lack of substantial differentiation among the 14 designated cities and four showcase areas. Investors often feel confused when selecting a delivery location and fierce competition between cities and industry parks vying for investments compounds the problem. As a result of these hindrances, it may take a long time for China's outsourcing industry to achieve truly diversified development.

Talent: situation and policies

Outsourcing is a talent-intensive industry: its forward development is contingent upon the appropriate talent supply. Yet, according to the Accenture-CCIIP survey, the lack of suitable talent has become a bottleneck in China, and respondents considered it one of three major barriers to the development of service providers, the others being lack of a strong brand and lack of capital (see Figure 3.8).

Although China produces numerous graduates every year (according to data from the Ministry of Labour and Social Security, the number of college

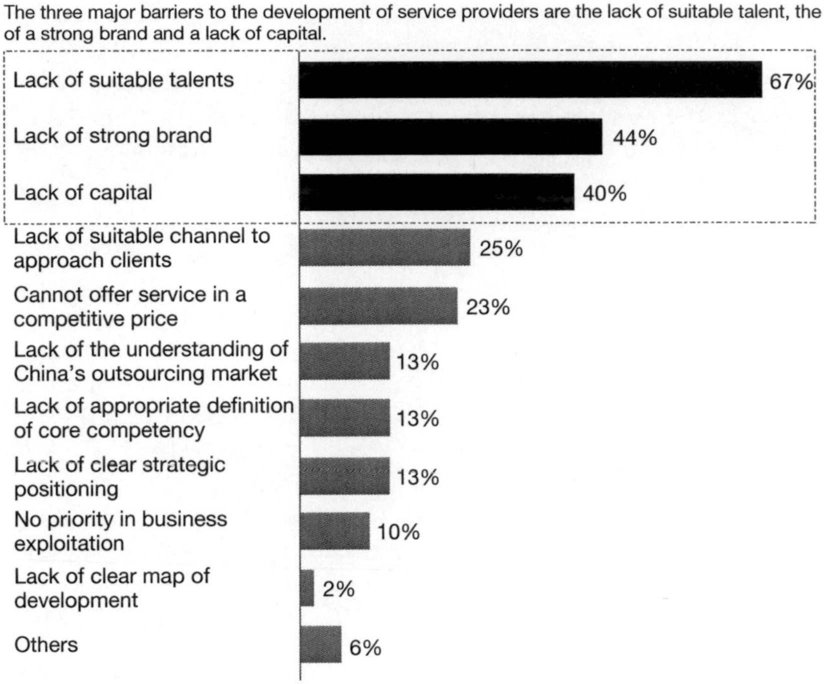

The three major barriers to the development of service providers are the lack of suitable talent, the lack of a strong brand and a lack of capital.

Lack of suitable talents	67%
Lack of strong brand	44%
Lack of capital	40%
Lack of suitable channel to approach clients	25%
Cannot offer service in a competitive price	23%
Lack of the understanding of China's outsourcing market	13%
Lack of appropriate definition of core competency	13%
Lack of clear strategic positioning	13%
No priority in business exploitation	10%
Lack of clear map of development	2%
Others	6%

Figure 3.8   Barriers to the development of service providers (N = 48)

graduates was over 4.9 million in 2007) and has achieved progress in reforming its higher education sector, problems still remain, especially in its curriculum design and teaching methodology. A gap exists between what is taught in universities and what is required by the market. This burdens employers with extra training costs. In fact, for the majority of respondents, employee training absorbs from 5 per cent to 20 per cent of their total operating costs. The survey respondents also indicate that, in terms of talent management, lack of language skills and high retention costs pose major problems (see Figure 3.9) Moreover, as noted previously, 55 per cent of respondents are considering shifting their low-end delivery centres to inland and western areas in order to reduce their talent retention costs.

To overcome the shortage of talent, the Ministry of Commerce has included in its 1000-100-10 Project a goal to train 300,000 to 400,000 people for the outsourcing industry and create outsourcing jobs for 200,000 to 300,000 graduates within five years. Starting in 2007, the Ministry of Commerce, in association with the Ministry of Finance, began to allocate funds from the Central Development Fund for Foreign Trade to support the training of outsourcing talent. Through this initiative, service providers in outsourcing delivery

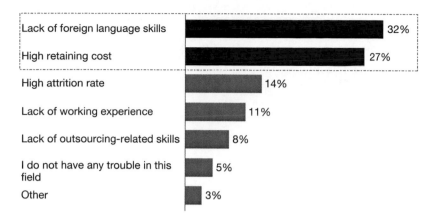

Figure 3.9 Talent management challenges

hubs, as well as qualified companies listed in the Ministry of Commerce's key outsourcing enterprises directory, receive government support to reduce their training costs. In addition, training institutions, including institutions of higher learning, are encouraged to train talent for the international outsourcing business.

In another government effort, qualified outsourcing enterprises may receive a fixed subsidy of not more than 4500 RMB for each new university graduate with whom they sign a labour contract for at least two years. Qualified training institutions will receive a fixed subsidy of not more than 500 RMB for each outsourcing trainee (college graduate or above) who passes a test of professional knowledge and skills and signs a labour contract of more than two years with an outsourcing enterprise.

In August 2007, the 1000-100-10 Project group of the Ministry of Commerce signed a cooperative agreement with the Tianjin Economic and Technology Development Zone to jointly establish a state-level outsourcing training centre in Tianjin. At present, other local governments also have submitted applications to the Ministry of Commerce to build state-level outsourcing training centres. The Tiajan training centre was designed to integrate various resources of the Ministry of Commerce, local government, MNCs, and leading enterprises in the industry; create and improve a customized training model; develop a talent training programme to meet China's needs; create a human resources network; and facilitate the operation of outsourcing HR pools. The centre is run on a non-profit basis and is open to the public. It enrols college students who will graduate in the current year as well as unemployed graduates for assessment and training in fields related to the outsourcing business. It also trains technical and management personnel for every level of the industry.

China and the global services market: Three trends to watch

Trend 1 – Knowledge process outsourcing (KPO)

The traditional outsourcing delivery model has been to disaggregate high volume and labour-intensive processes to offshore locations where they could be completed at much lower costs. However, with the growth of the MNCs and increased global competition for talent, the offshore outsourcing market has begun to move beyond the arbitrage of simple labour and capital to the offshore transfer of knowledge as well.

While cost reduction remains a major benefit of knowledge process outsourcing (KPO), it is not the primary focus. Unlike ITO and BPO, KPO extends an organization's reach to all parts of the world, where it may access talent in its various forms: creativity, experience, independent thinking and specialized skills. Instead of simply performing disaggregated functions, KPO teams directly support companies' core businesses. Therefore, it is critical that KPO services retain the benefits of data and IT integration, physical security, and legal protection typical of onsite services. Depending on the industry, licensing concerns may present a significant barrier to successful KPO.

Financial services and market research dominate the current KPO market, but significant potential awaits in animation, data, education, engineering, legal, pharmaceutical and tax services. Industry experts anticipate that India will capture the majority of the global KPO market, although the country's talent shortage is likely to hamper its progress.

As China moves up the value chain and expands its service economy, it faces the opportunity to enter the KPO market. However, significant challenges lie in its path. Although China is producing impressive numbers of university graduates, its education system still needs to adjust. To win a larger share of KPO contracts, China must cultivate creative, independent and critical thinking, as well as communication and teamwork skills, in its current and future workforce.

Trend 2 – Bundled outsourcing

Many enterprises have already achieved the vast majority of the performance improvements that can be obtained from a single-function approach to shared services and outsourcing. Scaling up and expanding the scope of outsourcing initiatives beyond single business functions requires an approach called "bundled outsourcing". Bundled outsourcing means consolidating multiple business functions and their underlying IT systems with a single service provider and guiding the whole approach with a common system of governance.

As organizations have matured in their experience with outsourcing, bundled outsourcing is fast emerging as a strategy used by business and government executives to drive greater value from their IT and business processes, and to

improve business performance and increase bottom-line savings as they jour-
ney toward high performance. Executives are seeing the need to gain economies
of scale across multiple business functions and to optimize end-to-end business
processes that cross functional boundaries.

One common example is to bundle the finance and procurement functions,
along with the applications supporting them, under a single provider. Other
companies may bundle finance and HR, learning and HR, or other key functions in different combinations appropriate to their needs, often bundling a
particular function or business process with the underlying applications and
infrastructure management. This trend suggests that China's provider commu-
nity will need to offer multiple services and technology capabilities to address
the needs of the largest global corporations. Certainly, bundling multiple functions into a single outsourcing contract can present its own unique challenges.
However, with new kinds of governance models and a more effective supplier
portfolio strategy in place, organizations can use bundled outsourcing as a
means to achieve high performance.

From the clients' perspective, the bundled outsourcing model enables executives to coordinate the outsourcing of disparate business functions by sharing
resources, applications and platforms. Providers may bundle BPO and ITO services to offer additional value to clients' operations through the rationalization
of the common underlying business applications and IT infrastructure. Bundled outsourcing also addresses the challenge of governance and eliminates the
need to manage various providers and contracts.

Trend 3 – Indian companies in China

Since Tata Consulting Services first entered China in 2002, other Indian
outsourcing companies have followed suit, building a solid and significant presence of Indian companies there. Since 2004, these Indian firms have set up their
own full-scale development centres across China, formed strategic partnerships
with both global MNCs and local players, built solid bases of support within
the various levels of Chinese government, and aggressively expanded their talent base. At present, Indian outsourcing companies employ several thousand
people in China and are planning to expand significantly by the year 2010.

The Indian players do not merely view China as a low-cost delivery location
from which to serve the local operations of many of their biggest multinational
customers from the USA and Europe. They also see China as a springboard
for the Japanese and Korean markets. And they have identified the value of
Chinese corporations with global operations as potential clients, such as the
Bank of China, China Mobile and PetroChina. Tata Consulting Services, Infosys
and Wipro provide a glimpse of the China activities of three leading Indian IT
outsourcing providers.

Tata Consulting Services

Tata Consulting Services (TCS) was the first Indian outsourcing firm to launch its China strategy by establishing a Shanghai office in 2002 (TCS Overview, 2008). A year later, TCS set up a Global Development Centre in Hangzhou, a representative office in Beijing, and an Oracle 11i technology centre in Shanghai. Then, in 2007, TCS partnered with Microsoft and three local, government-backed software companies to set up TCS China, which focuses on the financial services, telecom and government sectors. The total cash investment of the joint venture is estimated to be US$14 million.

TCS China follows a "research first, business second" approach: invest in research and technology centres to build a solid foundation, then leverage this foundation to obtain global contracts and local business (China Tech News, 2004). Since 2006, TCS has invested more than $10 million in China. This outlay has not only served as an indication of the company's ambitious strategy, but it has also proved to the Chinese government that TCS is committed to the Chinese market.

Over the next few years, TCS plans to expand its Chinese operations, increasing the number of employees to 5000 and setting up subsidiaries in new cities, with Tianjin, Guangzhou and Xi'an named as contenders. It will expand its vertical industry roster beyond financial services and telecom to include airlines, automotive and general manufacturing. TCS also hopes to enhance its position in the Japanese and Korean outsourcing markets, despite facing difficulties in hiring Japanese and Korean language speakers in Shanghai and Hangzhou. In addition to outsourcing, TCS plans to move into the fields of engineering and Six Sigma process consulting to serve China's large manufacturing base. TCS also will explore well established small, local, industry-oriented outsourcing companies (with 50 to 100 employees) as acquisition targets to drive its growth.

Infosys Technologies

Infosys Technologies (China) Co. Ltd (known as Infosys China) is a fully owned subsidiary of Infosys Technologies Ltd. Headquartered in Shanghai, Infosys China began operations in 2003 with the goal of building a world-class delivery hub in China. With development centres in Shanghai and Hangzhou and a representative office in Beijing, Infosys China now has about 800 consultants providing ITO and BPO services to global and Asia Pacific clients. The Shanghai centre focuses on IT services such as application development and maintenance, enterprise solutions and independent validation services. The centre in Hangzhou specializes in BPO services.

Infosys established its China operations with a relatively modest investment in Shanghai, but two years later, the company committed $65 million to build additional software development centres in Shanghai and Hangzhou. The new facilities are designed for onsite training – a key asset as Infosys China looks to tap the nation's deep talent pool. For its global offshoring work, Infosys China offers a cost-competitive delivery hub for customers interested in alternatives to India-based outsourcing. The company handles large enterprise solutions using SAP and Oracle platforms, and it offers Infosys's own core banking solution, Finacle, which can be deployed in large and mid-sized banks. In 2007, Infosys China became the first company in China to achieve CMMI® Level 5 (V 1.2). In the same year, the company was certified to ISO 27001 standards in order to alleviate the security and intellectual property concerns of its global customers.

Wipro Technologies

Wipro got its start in China in 2004, establishing a 50-seat development centre in Shanghai. Its initial customer base consisted of the Chinese offices of many of Wipro's global customers, with an emphasis on the localization of software, implementation and support services. But Wipro has consistently taken the long view toward serving China's domestic markets and addressing the needs of its Japanese customers in China. For instance, since 2004, it has completed two pan-China roll-outs of SAP applications in multiple cities for Olympus and for Sanyo.

Wipro has moved rapidly to expand its footprint in China. Its multiple delivery centres in the Shanghai area and Beijing cater largely to the growing needs of multinational customers' China operations. The company is currently planning a major expansion of its China operations and is likely to grow from a few hundred people based in China to 2,000 by the end of the decade. But Wipro's long-term plans call for capitalizing on China's enormous base of talent, setting up software development centres, and pursuing Chinese clients (IDG, 2008).

Conclusion

For China's outsourcing providers, today's multi-polar world presents two windows of strategic opportunity. First, providers may benefit from the influx of MNCs that have been drawn to China by its impressive economic growth. China already rules as the world's largest market for mobile phones, televisions and cars, and the nation is poised to become the biggest consumer market overall by 2025 (EIU 2008, Accenture analysis). MNCs come to China with deep experience and sophisticated operations, and they bring with them the capacity and desire to outsource services on a large scale. The Chinese outsourcing industry has the opportunity to capture a significant portion of these contracts.

Chinese vendors also may add value for MNCs by supporting their other Asia Pacific operations. The Asia Pacific markets are expected to continue to demonstrate the fastest ITO and BPO growth of any region, and China already enjoys geographic, cultural and linguistic advantages in serving the Japanese and Korean markets. China's outsourcing providers may use these opportunities as a springboard for regional expansion. And if they can translate and scale those experiences, effectively matching world-class standards, they will be perfectly positioned to compete worldwide.

Second, China's outsourcing providers may grow by serving domestic companies that conduct business abroad. Just as MNCs seek new opportunities in China, many leading Chinese companies are entering overseas markets. The Fortune Global 500 list contained 24 Chinese companies in 2007, up from 20 in 2006 and 16 in 2005. China's outsourcing vendors have a golden opportunity to leverage their existing relationships, local experience and resources to partner with these Chinese companies and serve overseas markets from their base at home.

These factors create unique prospects for short- and mid-term growth in China's outsourcing market, which are unequalled by any prospects enjoyed by its global rivals. To succeed in both of these scenarios, Chinese providers must develop capabilities that align with their clients' specific needs. They must evolve the ability to provide bundled services and end-to-end process management offerings that are tailored to the breadth and sophistication of their clients' operations, in areas such as application management, customer relationship management, finance and accounting, HR management and procurement.

Despite its bright prospects, China must uphold its end of the bargain in order to realize its potential. Already, China has begun making massive investments in public education and infrastructure and is reaping the dividends of a decade of support for English and technology education. By contrast, competitor India faces basic infrastructure bottlenecks and struggles to manage a limited supply of labour and salaries driven up by unmet demand. NASSCOM, an Indian software industry association, predicts an IT industry labour shortage of 500,000 by 2010. With the benefit of steady government backing, Chinese universities produced 575,000 engineering graduates in 2006 alone – almost twice as many as India's universities, allowing China to steer clear of labour problems at this stage.

Significant challenges remain for China's outsourcing industry. In an era of increasing economic openness, China will not be able to rely solely on its cost advantage. Its lower-end manufacturing companies are in the midst of learning this sobering lesson. China's ability to scale hinges on the quality, not the quantity, of the output from its education system. Despite increasing numbers of graduates, China's workforce must continue to improve its English language and management skills as well as gain a better understanding of the contract, legal and sourcing frameworks of Western MNC operations. In addition, while due diligence and security measures can limit risk exposure and help to persuade reluctant MNCs to outsource to China, the country also must continue to strengthen its legal system, improve intellectual property rights protection, and encourage service providers to obtain international standards certification.

China's success also depends on a political climate that favours continued economic liberalization, allowing labour and capital to move more freely. A slowdown in the Chinese economy may disrupt the country's social development and governance. If economic opportunities raise the nation's fortunes, however, an unintended consequence might be sky-rocketing incomes in Tiers Two and Three Chinese cities, which would have a significant impact on operating costs in businesses across the country.

As always, outsourcing investments are only as safe as the risks inherent in the host country and its market. If China can meet its opportunities with excellence in quality and a strategic commitment to growth, it can avoid the fate of becoming a destination for simple labour arbitrage. Success in the new global economy will not be easy. But China has the potential to become one of the world's leading outsourcing hubs.

Appendix 3   A note on methodology

In tandem with the 1000-100-10 Project, the China Council of International Investment Promotion (CCIIP) formed a partnership with leading global management consulting, technology services and outsourcing company Accenture to sponsor a wide-ranging research programme. The programme was launched with three key audiences in mind: potential customers that may outsource more to China; service providers, both Chinese-owned and foreign; and China government officials. The research programme had these key objectives:

- to provide a strategic review of China's outsourcing market, with data on market size and growth opportunities over the next five years;
- to assess and compare the roles of both China-owned and multinational outsourcing providers in China's domestic market;
- to assess and compare the roles of China-owned outsourcing providers in global markets;
- to showcase some of China's leading outsourcing providers using in-depth case studies.

The research was designed and led by an Accenture team of industry researchers and outsourcing experts. It involved two multiple-choice surveys. The first survey, asking 43 questions of outsourcing clients, queried senior managers at local Chinese companies, MNCs' China operations and the global headquarters offices of MNCs. MNCs were defined as companies in which foreign investment comprises more than 50 per cent of the companies' capital structure. A separate 37-question survey was sent to senior managers at locally owned and multinational outsourcing service providers across China.

Altogether, client companies received 140 questionnaires, and 37 (26.4 per cent) responded. Two hundred questionnaires went out to service providers, and 53 (26.5 per cent) responded. The questionnaires were sent by direct mail or email and were followed up by phone calls. All survey responses were confirmed in follow-up phone calls. To supplement the survey findings, Accenture researchers also conducted 15 in-depth interviews with executives across China's outsourcing industry.

References

BBC News (2005), "Rover Sold to Nanjing Automobile," 23 July. http://news.bbc.co.uk/2/hi/business/4708739.stm.

China Tech News (2004), *TCS Focuses On China Market*, 22 September. www.chinatechnews.com/2004/09/22/1829tcs-focuses-on-china-market/.

Eltschinger, Cyrill (2007), *Source Code China: The New Global Hub of IT (Information Technology) Outsourcing*. New Jersey, John Wiley & Sons.

Gartner Group (2008), *Forecast: Outsourcing, Worldwide, 2007–2012*. Gartner Group, New York.

Gartner Group (2008), *Market View Database, IT Services Market Metrics*. Gartner Group, New York.

Huawei (2006), *Huawei accepts 3Com's bid offer to purchase its stake in H3C*, 29 November. www.huawei.com/news/view.do?id=2332&cid=42.

IDC (2007), BPO, Offshore, "Worldwide offshore key horizontal business process outsourcing services 2007–11 Forecast and Analysis."

IDG (2008), "India's Wipro plans big expansion in China," 26 February 2008. www.networkworld.com/2008/022608-indias-wipro-plans-big-expansion.html.

TCS Overview (2008) Worldwide Locations, "China". www.tcs.com/worldwide/asia/locations/china/Pages/default.aspx.

4
Outsourcing in China: Lessons Learned

Wendell O. Jones

Introduction

This chapter is more management focused and provides an additional perspective on the management practices that promote outsourcing success. It evaluates the cultural dimensions that complicate the management of outsourcing in China, identifies the strengths and weaknesses of Chinese IT workers and managers and provides guidelines on how to evaluate, select and manage Chinese suppliers.

On some counts, information technology outsourcing (ITO) exploded from $9–$12 billion in the early 1990s to an estimated $200–$250 billion in 2008. Business process outsourcing (BPO) is estimated to grow from $140 billion in 2005 to $350 billion by 2010 (Willcocks and Lacity, 2009). Information technology is still the function outsourced the most, but if the estimates come true, BPO – now the fastest growing – will soon overtake ITO. Combined, they are estimated to approximate $600 billion at the end of 2010. The business processes most often outsourced offshore and nearshore include finance and accounting, call centres, human resources, legal services and related business processes. IT-enabled services (call centres and help desk services) lead the BPO segment (Willcocks and Lacity, 2009; Lacity, Willcocks and Rottman, 2008).

China and India are two of the more popular destinations for offshore contracts, but lately a number of other countries have entered the market. The Philippines, Singapore, Vietnam, Russia, Ukraine and other Far East countries have emerged as interesting alternatives to China and India. Clients in the USA use Central American suppliers in Costa Rica, Nicaragua, El Salvador, Guatemala, Honduras and the Dominican Republic for Spanish-speaking call centres and help desks. European companies are outsourcing to Eastern European countries, particularly the Czech Republic, Hungary, Poland and Slovakia (Lacity, Willcocks and Rottman, 2008). One of the latest types of outsourcing is knowledge process outsourcing (KPO). KPO requires a significant amount of domain knowledge and analytical skills. KPO suppliers collect data, mine and analyse data, write reports, and perform similar knowledge-based functions. The KPO market is still small, but industry analysts are predicting considerable growth (Lacity, Willcocks and Rottman, 2008).

This chapter explores what to consider when evaluating outsourcing opportunities in China. We extract lessons from information collected during two ten-day trips to China with delegations of business executives from the USA and Europe. Both delegations visited software centres in various metropolitan locations, mainly in Beijing and Shanghai areas. During both trips, we engaged in formal and informal discussions with Chinese executives, government officials, and American executives doing business in China. We visited 20 Chinese software companies and attended formal presentations by 34 Chinese software executives. Information for this chapter was also extracted from research papers, business articles and other sources produced by an extended network of outsourcing researchers, advisers and practitioners. Finally, this chapter draws on the author's 20 years of experience as an outsourcing buyer, supplier, writer, analyst, adviser, speaker and trend watcher.

Overview of outsourcing in China

China appears to devour Western know-how and technology while simultaneously behaving like the world's largest start-up and turnaround. Typical of a start-up, many actions are trial and error: making it up on the run, copying products and practices, and sprinting to capture the market first. But China is also a turnaround in that entrepreneurial power has been unleashed in a nation formerly smothered by Communism. Some China observers have compared the country's recent changes to what the USA experienced over several decades, starting with the robber barons of the 1800s and extending through the speculative financial mania of the 1920s, the rural–urban migration of the 1930s, the middle-class consumerism of the 1950s, and the social upheavals of the 1960s. In a way that is similar to the USA in the 1950s, this is the time for the first car, first college graduate, first owned home and first vacation for increasing numbers of Chinese families.

The Everest Group estimated that the Chinese offshore services market was $2 billion in 2006 and expected to reach $7 billion by 2010 (Bahl, Arora and Gupta, 2007; see also Chapter 3 for other sources). China is increasingly attractive as a destination for ITO and BPO because China has proved that its manufacturing capabilities are among the best and the cheapest in the world, and the Chinese government has made huge investments in information technologies and communication infrastructure (Lacity and Rottman, 2008). Meanwhile, companies around the world see a huge market opportunity with China's population growth and shifting demographics.

The demand for IT services in China is magnified by the huge internal requirements for skilled service workers to meet the needs of the country's booming economy, modernize the government, and fulfil the service needs of thousands of multinationals that have set up manufacturing bases on the mainland. Since the adoption of favourable industrial policies by the government in the turn of the 21st century, the core of China's software industry has grown with the development of national software bases, national software export bases and more than 170 national key software enterprises. During our first delegate visit to China in 2000, many of the modern software parks were ready for occupancy but vacant. In the ensuing years, Chinese software companies grew in number and revenue, gained experience working with customers in Japan and other Asian countries, and improved their software engineering skills.

At time of writing, in 2009, most of the Chinese software companies have reached CMM levels 3–5 of the maturity model, but much of the Chinese outsourcing experience has been limited to providing software and back office support for neighbouring Asian countries. Chinese call centre operators can talk to people in Hong Kong and Taiwan, and many workers speak Japanese and Korean. Owing to a large concentration of Japanese-speaking people in Northeastern China, most outsourcing clients for China are from Japan. On some estimates, more than 60 per cent of China's offshore software revenue is from Japanese companies. China's software companies specialize in modular programming and testing for the high tech and financial services industries, and a growing number of BPO companies provide back office processes, such as call centres, accounting and other financial functions.

Differences in offshore outsourcing

A number of important factors must be considered when outsourcing to any foreign country. The types and levels of risks with offshore sourcing are one such factor. Geopolitical risks and disaster recovery, for example, are more important considerations when planning to take work offshore. Differences in the business environment, cultures and values also call for different styles of management and ways of communicating across cultures.

Typically, few resources and assets (people and infrastructure) are transferred to the offshore service provider. This means that the customer company is not likely to get cash infusion for the "sold assets". Similarly, for the service provider, the upfront investment can be higher, as fewer assets are transferred, and both parties are faced with training and documentation requirements for knowledge transfer. Additionally, intellectual property and privacy protection, labour and employment laws, and legal requirements for cross-border data transfer further complicate the legal issues and introduce more risk. The operating model for offshoring is different, due also to the possibility of 24/7 operation and the implications for changing the working hours of the onshore people engaged with the offshore delivery team (Carmel and Tjia, 2005).

Potential differences in the quality of offshore infrastructure and resources mean that due diligence is even more important for offshore locations and offshore service providers. Similarly, because the processes and methodologies for managing offshore outsourcing are immature and less understood, the skills required to manage offshore outsourcing are in shorter supply. Lastly, there is the need for more direct involvement of senior management for both management effectiveness and public awareness. Offshore outsourcing may, for instance, engender adverse publicity that only senior management is positioned to address with the advice of public relations specialists.

Features that distinguish offshore outsourcing

Offshore and domestic outsourcing, then, are different. The features that distinguish offshore outsourcing are culture, distance and time zones. National culture includes language, traditions, customs and norms of behaviour. Distance and time zones refer to the geographical dispersion of the offshore and onsite workers and the corresponding differences in time zones (Carmel and Tjia, 2005; Jones, 2005).

A broad definition of national culture encompasses customs, norms of behaviour, ethnic traditions, national traditions and language. Cross-cultural outsourcing presents opportunities for increased productivity, but also the possibility of more problems. The potential problems are usually poor communications and lack of cohesion, while the positive is increased productivity with a 24/7 working week. According to most communications specialists, non-verbal cues (posture, gestures, eye contact and greetings) and contextual information provide most of the meaning in communications, and the actual spoken words account for a small part of the total. This presents outsourcing managers with a challenge – non-verbal cues rely on culture to convey meaning, but non-verbal cues are difficult to convey electronically over the Internet, telephone, or office video. On the positive side, however, diversity offers the potential to blend ideas, encourage fresh perspectives, develop new ways of thinking and produce better solutions. This is the energy and synergy that offshore outsourcing managers need to harness.

The geographical dispersion between offshore locations and other sites directly impacts on communications in a number of ways. Communication is less spontaneous and less frequent. Distance affects communications between the supplier's managers and the customer's managers, between remote workers and their managers, and between the developers and the users and business analysts. Distance affects all aspects of coordination and control. A traditional team of IT workers in the USA usually relies on informal coordination without many commands and formal controls. Since informal coordination is communications intensive, dispersion of the team members offshore means that face-to-face communication and coordination and informal controls no longer fit. Dispersed teams cannot build cohesion when separated by thousands of miles. Managers can no longer manage by walking around talking to team members. Distance forces communications into electronic channels, which are less rich than face-to-face methods. Americans appear comfortable building relationships electronically, but some cultures are uncomfortable about relationships over electronic media unless a personal relationship already existed (Carmel and Tjia, 2005).

Time-zone differences add more problems to the communications process. Normal working hours in certain parts of the USA do not overlap with normal working hours in China. This requires one location or the other to compromise, as a phone call, conference call, or video conference poses impositions for one of the parties. When I managed operations in Europe, my US boss would invariably schedule calls at a time convenient for everyone in California, but during my normal evening hours to relax and prepare to go to bed. Rotating the times to share the inconvenience is a better approach, but my hints never seemed to sink in, or if they did, the headquarters people were more influential. The persons who are not near to the centre of power are usually inconvenienced, and invariably they are the same people responsible for getting the work done.

Lessons learned

This section explores lessons learned about offshore outsourcing in China, taking a North American perspective. The central focus is what North American and Western European companies need to know when evaluating China as an outsourcing destination. Companies already involved in an outsourcing arrangement in China should also find the lessons informative and useful. The references are important sources for more in-depth information, as most lessons require more detail that can be covered in one chapter.

Lesson One: Chinese culture is different

Language, values and other differences in national cultures come powerfully in to play when outsourcing in China or any foreign country. Cultural differences complicate communications and often lead to misunderstanding. Hofstede (1980, 1983, 2009) was the first researcher to identify the dimensions of national cultures. He found that there are significant differences in cultural environments between the USA and other national cultures. He surveyed 116,000 IBM employees in 40 countries and concluded that national culture has a major impact on an employee's work-related values and attitudes. Hofstede concluded that people vary on five dimensions of national culture – power distance, individualism vs. collectivism, quantity vs. quality of life, uncertainty avoidance and long-term vs. short-term orientation.

Hofstede defined power distance as the degree to which people in a country accept that power is distributed unequally. It ranges from relatively equal (low power distance) to extremely unequal (high power distance). High power distance means that the people revere hierarchy, or if it is not revered, the people are careful to show proper respect to the boss and careful about sharing their opinions with superiors. In some cultures, people see large gaps between levels of the organization.

A personal experience that serves as an example of the differences in power distance was the offshore contract of NASD with an Indian supplier, TCS, in the late 1990s. Our delivery model called for locating about 30 Indian employees on site in Maryland, and another hundred or so in India. As an American senior vice-president, it was my habit to walk around the buildings on Thursday afternoons talking to employees and encouraging people to express their concerns or speak their mind. Our American employees were accustomed to freely letting the managers know what they were thinking, and/or sharing work-related ideas. But what seemed natural with Americans, failed with the Indian employees. My informal conversations with the Indian programmers were guarded, and clearly uncomfortable for the employee. After we chatted, the worker would immediately report the exchange to his supervisor and so on up the chain. As soon as possible, the senior TCS manager would rush to my office to "understand the concerns and document the requirements". Needless to say, senior management ceased wandering around and having informal conversations at the workplace with the Indian employees. We learned that in India power distance is much greater than in the US culture.

Individualism is the degree to which people in a country prefer to act as individuals rather than as members of groups, while collectivism is low individualism. *Quantity of life* is the extent to which assertiveness, acquisition of money and material goods and competition prevail. *Quality of life* is the degree to which people value relationships and show sensitivity for the welfare of others. *Uncertainty avoidance* is the extent to which the people prefer structured rather than unstructured situations. People in countries with a long-term orientation look to the future and value thrift and persistence. Short-term orientations value the past and present and emphasize respect for tradition and fulfilling social obligations.

There are important differences between US and Chinese cultures. The USA has a short-term orientation, places high values on individualism, emphasizes quantity of life, tolerates some uncertainty and perceives a short power distance. China and most Asian countries are exactly the opposite. Asians value collectivism and quality of life, demonstrate a strong need to avoid uncertainty, maintain a long-term orientation, and view power distance as very unequal.

With domestic outsourcing, differences in organizational cultures often introduce issues. Offshore outsourcing further introduces differences in religious beliefs, cultural values and standards of behaviour that often confuse people and complicate the relationship. Mixing a conflict-avoiding, consensus-oriented culture like China with a hard-driving, individualistic culture like the typical US company is a recipe that is ripe for misunderstanding and conflict. Different values, customs and languages make clear communications difficult. Cross-cultural training is essential for the people in both companies.

Lesson Two: Chinese business practices are different

In his book, *One Billion Customers: Doing Business in China*, McGregor (2005) contends that business practices in China are unlike accepted business practices in Western countries. He cautions Western executives to remain alert and wary, as there are significant differences in Chinese business ethics and accepted behaviour. The typical Chinese executive or politician is adept at avoiding accountability for their actions or inaction; a conflict of interest for some government officials is considered a competitive advantage, not a constraint; and it is accepted practice for government officials to use their power and influence for personal gain.

Two other differences are the importance of the relationship and the relative unimportance of a written contract. A contract in China may not be enforced, while the relationship is considered the foundation for everything. Relationships develop slowly in China, which means that the Westerner must be patient and avoid the temptation to "sell his or her soul". The Chinese are usually bold enough to ask for anything, which may tempt the typical Western executive to give too much too soon. According to McGregor (2005), a company considering a business arrangement in China needs to understand that a so-called "partnership" usually means that the Chinese attempt to take without giving and to gain access to the technological know-how and intellectual capital of the "partner" company.

It is a misconception to consider China as one monolithic market. China is a collection of many local and regional markets. This suggests that the best strategy is to launch the business at the provincial level and concentrate on developing relationships with local officials. Local contacts may then lead to stronger relationships and supportive advocates.

Lesson Three: People are the key to outsourcing success

Human emotions and feelings are highly important and among the most difficult issues to deal with during an outsourcing process. Everyone is beset with conflicting emotions and differing concerns. Employees with a strong attachment to the current organization and industry may find it hard to think of working for, or with, an outsourcer. The best and most experienced may take their knowledge and skills to another employer immediately. Still others may welcome the transfer and shift loyalties before transferring. Another group may feel inadequate or afraid of change and oppose outsourcing at every opportunity. Therefore, it is important to specify the criteria for the various groups of people, apply the criteria fairly, to decide who should stay, transfer, or terminate, and inform people as soon as possible. Consider incentives for retaining people in the organization either permanently or during the transition. The impact on employees not directly affected by outsourcing also needs to be considered. Remaining staff in other departments may worry that the outsourcing of additional functions is next.

The employees affected by outsourcing deserve frequent and candid communications using various means and media – town hall meetings, small group question and answer sessions, videoconferences, email notes, printed materials, and one-on-one sessions with individuals. As an example, when outsourcing the IT function in a large urban hospital, we prepared and distributed briefing packages for managers in every business and clinical unit to use for presentations to employees. We kept business unit managers, employees and other stakeholders involved on steering committees and teams. We used a hotline and an email facility to respond to employee questions and an Intranet website, which was frequently updated with the latest information. We conducted town hall meetings, led small group question and answer sessions, used videoconferences, sent email blasts, and scheduled one-on-one meetings with employees.

Effective relationship management requires retaining people who can communicate and negotiate inward across organizational boundaries within the company and outward across organizational boundaries and national borders. The dominant descriptors of the best relationship managers are team players, strategic thinkers, negotiators, communicators, consensus builders and analytical problem solvers who understand and appreciate different cultures. The best can think "big picture" and still focus on the details, while consistently fostering a "we", not a "we–they" attitude.

Lesson Four: Disciplined evaluation and selection processes are essential

Working principles for outsourcing foundation, evaluation and selection are provided in Appendices 4a and 4b. The outsourcing process usually begins with detailed planning of the evaluation, selection and implementation actions and responsibilities. A good plan includes detailed milestones and deliverables, clear objectives agreed to by the key stakeholders, profiles of stakeholder expectations, early and continuous involvement of human resources specialists, public relations and legal professionals and the advice and consultation of outsourcing experts. HR professionals reassure and help keep the staff informed; attorneys navigate the complexities of employment and contract law; outsourcing consultants advise, assist and/or programme manage the outsourcing evaluation, negotiation and implementation project; and public relations specialists deal with internal and external constituents (see Cullen, Seddon and Willcocks, 2005).

The major issues for the core team and the steering committee before and during the evaluation include defining the objectives, scope, desired results and metrics; determining the change management process, which can be particularly difficult across borders with multiple work sites; describing which company will be responsible for what work and identifying what work could be performed onsite, nearshore and/or offshore.

The best time to inform the employees that offshore outsourcing is under consideration, and why, is early in the evaluation process. Openness and candour are better than trying to maintain secrecy. Keeping a secret in most organizations is an impossible, and once "the cat is out of the bag", employees lose confidence in anything management says at a time when employee and management involvement are critical.

Senior management needs to agree on the outsourcing objectives, the scope of what is included and excluded, and what work seems best suited for offshore, nearshore, and/or onshore service delivery. Clear outsourcing objectives approved by senior management are necessary for setting the parameters of a detailed analysis, collecting appropriate information for the analysis, developing a request for proposal (RFP), and evaluating supplier responses. Clear objectives are also necessary for analysing and making trade-off decisions. Companies that rush into outsourcing without understanding why, or taking time to identify specific objectives are, usually on a path that leads to a strained relationship and unmet expectations (Klepper and Jones, 1998; Jones, 2008).

One of the early responsibilities of senior management is to identify an executive sponsor who will assume senior leadership, oversee the work of the evaluation and selection teams, and recommend the decision to outsource or not to outsource. The evaluation and selection team requires a mix of managerial and technical skills and people representing user areas whose services will be directly impacted by outsourcing. User perspectives and objectives are essential for setting scope, defining requirements, understanding stakeholder expectations and assessing risks.

The size of the evaluation and selection team depends on the scope and size of the project, but smaller teams (5–7 members) are generally more effective. The team can be small in the planning phase and expanded into multiple subteams when analysis begins. Teams with full-time members are often more focused and effective than teams composed of people who work part time, although full-time allocation may be impractical for small companies. If available, persons with prior outsourcing experience can be invaluable members of the team.

Internal baseline performance data and an understanding of the function under consideration for outsourcing are required to develop the RFP, evaluate supplier proposals and make an informed outsourcing decision. The RFP should not give detailed process flows or suggest approaches, but it should instead encourage the Chinese suppliers to demonstrate expertise and experience in what they propose. After evaluating the responses and deciding if outsourcing in China is still feasible and desirable, the next step is to select two finalists.

Lesson Five: Limit the scope of work to well-defined technical tasks

The projects that Chinese software companies can effectively undertake are limited, as the software workers are primarily coders without business domain knowledge. Many Chinese managers and workers do not understand business terminology and cannot easily communicate in spoken English. If provided with detailed technical specifications and clearly written requirements, the Chinese software engineers can deliver excellent code, but until their English language skills are more fully developed and they gain business experience, it is advisable to assign work that does not require business knowledge and interaction with users or functional analysts, and to limit the scope of work to projects with modular programming, coding, testing and related technical work.

It is essential to fully reference check the Chinese companies with past and current customers and to spend time at the companies observing and asking questions before deciding which to include on the shortlist. Interviews of companies that have previously outsourced to Chinese supplier companies can be a source of valuable information. China has limited experience doing business with American and European companies, and inexperience is fraught with potential problems and misunderstandings. Despite the boundless optimism of Chinese software executives and government officials we met on both trips, many executives in our trade delegation were concerned about intellectual property (IP) piracy. There are some indications that the Chinese government is beginning to take this problem seriously and may enforce laws that protect IP. Considering that most Chinese software outsourcing is low-level programming, however, the threat of IP piracy is probably exaggerated.

The weak English-speaking proficiency of Chinese workers and managers, however, is a serious and legitimate problem for US and Western European companies. Students graduate from Chinese universities with written English training, but few are fluent English speakers. The Chinese government is investing in English-language training to target the ITO/BPO markets. Nonetheless, for the time being, language barriers, cultural differences, and fears about IP piracy remain significant obstacles for Western companies. Once China removes these obstacles, more US and European companies may consider China as a viable and desirable offshore destination.

Shortage of experienced and skilled management of the sort detailed by Feeny, Lacity and Willcocks (2005) is another problem (see also Chapter 3). As the demand for business leaders and project managers increases, many Chinese middle managers remain overwhelmed by the fast-changing environment and the harsh realities of a market economy. Chinese managers grew up expecting never to change careers or locations. Meanwhile, economic progress is touching most business sectors in China and stimulating further change. The combined effects result in powerful forces that make it difficult for Chinese managers to keep pace with the change. This applies as much to the client as to the supplier, so retained client capabilities such as those detailed by Feeny and Willcocks (1998) need strengthening in the Chinese client context (see also Willcocks and Feeny, 2006).

Lesson Six: Effective relationship management is the pathway to sustained benefits

Paying insufficient attention to building a relationship foundation is a common mistake as American companies have a short history of positive supplier relationships. In the not too distant past, customer companies tended to keep an arm's-length relationship with suppliers by awarding short-term contracts to supply items or services according to precise specifications. No thought was given to using suppliers as a source of ideas for improving the business. Supplier relationships in the 1970s and 1980s were tense, if not outright adversarial. The buyer company might engage the same suppliers repeatedly, but there was no assurance of repeat business. Price was usually the determining factor for getting the contract or order, and companies manoeuvred among suppliers to squeeze out the lowest possible price. The threat of switching to a different supplier was the company's primary weapon, and short-term contracts with multiple suppliers were used to promote lively competition.

When outsourcing arrived in a major way in the 1990s these old "arm's length", "give-them-hell" ways of dealing with suppliers were carried forward into how companies dealt with outsourcers. Incomplete outsourcing contracts were written in haste, and the outsourcer usually assumed responsibility for a distressed function for which a scope description or meaningful past performance levels often did not exist. Useful metrics were not specified in the contract and relationship management practices were woefully inadequate. "Keep an eye on them and check the invoice carefully" was the prevailing attitude about how to manage the outsourcing suppliers.

Without metrics or a process in place, the supplier did not feel compelled to report on performance, and the customer managers usually avoided taking joint responsibility. These ways of dealing with suppliers usually resulted in unsatisfactory performance, disagreements over pricing and complaints of underperformance. In the worst cases, these failing relationships degraded into a pattern of complaining, blaming and inflaming (Lacity and Willcocks, 1998, 2001, 2003). Outsourcing researchers discovered, and practitioners eventually learned, that the most successful outsourcing managers valued their outsourcing relationships and treat the supplier as a source of sustained value. Time and resources are devoted to managing the relationship in a manner that builds mutual trust.

Lesson Seven: Barriers to effective communications are amplified across national cultures

The barriers to effective human communications are significant, even among people from similar backgrounds. The most common barriers are filtering, selective perception, information overload, emotions, language and gender.

Filtering refers to the way a sender manipulates information so that it will be seen more favourably by the receiver. Telling the boss what one thinks he or she wants to hear is an example of filtering. Factors which tend to increase filtering include number of levels in the organization and the extent to which organizational rewards emphasize style and appearance, and thereby encourage managers to filter communications in their favour.

Selective perception is selective hearing of communications based on one's own needs, motivation and other personal characteristics. People from different cultures and backgrounds perceive the same events and messages differently.

Information overload is the result of information available exceeding one's processing capability. Information overload causes people to ignore, select out, pass over, forget information, and/or just stop processing it all together. In any case, the result is lost information and ineffective communication. Emotions also play a part. How a person feels when a message is received or sent influences the way it is interpreted. Feeling happy or depressed changes the way a message is received and interpreted.

Gender and language are two other barriers to effective communications. Men and women in the same culture often communicate differently. American women usually communicate to develop a relationship with the other person, while men tend to communicate to solve a problem or demonstrate power. *Language* refers to the different meanings for words. Age, education and cultural background are three obvious variables that influence the language a person uses and the definitions he or she applies to words. The meanings of words are not *in* the words, they are *in us*. Jargon and technical language are two other examples. Senders of messages should not assume that the receiver interprets words and phrases with the same meaning. It is important to avoid slang and jargon when communicating with offshore counterparts. Indians learn British English, not American English; Chinese software workers learn the formal written language, but usually not the jargon, acronyms and slang.

Given that these communications barriers are possible wherever two or more humans gather together, outsourcing managers need to know how to overcome the barriers. *Feedback* is one technique, which is checking the accuracy of what has been communicated or what was heard by restating the words. *Simplifying the language* is a second way. It is essential to use words that the Chinese understand and are less likely to misinterpret. *Active listening* is a third approach, which involves listening actively and attentively for the full meaning of the message without making premature judgements, arriving at quick interpretations, or thinking about what to say in response while the other person is still talking. A fourth technique is to communicate only when *neither person is emotionally charged*. If emotions or tensions are running high, it is best to calm down before attempting to communicate.

Lesson Eight: China is not the only viable alternative to India

In her book, *The Elephant and the Dragon*, Meredith (2007), a foreign correspondent with *Forbes* magazine, describes China and India as the fastest growing big economies on their way to becoming economic giants within a generation. Other China watchers predict that China will become the IT centre of the world in less than a generation, while still others argue that China has too many barriers to overcome. Longer term, China might overtake India and emerge as the dominant offshore powerhouse, but that ascendancy seems unlikely anytime soon. China needs to convince more Western companies that the government is enforcing IP protection, developing enough workers with English-speaking proficiency, and producing project managers with leadership and communication skills.

But even after China makes the needed improvements, India may still hold a commanding lead in skills and experience. Today, ITO and BPO revenue in India is more than 20 times that of China. Applying any objective measure, China lags behind India by 5–10 years, or more (see also Chapter 3).

The trend so far is for the nations of Latin America, Eastern Europe and other regions to offer a wider choice of destinations for offshore outsourcing. The Philippines, Singapore, Vietnam, Russia, Ukraine and other Far East countries have surfaced as interesting alternatives to China and India. ITO and BPO markets are now active in Costa Rica, Nicaragua, El Salvador, Guatemala, Honduras and the Dominican Republic. Many US clients use Central American suppliers in the same time zones for Spanish-speaking call centres and help desks. European companies are outsourcing to Eastern European countries, particularly the Czech Republic, Hungary, Poland and Slovakia (Willcocks and Lacity, 2009).

But regardless of the outsourcing destination, offshore outsourcing is high risk by any standard or measure. Outsourcing failures are inevitable where client companies do not plan well, do not contract wisely, or manage relationships ineffectively.

Conclusion

This chapter explored the rewards, risks, challenges, opportunities and short-comings of outsourcing in China and examined the differences in cultures and business practices that complicate the process. China's major attraction is the potential for significant cost reductions, but other advantages include filling gaps in a client company's capabilities and gaining access to infrastructure and other resources in mainland China. With a market as large as China's, companies are highly motivated to work cooperatively and establish a foothold in the Chinese market.

The worldwide demand for outsourcing and the Chinese government's investment in its domestic software industry are fuelling growth of the outsourcing industry. However, working with China is not like doing business in Western countries, and Western managers must be aware of the differences and wary of the potential pitfalls. The most likely mistake for a Western company is misunderstanding Chinese business practices. Relationships are everything in China, and they cannot be developed hastily. The complexity of the Chinese market is another factor. The Chinese understand the outside world much better than the outside world understands China.

In the author's view, perhaps the most serious shortcoming is the gap between requirements and the skill level of Chinese IT workers. China offers a large number of coders, but most cannot easily communicate face-to-face in English with business analysts and users. If they are provided with detailed specifications and requirements, the Chinese can understand the technical requirements and write the code. Nonetheless, until their English language skills are more fully developed, it is advisable to avoid assigning work that requires business analysis or extensive interaction with users. Programming and related technical skills, rather than functional domain knowledge, are the strengths of the Chinese workers. Another significant weakness is the shortage of experienced project managers (see Chapters 1 and 3 for other perspectives on these issues).

With continued training and heavy Chinese government backing, China may eventually surmount the obstacles and gain more customers outside Asia. Meanwhile, expertise in written and spoken Asian languages gives a competitive edge for China in that region of the world. As Chapter 2 argued, after honing skills in the Asian market and gaining extensive experience from domestic software work close to home, China's outsourcing services capabilities should mature and the industry should attract more global customers. In the final analysis, however, the question should not be whether to outsource to India, China or other countries, but rather how to pursue a global outsourcing strategy that provides the right mix of scale, quality service and cost savings. Unless there are compelling reasons for establishing a foothold in the Chinese market that only outsourcing in China can make possible, companies considering offshore outsourcing are advised to objectively compare China's potential advantages and disadvantages with other nearshore, onshore and offshore destinations.

Appendix 4a   Foundation principles for outsourcing in China

Appoint a core team	Once the decision is made to outsource, identify who will be assigned responsibility for supplier management. These people should be part of the team that crafts the contract. Their inclusion is important, as there is no better way to understand the issues than to be involved in all aspects leading up to the decision. A relationship starts at the moment discussions begin. Remember that the relationship is everything to the Chinese. Similarly, it is a good idea to avoid changing team members. The team that negotiated the contract needs to stay engaged. The Chinese highly value personal relationships developed over a long time.
Establish Executive Steering Group	Early in the evaluation, it is important to establish a steering committee that will take leadership responsibility, evaluate the analysis, approve the decisions, and make recommendations to senior management team and the Board. An executive sponsor usually chairs the steering committee, and those serving on the committee should represent the business units that will be using the outsourced services. An outsourcing initiative driven by the Board of Directors requires the highest possible level of executive sponsorship, even if the scope is narrow.
Understand differences in Chinese business practices	Be aware and wary when doing business with the Chinese. A Chinese executive or politician succeeds because he or she is adept at avoiding responsibility for bad decisions. A conflict of interest is viewed as a competitive advantage. A government official may use power and influence for personal gain.
Develop a clear, complete RFP	A complete, unambiguous RFP is essential to avoid misunderstanding and to clearly define the scope and responsibilities of both parties.
Start locally	The Chinese understand the outside world much better than the outside world understands China. China is not one national market but rather a collection of many local markets. Normally, it is best for foreign companies to first establish

(Continued)

	relationships at the provincial level before concentrating on the national level. The Chinese market is best understood as markets that differ in each province.
Avoid one-sided "partnership"	The Chinese may ask for anything. Accordingly, a company doing business in China must understand that the so-called "partnership" means that China will be trying to obtain the company's technology, know-how and capital while maintaining Chinese control.

Appendix 4b   Outsourcing evaluation and selection process

Define outsourcing objectives and requirements	Develop and gain stakeholder agreement on the outsourcing objectives and why China is a potential offshore location. Define requirements that are detailed and measurable. State requirements in terms of the performance of the customer's organization and its business units, such as how the outsourcing will contribute to business performance.
Link outsourcing performance to compensation	Link the Chinese executive's compensation to the customer's business performance. Align the supplier's objectives and performance compensation with customer objectives wherever possible.
Baseline current and future client company costs	Determine the relevant baseline costs and estimate future costs based on the requirements and baseline. Without a good idea of future needs and the costs of meeting them, it is not possible to outsource effectively and efficiently. Identify all the costs. Some costs may be in user budgets or in multiple supplier charges. Remember that size, complexity, the need for flexibility and newness to Chinese outsourcing raises the costs of managing a Chinese outsourcing relationship and raises the risks.
Use disciplined outsourcing decision process	Prevent the suppliers from short-circuiting the disciplined evaluation and decision-making process by going directly to senior managers or user managers for quick decisions. Be clear and complete in the RFP; you get what you ask for, and no more. Keep the process simple but rigorous. Give each supplier the opportunity to present its proposal in person and answer questions. Set deadlines and enforce them on both parties. Tell the suppliers what they need to know to understand the requirements and effectively respond to the RFP, but do not give them the solutions.

Relationship management best practices	Foster a professional relationship between and with suppliers from initial contacts through contract signing and ongoing. Develop the foundation for an effective relationship and build trust in all dealings with suppliers from the outset. Require suppliers to respond to everything you need to know in order to make a sound decision. Emphasize a win-win attitude from the outset. Set a schedule and insist that all parties stick to it.
Check references and require full disclosure	Check supplier references completely. Require the Chinese suppliers to provide customer contacts with which they have less than an excellent relationship, and check them too. Require full disclosure from both sides.
Qualify the suppliers	Determine if the vendors have domain knowledge – are they financially viable, are contractual safeguards in place to protect IP; can they communicate effectively?
Assign a top programme/ project manager	Assign one of your best. Just like the supplier's project manager, an internal PM/relationship manager is essential to manage the supplier, control hand-offs, ensure accountability, etc.
Concentrate on continuous development of the Chinese service provider's staff	Train the service provider's staff. They need to know the client's culture, how the product or application will work and understand the business context in which it is intended to work.
Implement effective change management processes	Establish a joint change management process. With work taking place on site and offshore, it is essential that a clear and well-controlled change process ensures that only desired and necessary changes are made.
Use disciplined and structured process	Assign work that the Chinese are best qualified to perform. Documented requirements, non-volatile requirements, minimal user interaction and iteration and systems without multiple interfaces to other systems are all best candidates for offshore work.
Plan for each project to take longer and cost more than original estimates	Develop a project schedule then plan for it to take longer. Just like internal projects, the first one or two will invariably exceed estimates. A good guideline is to increase the estimation for the first project by 25–30 per cent.
Encourage the same people to remain with the project from the beginning through implementation	Verify that the supplier people planned to work on the project are the actual persons working on the project. The time spent on training is wasted, the rework will increase and the project schedule will suffer if project staff is permitted to come and go.
Provide the tools, processes, methodologies to support the project	Provide the tools, structure and discipline required for both companies. The offshore and on-site developers need access to source code, defect tracking system, platform applications, structured tools, office video conferencing, etc.

References

Bahl, S., Arora, J. and Gupta, A. (2007), *What's Happening in China*. The Everest Group, ERI.2007,2.W.0172.

Carmel, E. and Tjia, P. (2005), *Offshoring Information Technology: Sourcing and Outsourcing To A Global Workforce*, Cambridge University Press, Cambridge.

Cullen, S., Seddon, P. and Willcocks, L. (2005), "Managing outsourcing: The life cycle imperative," *MIS Quarterly Executive*, 4 (1): 229–246.

Feeny, D., Lacity, M. and Willcocks, L. (2005). "Taking the measure of outsourcing providers," *Sloan Management Review*, 46 (3): 41–48.

Feeny, D. and Willcocks, L. (1998), "Core IS capabilities for exploiting information technology," *Sloan Management Review*, 39 (3): 9–21.

Hofstede, G. (1980), *Culture's Consequences: International Differences in Work-related Values*, Sage. Beverly Hills, CA.

Hofstede, G. (1983), "National Culture in Four Dimensions," *International Studies of Management and Organization*, 13 (2): 46–94.

Hofstede, G. (2009) *Cultural Dimensions* Available at: www.geerthofstede.com/hofstede_dimensions.php.

Jones, W. (2005), "Offshore outsourcing: Trends, pitfalls, and practices (Part I)", and "Outsourcing: Strategies, processes and responsibilities (Part II)", *Cutter Consortium*, 4 (4).

Jones, W. (2008), "Outsourcing: The Critical First Steps," *Outsourcing Magazine*, June, 12–14.

Klepper, R. and Jones, W. (1998), *Outsourcing Information Technology Systems and Services*, Prentice Hall, New Jersey.

Lacity, M. and Willcocks, L. (1998), "An empirical investigation of information technology sourcing practices: Lessons from experience," *MIS Quarterly*, 22 (3): 363–408.

Lacity, M. and Willcocks, L. (2001), *Global Information Technology Outsourcing: In Search of Business Advantage*. John Wiley & Sons: Chichester.

Lacity, M. and Willcocks, L. (2003), "Information Technology Sourcing Reflections," *Wirtschaftsinformatik*, Special Issue on Outsourcing, 45 (2): pp.115–125.

Lacity, M. and Rottman, J. (2008). *Offshore Outsourcing of IT Work*. Palgrave, London.

Lacity, M., Willcocks, L. and Rottman, J. (2008), "Global outsourcing of back office services: Lessons, trends, and enduring challenges," *Strategic Outsourcing: An International Journal*, 1 (1): 13–34.

McGregor, J. (2005), *One Billion Customers: Lessons from the Frontlines of Doing Business in China*. Free Press: New York.

Meredith, R. (2007), *The Elephant and the Dragon: The Rise of India and China and What It Means for All of Us*. W.W. Norton: New York.

Willcocks, L. and Feeny, D. (2006), "The core capabilities framework for achieving high performing back offices," in Willcocks, L. and Lacity, M. (eds), *Global Sourcing of Business and IT Services*. Palgrave: London.

Willcocks, L., and Lacity, M. (2009), *The Practice of Outsourcing: From Information Systems to BPO and Offshoring*. Palgrave: London.

Part II

Research Studies on China's Emerging Outsourcing Capabilities

5
Mediated Offshore Software Services Models in China: A Two-stage Study of Operational Capabilities Development

Sirkka L. Jarvenpaa and Ji-Ye Mao

Introduction

Offshoring of information technology (IT) services involves contracting beyond national boundaries. When services are contracted to independent third parties abroad, the client is critically dependent on a supply of providers (vendors) that have operational capabilities to offer comparative cost advantage, satisfactory quality and on-time delivery in spite of the differences in distance, time zones and culture (Carmel and Tjia, 2005).

China represents an understudied setting, yet an important one for software services offshoring. The Chinese software services industry has been growing and is expected to continue to grow in the coming years (Qu and Brockle-hurst, 2003; Carmel et al., 2008). China's software services outsourcing reached RMB 2.6 billion (about US$340 million) in the first quarter of 2006. During the same quarter in 2007, the market increased to RMB 3.3 billion (about US$430 million) (Analysis International, 2007). The first quarterly revenue increased to RMB3.9 billion (US$570) in 2008 (China Sourcing, 2009).

China-based providers are also an important focus because many of them use business models that are different from those presented in much of the off-shoring literature. The Chinese software services export firms are largely small and medium-sized with heavy reliance on the mediated offshoring business model, whereby a Chinese vendor delivers offshore software services to a larger foreign-based information technology (IT) contractor (vendor) that interfaces with the end-client firms. The mediated business model has both theoretical and practical implications for the development of the operational capabilities in the Chinese software services firms. To survive and grow, these firms must be able to develop operational capabilities that go beyond country-level comparative low labour costs, which are shared by all the Chinese firms and by firms in many other low-cost countries (Qu and Brocklehurst, 2003). Yet, the development of those capabilities is impeded by the business model the firms deploy. Among the limiting factors are small-sized projects, low-value-adding tasks, and limited opportunities to interface with the end-client. The question we explore in this chapter is: How are Chinese firms developing their capabilities in spite of the constraints of the mediated model?

Prior literature has found IT vendor success to be reliant on three types of operational capability: client-specific capabilities, process capabilities and human resources capabilities (Rajkumar and Mani, 2001; Levina and Ross, 2003; Ethiraj et al., 2005). However, all of these studies focused on *large* vendors. The current theories on the development of capabilities also relate mainly to large firms or firms in mature economies (Zollo and Winter, 2002; Zahra et al., 2006). Deciding on what capabilities to build and how to build them are critical managerial choices for any firm, but the decision is especially crucial for small and middle-sized offshore software services firms with a limited resource base. Many capabilities reflect an evolutionary learning process in which an organization needs to invest financial, cognitive and emotional resources for an extended period (Zollo and Winter, 2002). Capabilities development can sap critical resources without commensurate returns and undermine not only firm growth but also survival (Sapienza et al., 2006). Hence, the context of small firms in an emerging economy can benefit both theory development and practice of global services offshoring.

The rest of this chapter is organized as follows. In the next section, we present the background on the mediated model in China, operational capabilities in IT offshoring, and the learning perspective to the development of capabilities. Then, we present the case study research methods. In the fourth section, we present the case analyses, and in the last section, we suggest some theoretical and practical implications.

The mediated business model, operational capabilities and capabilities development

The extant literature on IT service outsourcing covers a broad range of issues but it comes largely from the customer perspective (e.g., Willcocks and Lacity, 2000; Goles, 2001; Willcocks and Lacity, 2006; Tanriverdi et al., 2007; Cha et al., 2008; Gewald and Dibbern, 2009). Much of the literature focuses on client capabilities to manage offshore vendors (e.g., Nicholson and Sahay, 2001), client decision processes of what, how and when to offshore (Carmel and Agarwal, 2002; Aron and Singh, 2005; Rottman and Lacity, 2006; Tanriverdi et al., 2007; Gewald and Dibbern, 2009), managing the client-vendor relationship (Kaiser and Hawk, 2004; Koh et al., 2004; Cha et al., 2008; Dibbern et al., 2008; Levina and Vaast, 2008), organizational form and location decisions (Aron and Singh, 2005; Vestring et al., 2005; Levina and Su, 2008), and the deployment of advanced software process approaches (Pries-Heje et al., 2005).

The extant literature on vendor capabilities is more limited (e.g., Levina and Ross, 2003; Feeny et al., 2005; Borman, 2006). Few empirical studies have examined offshore vendor capabilities development. These studies are from the vantage point of the India-based providers and the business models they use with their US and European customers (e.g., Kaiser and Hawk, 2004; Ethiraj et al., 2005). The offshore literature is generally dominated by the perspective of India-based vendors (Nicholson and Sahay, 2001; Rajkumar and Mani, 2001; Aron and Singh, 2005; Vashistha and Vashistha, 2006; Levina, 2006; Rottman and Lacity, 2006; Oshri et al., 2007; Vlaar et al., 2008). Other regions have been much less studied, such as Russia (for exceptions see Pries-Heje et al., 2005; Levina, 2006), Taiwan (Wu 2006) and China[1] (Qu and Brocklehurst, 2003; Carmel et al., 2009; Mao et al., 2008; Su, 2008).

Transaction cost economics has been a popular theoretical paradigm in offshore sourcing (e.g., Qu and Brocklehurst, 2003). Recently, the theoretical frameworks have become more diverse encompassing the systems dynamics approach (Dutta and Roy, 2005), knowledge systems perspective (Garud and Kumaraswamy, 2005), the modular systems approach (Tanriverdi et al., 2007), trust and control theory (Mao et al., 2008), and the resource-based view of the firm (Wu, 2006). The resource-based view of the firm (Penrose, 1959; Barney, 1991) is still debated, although largely through an accepted theoretical lens in information systems research to examine how firm-specific capabilities are developed and how the capabilities contribute to firm performance (Gonzales et al., 2006).

Mediated business model in Chinese software services firms

Our focus is on the capabilities development in a mediated business model. The mediated business model is recognized in the literature (e.g., Rajkumar and Mani, 2001; Ethiraj et al., 2005). It is seen to compete primarily with country-level comparative low labour costs and less with skill or competence advantage (Carmel and Tjia, 2005). It is largely viewed as a transitory model during the early phases of a vendor's life. For example, Morstead and Blount (2003) associate the mediated model with Tier 2 vendors that have yet to mature to Tier 1 vendors.

The mediated model is pervasive in the export business of Chinese software services to Japan (Qu and Brocklehurst, 2003). Japan represents the largest market to Chinese firms (Hu et al., 2007). In the first quarter of 2008, the Japanese market accounted for 51 percent (China Sourcing, 2009). Similarly, China constitutes the main offshoring destination to Japan (OECD, 2007). According to Qu and Brocklehurst (2003, p. 62), "China has at least managed to compete with India on an equal footing in the Japanese market."

In the Chinese-Japanese offshoring services, the mediated business model developed over time. Initially, the Chinese firms provided onsite staffing to

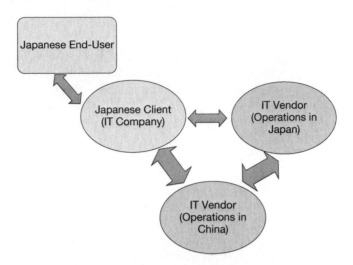

Figure 5.1 Business models in Chinese-Japanese software services offshoring

alleviate the cost pressures that Japanese firms faced in early 1990s, but over time, the staff augmentation model was complemented or substituted with offshore development to deliver greater cost reduction to the Japanese firms. Expatriate Chinese who had worked in Japan started to set up offshore facilities in China.

In the mediated model, the *client* is not the end-user of the software, but a Japanese IT company (see Figure 5.1). The Japanese IT firm (client) contracts work with the Chinese software services firm (vendor) to carry out tasks such as program design, coding and unit-testing. The Japanese IT firm (client) performs the high-level functional design, and it might break up the application into several different projects to be subcontracted to different Chinese vendors. It is also the client who integrates the different deliverables into a functioning system and manages the interactions with the *end-client* (end user of the software such a bank) (Qu and Brocklehurst, 2003). In the mediated model, vendors tend work with projects of small size, low-value-adding tasks, and limited interaction with the end-client. The project price is based on man-month expended. To make any profits on a project, the vendor needs to engage in tight cost control (Mao et al., 2008).

Drivers of Mediated Model. The mediated model accommodates the broader industry environment in which Chinese software services companies operate. The primary drivers include lagging maturity in process capabilities and the fragmented market comprised of small sized firms (OECD, 2007). The mediated model allows firms of small size and with limited process capabilities to enter the market. Indeed, the low entry barriers have triggered high levels of entry by new firms (Vashistha and Vashistha, 2006). The growth has occurred despite the limited supply of managerial resources with experience in software industry and prior experience in client industry (Ju, 2001).

The mediated model also helps to overcome the lack of robust partnership networks overseas. Fairly recently, Chinese software firms were argued to have weak overseas connections compared to their Indian counterparts (Wu et al., 2005) although this driver is becoming less important as managers increasingly have overseas education and or work experience (Carmel et al., 2008).

The mediated model also overcomes obstacles related to work culture. Although geographically, culturally and linguistically, Chinese firms have an advantage with the Japanese clients compared to the Indian or Western firms, there are still major differences. The Chinese mentality of "cha-bu-duo" (close enough is good enough) promotes ad hoc work practices. The mediated model lowers the client risk from the ad hoc work practices. Gupta and Raval (1999) suggest that cultural issues can "make or break an offshore project".

Finally, the mediated model protects clients against what is characterized as a weak contract and intellectual property system in China (Kennedy and Clark, 2006; OECD, 2007). The Chinese legal system, while improving, is a major impediment to China's growth as an offshoring destination (OECD, 2007). Rottman and Lacity (2006) report that firms break projects into smaller ones to protect intellectual property. By distributing smaller segments among different suppliers, no one vendor sees enough of the project at any one time to be able to understand it fully or it exploit that understanding opportunistically.

Operational capabilities in software services firms

Little is known about operational capabilities that allow firms to succeed with the mediated model. Prior literature on IT outsourcing has identified three classes of capabilities with vendor success (Levina and Ross, 2003): client-specific capabilities; process capabilities; and human resources (HR) capabilities.

Client-specific capabilities focus on relational routines and resources that align vendor activities with the client's goals and priorities on a short-term and long-term basis (Levina and Ross, 2003; Ethiraj et al., 2005). The vendor must develop an understanding of the client's business and design cost-effective communication and interaction patterns (Rajkumar and Mani, 2001). The vendor must have sufficient knowledge of the business (e.g., banking), functional domain (e.g., stock trading), and the specifics and idiosyncrasies of the client's operating environment. The vendor's interactions with clients must help clarify expectations and establish a sense of client trade-offs (user needs versus budget limits). Ongoing communication must clarify priorities, anticipate resource requirements, and report on issues and changes in project status.

Process capabilities relate to service delivery routines and resources that accomplish software design, development and execution (Levina and Ross, 2003; Ethiraj et al., 2005). The capabilities reflect technical competences, skills, and resources in systems and software development processes. The capability maturity model (CMM) developed by the Software Engineering Institute (SEI) at Carnegie Mellon University is commonly used to improve software development processes. However, improving the process maturity requires substantial discipline and explicit learning investments in infrastructure, systems and training programmes (Ethiraj et al., 2005). Although Chinese firms' process management capabilities lag behind, their clients, Japanese IT firms, maintain arguably the best quality control and most sophisticated process management in the world.

Human resources capabilities are associated with recruiting practices, training and mentoring programmes, designing jobs with a balanced mix of specialization and exposure to a variety of tasks, and developing performance appraisal and compensation systems (Ferratt et al., 2005; Levina and Ross, 2003). Rotating employees across projects gives them opportunities to learn new skills and interact with different team members (Argote, 1999). Individual career development plans, promotion from within, and alternative career hierarchies are all associated with beneficial effects on human resources capabilities (Levina and Ross, 2003).

According to the Levina and Ross (2003) study of a large US vendor, all three operational capabilities have to be simultaneously present and mutually reinforce each other to gain performance improvements. Their findings imply that making choices among the three capabilities might be misguided, as all three capabilities must be developed in concert. In the offshoring context, Ethiraj et al. (2005) examined client-specific and process management capabilities in the context of a large Indian offshore vendor. They found both capabilities to be associated with firm performance. The project management capabilities helped to maximize internal operational efficiencies, and improve quality and profitability in rapidly maturing Indian software industry that targets offshore markets. In the software development literature, more broadly, many have found that the increased levels of formalized routines improve quality and productivity (e.g., Herbsleb et al., 1997; Krishnan and Kellner, 1999).

For client-specific capabilities, Ethiraj et al. (2005) note the key role of personnel used by offshore vendors at the client site. A similar finding was reported by Kaiser and Hawk (2004) who examined the development of vendor and client capabilities among a large Indian vendor and US financial services clients. The on-site personnel were critical to ensure robust communication channels and develop a long-term relationship between the firms. In her study of a small Russian and Indian provider, Levina (2006) found the boundary spanning practices of middle managers at the client organization to be more critical for effective collaboration than the middle managers at the provider organization. Outside the offshoring and outsourcing literature, such middlemen are often labelled as relationship managers, account managers, client executives, or consultants (Iacono et al., 1995; Brown 1999).

In terms of human resources capabilities, Ethiraj et al. (2005) only mentions the need to invest in training programmes in new technologies and software processes for both developers and managers. Others, not specific to the offshoring literature, have noted that human resources practices are closely aligned with firm strategy (Youndt et al., 1996). Ferratt et al. (2005) review two human resources archetypes. Archetype 1 has a short-term transactional orientation that puts lower emphasis on firm-specific investments in terms of formal training and mentoring. Archetype 2 has a longer-term relationship orientation that puts greater emphasis on worker participation in firm decisions, significant investment in formal training and mentoring. Following the notion of "fit" (see Ferratt et al., 2005), firms competing primarily on comparative labour cost advantage would be expected to emphasize Archetype 1.

Development of operational capabilities in mediated offshoring model

The mediated model has implications for the development of operational capabilities. Qu and Brocklehurst (2003, p. 64) note that "most Chinese suppliers are not even aware who the end-users are". Others have noted that Chinese firms have little contact with the end-user's business except for certain stages of project, such as field support. This limits the acquisition of client-specific capabilities particularly business domain knowledge and the development of robust communication routines. The high-level and high-paying work is retained by the Japanese IT firms, which leave low-level work to the Chinese vendors. The low-level work demands low technical skills from the Chinese developers. Therefore, the mediated model can also impede the development of human resources capabilities. Small sized projects, low-value tasks, and limited end-client interaction limit the degree of employee specialization as well as the variety of tasks that they are exposed to. In such an environment, the firms are challenged to develop meaningful career paths.

Although the mediated model can be constraining in terms of capabilities development, we counter argue that Japan–China offshore outsourcing presents an environment where Chinese vendors are able to overcome – at least partially – some of these constraints and develop their capabilities incrementally. Since the Chinese vendors work with Japanese clients (Japanese IT companies), which tend to possess strong process capabilities, it is an opportunity for the Chinese firm to learn and gain maturity. Also, the contracts are generally incomplete and require substantial knowledge transfer from the client to the vendors in terms of business knowledge and project management know-how. Furthermore, the offshored work involves frequent changes in client requirements. Japanese clients maintain a hands-on approach to project management, which allows them to assess quality, progress and costs, and to take intervention actions, if necessary, as they do in other industries (Liker and Choi, 2004). The client's technical experts often remain on the vendor site for extended stay to introduce business requirements to the project team, perform design reviews and monitor quality.

Learning mechanisms for developing capabilities

Zollo and Winter (2002) distinguish between two types of learning mechanisms in capabilities development in large firms: deliberate and explicit firm-specific investments, and implicit "learning by doing". The deliberate investments involve explicit knowledge articulation and knowledge codification mechanisms and require greater managerial and financial resources than the passive experiential processes of learning by doing. The explicit investments involve time and energy to engage in collective discussions, performance evaluation processes and codification of knowledge in the form of manuals, blueprints and project management software. The implicit learning by doing involves repeated and cumulative experiences. Both implicit and explicit categories of learning mechanisms result in improved performance, although the degree of improvement can be impacted by a variety of factors such as internal organizational processes and structures (Eisenhardt and Martin, 2000).

The mix of learning mechanisms also depends on the characteristics of the capabilities to be developed (Zollo and Winter, 2002). Ethiraj et al. (2005) argue specifically that implicit and tacit experience by doing is the dominant learning mechanism for client-specific capabilities, whereas improvements in process capabilities requires explicit learning investments in infrastructure, systems and training programmes. By inference, Ethiraj et al. (2005) argue for explicit investments for human resources capabilities development.

Importantly, Ethiraj et al. (2005) focus on large firms. Zollo and Winter (2002) focused on large firms in mature economies and industries. We know of no study that has explicitly examined capabilities development in small and medium-sized offshore software services firms although studies exist on capabilities development in call centres (Pan et al., 2006) and IT hardware component sourcing (Wu, 2006).

Research method

We chose the case study method in order to explore the research question of how Chinese firms develop their capabilities in spite of the constraints of the mediated model. Case study research is appropriate in situations where the research question involves a "how", "why", or exploratory "what" question.

The investigator has no control over actual behavioural events, and the focus is on contemporary phenomenon (Yin, 1989). The research presented in this chapter fits all of these three criteria.

We selected three small and medium sized entrepreneurial firms as our case study sites. Unlike Chinese legacy firms (e.g., Neusoft), the new entrepreneurial firms do not have a captive client base and hence capabilities development is critical for their survival (Carmel et al., 2008). All three firms were located in Beijing, which represents the largest base for software development and export, as well as the most rapid pace of growth in China. We selected these three because the researchers had connections or could get referrals to the firms in Beijing. In addition, the firms were exporting software services, were founded by Chinese entrepreneurs, and were under the control of Chinese managers at the time of the study. However, the firms varied in terms of background, size and software services. One was a well-established service provider to Japan, whereas the other two were recent entrants to Japanese-Chinese outsourcing. One of the latter two was already established in American-European export markets (see Tables 5.1 and 5.2).

The unit of analysis is the vendor company. In each case, interviews were arranged through a senior executive of the target firm, and senior management including the CEO or president usually participated in the study (see Table 5.3). The interviews in each firm were scheduled in a top-down sequence, and this way assured open and active participation of lower-level personnel. Site visits lasted for one or two working days, with each interview taking one to two hours. Both researchers participated in the interviews, and extensive notes were

Table 5.1 Profile of the companies studied

Company	Primary Services to Japan	No. of Employees	Starting Time	Ownership	Market
A – high growth publicly held firm	Testing, coding, design, architectural design	In 2005: 1200 + (72)[1] In 2009: 2800+	1995	Public (initially management and Japanese minorities)	90%+ to Japan
B – Slow growth small firm	Testing/coding, some design	In 2005: 130 + (60) In 2009: 300+	2001	Management and Japanese minorities	96% to Japan, 4% in China
C – Established firm, new to Japanese market	Staffing, some development	In 2005: 700 + (20) In 2009: 4000+	1995	Management, and strategic investors lately	90% Euro-US, 10% to Japan

Table 5.2   General background of the companies studied

Company	Background
A – High growth publicly held firm	Started up by two former university classmates, previously an experienced developer in Japan and a software sales representative in China for a multinational. Publicly listed on Hong Kong Stock Exchange in 2004. One of the largest vendors in China, with over 10 subsidiaries in China, and one in Japan, in 2006.
B – Slow growth small firm	Founders previously worked in a Japanese joint venture company in China, or Japan. Worked with many different clients and various types of projects. Much of the initial work had been at the lower end of the value chain but increasingly moving up to higher value-adding work.
C – Established firm, new to Japanese market	Ranked among the top ten offshore vendors in China, founded by four former university classmates. Outsourcing business to the Japanese market since 2003. Initially staffing by internal people, and after some setbacks replaced them with Chinese developers with Japanese work experience.

Table 5.3   Interviewees' job title

Company	Job titles
A	President; senior manager for training; quality assurance engineer; project manager; senior developer; developers
B	Co-Founder and director, software development division; manager, quality assurance; project manager; developer; hr manager, internal training instructor
C	Chairman & CEO; VP marketing; GM Japanese business; marketing manager; Japanese business manager; PR manager

taken. In one of the companies, a research assistant was also present at the interview to help transcribe the interviews. The two researchers then compared their notes, and combined a consolidated version. In addition to interview data, relevant information in the public domain, such as company websites, news releases, publicity in the media, and financial statements of public company were all collected and used.

The data collection, took place in two stages, during the summers of 2005 and 2007 in the same three companies. Essentially, the same data collection procedures were used in both stages, except that in 2007 we got permission to record the interviews, which were transcribed for analysis.

An interview guide was prepared prior to visiting the sites. For qualitative research, some (Eisenhardt, 1989; Yin, 1989) recommend predetermined research questions, themes and data collection plans. Having predetermined data collection plans is helpful, especially when multiple case studies are used, as this makes data collection more systematic and enhances the comparability of results. Following these recommendations, the relevant literature in the area of capabilities management was reviewed and the interview guide developed.

Qualitative case analysis involved individual case write-ups based on the interviews and the archival data. These individual case write-ups were then "coded" in terms of the client-specific, project management and human resources management capabilities. The second author did the first round of the coding and the first author did the second round. The cross-case comparison of data explored the commonalities and differences in capabilities and in their development (i.e., learning mechanisms).

Results

All three companies showed signs of enhanced capabilities and maturity in the client-specific and process capabilities. All three firms relied heavily on tacit knowledge accumulation in building client-specific capabilities, although deliberate investments in firm-specific structures and processes were also evident in the case data, but to a lesser extent. The accumulation of learning about the client's business domain and hence the development of client-specific capabilities were strongest at middle and top management levels. The top management brought years of experience in responding to clients' needs and their business networks, or lack of thereof, in Japan. The repeated interactions had developed high levels of familiarity between the management of the vendor and the client. Lower levels of the firms had much fewer opportunities to gain customer-specific capabilities, including the domain knowledge (See Table 5.4 and Figure 5.2).

Similar to client-specific capabilities, process capabilities were developed from both deliberate investments and experience accumulation, although here, the explicit investments were more apparent, particularly in 2007. Most of the firms made proactive investments in the deliberate learning of project management tools and methodologies. The firms had pursued CMM process maturity competences to varying extents, and more importantly each firm adapted the standard processes to their circumstances.

The lesser focus on human resources capabilities development was a response to the constraints of financial and managerial resources as well as the turnover of lower level staff. Skill development, promotional policies, encouragement and incentives remained somewhat ad hoc except in company C. Most visible

Table 5.4   Learning mechanisms of the capabilities

Capabilities	Learning mechanisms
Client-specific	Top management's overseas work experience, familiarity with the client culture, focus on long-term relationship with clients, and ability to creatively adapt client procedures to the suit the Chinese context; Infrastructure development to cater client needs in safety and security measures, separate venues and work units, and communication channels for client; Extensive use of on-site staffing and bridge engineers, including native Japanese; decentralized quality control (QA) function to cater to client needs; Having client expert on-site; participating in training sponsored by clients.
Process	ISO 9000:2000,CMM certification and related training; employee work report; standardized requirements documentation, templates, and design review procedures; Adopting the client company's procedures, tools, QA systems, and philosophy. Deliberate effort in learning by doing, and then fixed as standard processes; extensive effort in "optimizing" ISO processes based on client needs; Learning from clients, e.g., by applying a US-based major client's sophisticated testing procedures for Japanese clients; managerial training.
Human resources	Middle managers received external training; hiring fresh graduates and providing training regardless of firm sizes, and experienced expatriates; systematic career development systems; Frequent visits by employees to the client firm; cultural blending activities; employees' self-driven learning; "People-oriented" philosophy; flat organizational structure and friendly work environment; Japanese language training, opportunity to work overseas on client sites, and raises to motivate employees; Adopting tools and platforms in Japanese language; team-building camps, and language training; employee development programmes.

learning and improvements took place at middle levels as companies tried to tighten cost and quality control and increase profitability.

Next, we discuss how the firms appeared to have overcome the constraints of the mediated model to be able to develop their capabilities. The nature of the projects and the interface with the client, who possessed not only domain knowledge but also process capabilities and technical skills, appeared to be determining factors. This is a unique feature of the mediated model, influencing the mix of learning mechanisms by the Chinese vendors.

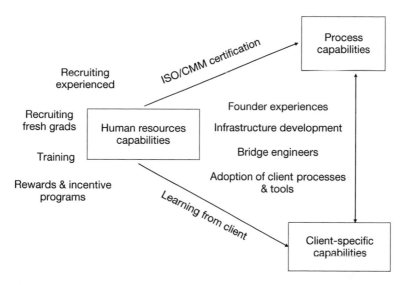

Figure 5.2   Learning mechanisms in the three cases

Company A – High growth publicly held firm

Company A was ranked among the top five Chinese firms providing offshoring software services to Japan (in terms of revenues).

Client-specific capabilities

In 2005, Company A's capabilities development largely occurred implicitly via close coupling with its clients. The majority of the company's business came from the bulk share of only a couple of very large Japanese IT firms that served end-user clients in the banking and securities industry (e.g., electronic trading solutions). Much of the work involved coding and unit testing. However, by 2007, the firm was more involved in design activities. The client base was more varied and including even end-clients. A manager reported, "Previously it was indirect outsourcing, via the integrator in the middle. Now our company has a considerable size of end-clients." One of the key indicators of enhanced capabilities is that "Our company's capabilities have grown, and we became more proactive, leading the client [in process and delivery]."

Initially, the president (and a co-founder) of the firm had brought with him years of experience in responding to the clients' needs and their business networks in Japan. The repeated interactions had developed high levels of familiarity in the business domain and practices of the client. In 2005, the president commented,

Trust with Japanese clients has evolved to such a stage over time that I can sign a contract without looking at the financial details. If I lose money on a particular project, they will make it up with extra in the next contract to me. If I bided 100 man-months and ended up using 80 only, we'd do more on usability and user interfaces, so that we are not too far off. If my client has to cancel a project, and asks me to share some of the loss, I'd do it because I know they'll pay me back in the next project.

The President continued, "This is hard for the Indian companies to do, coming from a Western contract-based culture. This is in the root of east agricultural economies, which is something common between Chinese and Japanese culture." Much of the learning of client-specific capabilities occurred implicitly at the project level through the Japanese technical experts whom the clients sent to the vendor to assist with frequently changing and ambiguously specified business requirements.

Company A had also made explicit investments to stay closely connected with the clients, but so also did their clients. Company A's divisions and departments were structured with direct correspondence to clients. In some cases, a client paid for a fixed charge to retain a department on long-term contracts for staff stability and guaranteed availability. This allowed the vendor to develop a workforce with a high level of domain knowledge in a client's business. The staff members for different clients were housed in different geographic locations as a way of managing security and protecting customer confidentiality. In some cases, the technical development environments were physically disconnected from the company's infrastructure but connected with that of the client's. Company A had also dedicated on-site personnel, so called "bridge engineers" for major projects at the client sites. Bridge engineers handled the day-to-day interaction between the client and the offshore site.

Investments in organizational structures and processes increased as the business growth intensified. In 2007, a division manager commented, "Our managerial sophistication has definitely progressed over the past two years. We have developed norms and principles based on the accumulation of prior experiences." For example, "as the scale increases, information securities become more important, involving client confidentiality and security checks, etc. Structural change of the organization have been continuous, to deal with the growing business scope."

Process capabilities

Initially, Company A's process capabilities originated from the creative adaptation of a methodology to local culture and client needs, which the president had learned in Japan. The company continued to develop process capabilities via learning from the technical experts sent to the vendor site and from "the bridge engineers". The project teams used the client's software design and build-ing platforms. Effort estimation was based on prior projects with the particular client.

Compared to learning from the clients via experience and by adopting their sophisticated processes, it was less important for the firm to invest extensively in standard processes and quality standards beyond certain degrees. Two of the company's departments passed CMM Level 2 in 2002, but the company had made a conscious decision not to pursue CMM Level 3. In 2005, one project manager remarked, "CMM is a reference point for us, the client requirements are our guiding principles." A developer remarked, "We do not practice quality here as a straightjacket." To be responsive to client needs, the quality assur-ance function was decentralized. Most of the quality personnel resided within the departments serving specific clients. There was only a small central quality assurance group.

By 2007, there was more focus on process capabilities although not in the form of certification. The process focus was seen critical for improved profitabil-ity and flexibility. A manager noted, "The company has progressed over the past few years, e.g., in processes and quality awareness, and employee sensitivity to quality. Procedures were created along with documentation, although commu-nication with clients on details of the processes is still needed." Now, "The way to complete tasks is similar to that of Japanese clients, except for minor differ-ences in details. Thus communication is bound to be smoother. There shouldn't be any difficulty if we switch to a different client."

Another manager summarized the progress: "There were radical changes to the processes in 2000 when we passed CMM Level 2, although we were certified by ISO 9000 earlier. However, our processes have gone through more major changes yet again. It was mainly driven by the desire to do better with the projects, and getting better contracts." For example,

> Each design document has a review with it. It is not acceptable to wait till the end to realize that the quality of the project is no good. Coding should go through some review and evaluation, which was mainly done by the team leader, people with good technical skills, and independent tests by the testing group, not by me. Assessment and evaluation are conducted in each stage by the client, so that it would be impossible to have serious problems at the end.

Human resources capabilities

The frequent changes in requirements and rigid process adherence dictated by the client were not always welcome by the developers, however. In 2005, one of them described how in one project, 90 percent of the team quit because of fatigue and the lack of recognition of individual contribution. The developers also resented that their development environments were locked by the client's needs and that they had little opportunity to gain skills on new platforms and new clients. One described the work environment as " 'blue-collar' style, equipped with basic furniture and crowded, and offices scattered in the city for cost-saving". The task features of projects imposed a challenge for human resources capabilities development, to identify and train the people with the right skill set and attitudes. In 2005, the company's strategy was focused on operational efficiency at the low-level coding and unit testing, which involved lower risks and required fewer capabilities. This meant low-level and low-value-adding work for developers.

In 2005, a key mechanism for human resources capabilities was recruitment. At the entry level, the company preferred to hire fresh college graduates as the main source of developers, and then provide initial training for them. It was believed that people who had worked for three to five years become hard to train and indoctrinate with the company values. Training was conducted in a centralized intensive mode for three months, consisting of Japanese language training and working on prior client projects. Through this explicit process, codified knowledge is shared and transferred to new employees. Much of the task-specific and client-specific training occurred on the job later on.

In 2007, there were signs of growing reliance on knowledge articulation and explicit learning, as employee training was increasingly done internally, as opposed to externally by the client or training-by-doing. A manager explained, "Department managers conduct training and coach their subordinates." Cross-division training was also provided on a reciprocal basis, and internal training within departments (to new hires and other employees below project managers)." A manager continued, "We place strong emphasis on discussion within the project team."

There was better cross-department coordination and personnel mobility within the company. "It is no longer a single team or department working on a project alone independently. Both personnel and business float inside the group company to a certain degree. [Our staff] could be transferred in from the company's Japanese subsidiary firm, or from other departments, etc." Nevertheless, the number of internal transfer remained small. Employee turnover was mostly external to other companies.

The management also acknowledged that human resources management was an area that much needed further development. A manager reported on some core areas, "The company is keen on keeping employees motivated, which is a good means of capability strengthening. Financial incentives (salaries and benefits, or bonus) play a role in this to a certain degree. It is more important to have individual career development plan, and to offer a bigger space for growth in the company."

Company B – Slow growth small firm

As the smallest and youngest company in our sample, Company B faced the biggest resource constraints in developing its capabilities.

Client-specific capabilities

Similar to the earlier days in Company A, a director of Company B attributed his firm's client-specific capabilities to "our senior management's experience in working with Japanese clients". The senior management had much tacit knowledge of the clients' operations and stayed in close daily contact with the client's project personnel. For middle and lower level personnel, developing client-specific capabilities was more challenging. In 2005, Company B acquired disparate and relatively small projects from a diverse set of clients. A project manager described their work as "hard bones with little meat to bite".

By the summer of 2007, things had improved significantly. The company deepened its ties with key clients. We were told: "The most significant change since 2005 has been in client relationship management. We do much better in this area now, having become a golden partner of a major client and upgraded the partnership." A manager explained, "We started with small projects, did them well with quick response. Probably it [upgraded partner relationship] was due to high customer satisfaction, related to their assessment of our teams." The partnership also meant financial support from the client for infrastructure development. A client provided funding for a leased communication line, telephone number, and backup switch.

Process capabilities

In 2005, the firm largely relied on ad hoc implicit learning. Many of the projects "came with tight schedules and changing objectives. As a result, there were many versions to manage, a modification might affect not only just one module, but all modules need to be inspected for the rippling effect." It was only through trials and errors and gradual accumulation of experience that the project teams figured out an approach in response. The teams' approach was to increase internal discussion aimed at thorough understanding of the design. This approach was also used to deal with the client's vagueness. As another example, individual programmers' first reaction to technical challenges was to get on the Internet or other forms of self-learning, rather than looking to formal institutional infrastructure for support.

The increasingly complex work put pressure on the company to move away from ad hoc practices to developing a more disciplined approach, noted by the quality manager. Some of the major clients, especially those that had developed closer relationships with the company through a history of successful past projects, had also sent their personnel to the company to train developers in process management.

To enhance its process capabilities, Company B augmented its learning from clients by investing in both standard processes and certification. The firm had achieved 1SO 9000 certification, and was planning for CMM Level 3 in 2005. Part of the task of the central quality group was to optimize ISO processes, understand CMM requirements, and consolidate CMM and ISO into the firm's processes. This work was very hands-on. The quality manager reported, "Right now, Q/A is involved in the full process of product development, but once the processes are mature, we [Q/A] might just follow the key points."

In 2005, Company B struggled to find the right balance between best-in-class processes and the client's tight delivery deadlines in order to improve the firm's profitability. A manager commented, "Indeed we have improved our competence through doing outsourcing for Japanese clients. Our clients have strict quality processes. We follow their processes as much we can and in the process, improve our own abilities." One of the founders noted that "Our Japanese clients do not care much about the level of CMM because Japanese companies have their own procedures and processes. We are building a quality system to develop our own processes, a uniformed system to respond to all kinds of requirements from Japan. It allows a common response to all scenarios."

By 2007, Company B completed CMM Level 3 certification successfully. A manager explained, "Through the one and a half years of certification process, we strengthened our management capabilities at the organizational level, in areas such as personnel and project managers' capabilities." The impact was perhaps most widely felt in quality management. "CMM has impacted on our client management, e.g., how to respond to requirements. For example, in collecting requirements, what levels of details should it arrive at? How to confirm the requirements? All of these are covered. Clients are invited to provide feedback after the project completion, and surveys of customer satisfaction, are all covered." They also intended, "to conduct cross-department technical exchange, and cross-platform exchange, through CMM or other means".

In 2007, the company was still grappling with the tensions between processes management and profitability goals. A manager noted, "At the moment CMM is challenging to handle. The ultimate goal is to increase productivity, including the creation of processes, strengthened personal training, human resources. We are not experiencing much of the productivity gain from CMM yet likely because we are not proficient yet. More labour is needed for project development, and flexibility has lost quite a bit".

Human resources capabilities

In 2005, the strategy to develop human resources capabilities was similar to that of Company A, especially in terms of recruitment practices. The company hired entry-level developers mostly from universities in Beijing, whereas the middle tier was recruited from job fairs. New candidates were asked to attend new employee training programmes and re-do a previously completed project in order to accumulate experience. As in Company A, Company B's human resource practices aimed to promote Japanese business customs that stressed the needs of the client company. Moreover, the company maintained a large percentage of the team on-site, and the opportunity to work in Japan was used as both a reward and employee development practice.

In 2007, the company anticipated much of the benefit from the CMM certification to be reaped in terms of improved human resources capabilities. A manager emphasized that the drive for certification was mainly internal as "we wanted to train the middle managers, project managers". A manager explained, "CMM certification helps to increase managerial competences. No other means is available for such substantial increases in managerial measures."

By 2007, one development in human resources was visible: namely improved training resources. A manager explained, "Through the dedicated line, the client beefed up training to us, education, including an entire series of training manuals in the client library on the network." However, exploitation of those resources remained ad hoc. There were few formal processes for training and development.

In 2007, the company continued their past practices of focusing on recruiting fresh college graduates every year, and starting the training from scratch. "This year, we hired more than 40. We also hire experienced hands with Japanese projects, but this is really difficult. We use another method, which is to send the promising ones to our Japanese subsidiary. Those dispatched two years ago are due to return at the end of this year."

The company's clientele and project composition constrained the development of human resources. The personnel was dedicated to the clients and some personnel found the work for Japanese clients to be repetitive and at low level, and wished to work on domestic clients' projects that involved a higher level of work such as requirements analysis. A manager acknowledged that the tight control on staff rotation "influences staff morale. No free flow is allowed at the moment. They have to apply for formal transfer."

Company C – Established firm, new to the Japanese market

Company C had built a strong reputation in servicing European and US clients. However, it was new to the Japanese market in 2005.

Client-specific capabilities

Having been used to conducting business with Western clients, learning client-specific capabilities in the Japanese market had been challenging. The CEO noted that it took two to three years of work with Japanese customers before gaining their confidence. Technological know-how was not an entry barrier, but trusting relationships, as "steady business comes after trust is established".

Because of the differences in business practices and customs, the firm was able to leverage little of its international reputation with European and US clients in Japan. To overcome this constraint, the firm used its human resources practices to build client-specific capabilities. The firm had hired several seasoned Chinese managers with work experience in Japan to develop client relationships.

Process capabilities

As in the other companies, process capabilities were also built via learning from the clients as well as deliberate investments in certification. Company C heralded its superior ability to learn from clients by sending its personnel to the client's training courses. One of the founders explained, "We send employees to our clients' project management training courses. We have adopted many procedures from our customers including their internal quality tools." Company C passed ISO 2000 quality certification in 2004 and CMM Level 3 certification in December 2006, partly because its US clients valued the CMM certification. Regarding Japanese clients, a manager explained, "Japanese have different methodologies, but still the general process thinking is the same. We can leverage our process management successes from the US and European side in our Japanese business." In practice, this meant meeting the internal quality frameworks of Japanese clients using the CMM and ISO reference points internally.

By 2007, the company had continued its focus on process management, by passing ISO 9001:2000, CMM Level 4, ISO 27001 certification and evaluation. These developments had helped the firm to increase the size of the projects as well as their profitability. The success of the company was recognized, and honoured with numerous industry and government awards, as one of the "Big three in US-European Outsourcing", "Global Top 100 Outsourcers in 2008", "Asia Top 100 Private Enterprises", "Chinese Top 50 High-Tech and High Growth Firms" and "Premier Software Firms Designated by the National Planning in China".

Human resources capabilities

Already in 2005, Company C had the most extensive and deliberate human resources capabilities among the companies. The CEO's motto was, "Great people come through good HR processes", which highlighted the central importance of human resources capabilities. The company had an extensive internal training programme that focused on not only technical skills, but also on cross-cultural and client management as well as process management. Such extensive training was exceptional in the software services industry in China. The company was known for its emphasis on learning and team-oriented culture. All of its senior managers had earned their EMBA degree on a part-time basis. After three years of service, employees were sponsored to study for a master's degree in software engineering from top software engineering schools.

Whereas the recruitment practice was similar to that of the competitors targeting fresh university graduates at the entry-level and veterans in the industry at the middle level, Company C invested more in formal training. For example, fresh graduates were given three months' training, conducted by two outside companies. Project managers hired from overseas would be brought back to Beijing for at least one week for orientation and cultural immersion.

To complement the deliberate learning mechanisms, the firm also created an environment to facilitate experiential learning. When asked for examples, the general manager of Japanese operations mentioned that despite the multimillion losses in his initial management responsibilities, he was still trusted by founders and given more opportunities. A junior employee compared his experience with his previous employer and noted how Company C went out of its way to assign work that leveraged his talents and strengths, because managers knew their employees really well through social and training camps, which are really exceptional in the offshore market.

In 2007, the firm continued to focus on training and team-building. It kept its commitment and continued its effort in deliberate learning. It sought opportunities for employees to gain overseas education and work experience. It offered opportunities for people to be trained by the native language speakers and become immersed in the clients' culture.

Of the three companies, Company C had grown the most during the two-year period. Company C managed to increase the number of employees to more than 4000, from a mere 700 plus in 2005. Companies A and B more than doubled their, size measured by the number of employees. The growth took place in what was seen as the rapidly expanding export software services industry in China. The growth was critical for the long-term survival of the firms as the offshore outsourcing industry was undergoing a consolidation process involving many merger and acquisition deals to create the necessary scale to compete internationally.

Discussion

Compared to previous studies involving large Indian vendors, our study focused on small and medium-sized China-based companies that do their business as subcontractors to Japanese IT firms, to carry out tasks such as software testing and coding. Our two-stage empirical study shows that over time, there were signs of enhanced vendor capabilities. There were even early signs of breaking away from the mediated model, which will most likely results in different projects and higher profitability. Company C had achieved the fastest growth, with the strongest emphasis on human resources development and deliberate learning.

The mediated model

The main finding from the case studies is that the mediated model affected the development of capabilities. Particularly early on, the mediated model shifts the development of capabilities from the vendor's organizational boundaries to the "extended organizational forms" (Aron and Singh, 2005). Long-term close relationships with clients facilitate the transfer of domain knowledge, IT technical knowledge and process management. This is in contrast to what has been found with large vendors in both offshore and outsourcing context. The most advanced IT technical knowledge and process management resides with the vendor (e.g., see Kaiser and Hawk, 2004).

Human resources capabilities development appeared to be the most constrained by the mediated model. In some of the firms, only low-level ("blue collar") work is assigned for the vendor. In such a model (as in manufacturing), scale and operational efficiency are important for the vendors. The work can be tedious and result in low staff morale. Some of the Chinese developers conveyed a sentiment that they feel that they are required to act passively doing everything according to the design specifications, without any need to think on their own.

The constraint on human resources put pressure for the firms to invest in recruiting, development, and appraisal processes that fit with their strategy. Whereas firms shared common recruiting approaches, they also exhibited different human resources practice archetypes in training and employee development. For example, Company A and B followed Archetype 1: short-term orientation, reliance on recruiting rather than developing personnel, and lower emphasis on firm-specific investments on ongoing employee training. In contrast, Company C was more of Archetype 2: longer-term orientation, promotion from within, significant investment in training and development. The finding might appear surprising given that the mediated model is seen to be primarily competing on efficiency and comparative low labour costs, which suggests Archetype 1. A closer examination of the cases reveals that the differences can be accounted for with the contingency factors such as task features, vendor scale and client relationship.

Similar to the prevailing offshore models described in the literature (Kaiser and Hawk, 2004; Ethiraj et al., 2005; Levina, 2006; Oshri et al., 2007), the mediated model accommodated vendor personnel ("bridge engineers") at the client site. However, the bridge engineers' role was "narrowed" compared to what has been described with the non-mediated offshore models. For example, Kaiser and Hawk (2004) describe how the on-site vendor personnel accomplished requirements determination for new applications and even conducted performance reviews for the client technical personnel. In a mediated model studied here, the bridge engineers' role seemed to be more limited in terms of functions as well as access. Particularly early on, the access was limited but widened as the project moved through testing and maintenance phases. The limited access was overcome by top management's prior experience in Japan and their ongoing close involvement in the projects.

The mediated model also required high levels of vendor flexibility and adaptive capability. The mediated model with Japanese clients had to manage frequent change to requirements, some of which were specified at very high levels. The vague requirements had to be further specified while the software was developed. This led to the client's sending their own technical personnel to the vendor locations to manage the frequent updates. The vendor visits promoted learning, but they could also lead to cultural conflict. China and Japan have different customer service cultures. This is not unique to software services firms. While Japanese clients tend to strive for perfection in customer services, which leads to the frequent changes in the requirements to satisfy their end clients, Chinese developers are under the influence of their "cha-bu-duo" attitude ("close enough is good enough"). Ever-changing requirements were seen by Chinese developers to cause work pressure and communication overhead. Human resources practices were needed to help employees to deal with these cultural conflicts.

Development of operational capabilities

Prior literature (e.g., Levina and Ross, 2003) has noted the complementary relationships among the capabilities. Our case studies extend their findings by particularly anchoring human resources as the foundation for the development of the two other capabilities (see Figure 5.2). In the mediated model, each company's success is tied to its recruiting various levels of talents, providing training in the client language, culture, technical skills, project management processes and instituting client-service mentality in the employees to cater to the clients' communication style, business requirements and processes. The importance of human resources capabilities development was stressed by all three firms and appeared to be most challenging to achieve.

In the mediated model, client-specific capabilities are manifested in the effective adoption of the client process, processes and procedures, communication styles and business knowledge. As one of the managers pointed out, the adoption of client processes and tools was important, and sometimes more so than ISO and CMM standards, because it could facilitate the mediating Japanese firm's effort to integrate the final systems, which maybe developed by several parties. In addition to training, client-specific capabilities gradually developed via bridge engineers, staffing on client site (e.g., for system integration and support), client representatives' visits, and regular communication between the vendor and client personnel. The accumulation and retention of such capabilities also hinged on human resources capabilities. The cases illustrated slightly different practices in retaining and motivating employees based on their circumstances.

In the mediated model, where the Chinese vendors operated at the down stream of the value chain featuring mostly coding and unit-testing, the work was relatively portable and modular, and revenue and productivity were based on fixed estimated man-months. Therefore, cost control was important, which requires operational efficiency via process enhancement and quality assurance to stay within project budget, schedule and allowed bug rate. Scaling up was key for the vendors to obtain larger and more profitable contracts, which in return secures resources for explicit learning mechanisms such as CMM certification and richer forms of client engagement, e.g., bridge engineers, visit to client sites, and video conferencing and phone calls. Interestingly, Company B had its multi-year projection of head-count growth on its website, as a management objective. Figure 5.3 illustrates these interdependencies among the operational capabilities.

Contingent nature of the learning mechanisms

Our case data also allowed us to go beyond Zollo and Winter (2002) by specifying the impact of the capabilities development on the contingency factors in an interactive relationship for the mediated business model. Three factors appeared to influence the adoption of learning mechanisms (see Figure 5.3).

First, the scale of the company is a factor. Larger ones possess more resources, bigger bargaining power, and internal specialization of organizational units and individuals (e.g., dedicated QA personal), which led to bigger and more

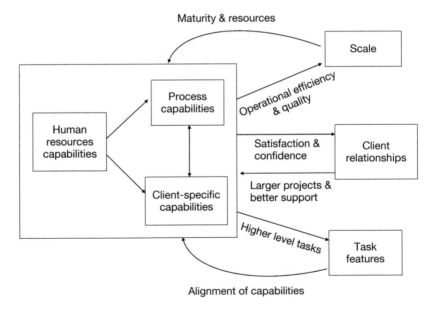

Figure 5.3   The full model of capabilities development

profitable projects. Only after firms became larger could they afford the certification (CMM and ISO) and other forms of deliberate learning. Smaller firms such as Company B had to rely more upon experience accumulation. One of Company B's teams had a lot of problems with the evolving client requirements, and it was only through trial and error that they gradually figured out their own way to deal with it.

Second, the strong orientation to long-term client relationship was a key factor early on in capabilities development in the mediated model. Through repeated interactions with two to three of its largest clients in supplying software services, Company A had developed not only a better understanding of the client business requirements and customer service culture, but also efficient approaches to deal with clients' vague style of communication and incomplete specifications in terms of process capabilities. For example, the company had developed customer-specific development and review checklists. An interesting finding of the case studies is that in these companies the client relationship tends to grow tighter for mutual gains, along with vendors' capabilities development and maturity. At the same time, the improved capabilities provide greater profitability that can allow the firm to break away from the mediated model or possibly develop in parallel a second business model that is more targeted to end-clients. By 2007, Company A was broadening its client base while maintaining tight relationships with its long-term clients.

Third, as predicted by Zollo and Winter (2002), a firm's task features (originating from its strategy) tend to exert influence on the learning mechanisms. A comparison between Company A and Company C lends support to this assertion. Company A was a low-cost and high efficiency firm, achieving its high profitability via a combination of focus in financial services, working with few clients with many big projects, and effective cost control. Both client-specific and process capabilities resided with senior and middle managers, whereas low-level staff had to rely on the accumulation of personal experience. In contrast, Company C had some unique capabilities in software product localization and a diverse range and levels of tasks, which required a more specialized work force. Company C exhibited the use of extensive deliberate learning mechanisms including human resources practices of the type associated with Archetype 2 (see Ferratt et al., 2005).

Conclusion

We conclude with limitations and implications.

Limitations

This research has several limitations. First, the sample is a convenience one, based on accessibility to vendors. All firms were headquartered in Beijing, where one of the authors is located and has industry contacts. However, our focus on Beijing-based vendors is appropriate, since Beijing is the largest base in China for software export. Second, as an exploratory study, this research is aimed at identifying issues concerning capabilities development, instead of quantitative evidence to prove or test any theory. Our qualitative analysis started out without a set of predefined constructs or coding scheme.

Implications

In spite of these limitations, our study makes three important contributions to the research literature. First, the results suggest that capabilities development is affected by the business model. The mediated model helps to overcome some of the challenges that small and medium-sized Chinese firms face because of their size, low maturity of process capabilities, and the weak legal environment, although the mediated model can also constrain the development of certain operational capabilities. Our results contribute to the stream of research that emphasizes capabilities being highly context specific, and need to be studied accordingly. In the mediated model, the human resources capabilities appear to play a particularly pivotal role.

Second, compared to the level and value of capabilities, the learning mechanisms can take on more generic mechanisms. Although the companies varied in the level of client-specific capabilities, interactions with clients were part of the mechanisms to develop the capabilities in the different firms. Of course, some mechanisms can be specific to firms as well. For example, Company A dealt with financial services firms that were particularly concerned with security and privacy. Security procedures that protected client confidentiality were a critical part of customer-specific capabilities.

Third, we have integrated the three types of capabilities and the contingency factors into a synthesized model (shown in Figure 5.3), and examined their two-way relationships between the capabilities and contingency factors.

In terms of practical implications, this study has obvious implications to offshore vendors. However, findings have implications for clients as well, especially for overseas IT firms seeking cost reductions. In managing relationships with vendors that lack both business domain knowledge and project management capabilities, deep relationships that embed knowledge transfer are critical. Deep relationships can evolve through escalation of project sizes via repeated interaction to reach co-dependence to maximize mutual gains. However, at least initially, it is the client that must make implicit and explicit learning investments to help develop the vendor's capabilities. The client needs to be sensitive to a vendor's personnel and their needs to upgrade their skills.

Acknowledgements

The authors would like to thank Chunping Deng and Xiaoyan Li for their contribution and support in data preparation, transcription and part of the data analysis.

Notes

1. The literature on offshoring to China (e.g., Kennedy and Clark, 2006; Feenstra and Hanson, 2005; Hsieh and Woo, 2005) focuses on manufacturing and product outsourcing, not services outsourcing.
2. The material was supplemented with interviews with various experts in the industry during July 2004.
3. The material is based on interviews with experts in the industry during July 2004.

References

Amit, R. and Schoemaker, P. J .H. (1993), "Strategic assets and organizational rent," *Strategic Management Journal*, 14(1): 33–46.
Analysis International, (2006), "China's Software Outsourcing Market Reached RMB 2.592 in Q1 2006." http://english.analysys.com.cn/home/index.php (last accessed 30 September 2007).
Analysis International, (2007), "Analysis International Says China Offshore Software Out-sourcing Market Reached RMB 3.315 in Q1 of 2007," http://english.analysys.com.cn/home/index.php (last accessed 30 September 2007).
Argote, L. (1999), *Organizational Learning: Creating, Retaining, and Transferring Knowledge*, KLuwer Academic Publishers, MA.
Aron, R. and Singh, J. V. (2005), "Getting Offshoring Right," *Harvard Business Review*, 83(12): 135–140.
Barney, J. B. (1991), "Firm Resources and Sustained Competitive Advantage," *Journal of Management*, 17(1): 99–120.
Borman, M. (2006), "Applying Multiple Perspectives to the BPO Decision: A Case Study of Call Centres in Australia," *Journal of Information Technology*, (21): 99–115.
Brown, C. Y. (1999), "Horizontal Mechanisms Under Differing IS Organization Contexts," 23(3): 421–454.
Carmel, E. and Agarwal, R. (2002), "The Maturation of Offshore Sourcing of Information Technology Work," *MIS Quarterly-Executive*, 1(2): 65–77.
Carmel, E., Gao, G. and Zhang, N. (2008), "The Maturing Chinese Offshore IT Services Industry: It Takes 10 Years to Sharpen a Sword," *MIS Quarterly-Executive*, 7(4):157–170.
Carmel, E. and Tjia, P. (2005), *Offshoring Information Technology: Sourcing and Outsourcing to a Global Workforce*, Cambridge.
Cha, H. S., Pingry, D. E. and Thatcher, M. E. (2008), "Managing the Knowledge Sup-ply Chain: An Organizational Learning Model of Information Technology Offshore Outsourcing," *MIS Quarterly*, 32(2): 281–306.
China Sourcing (2009), http://chinasourcing.mofcom.gov.cn/content2.jsp?id=15473 (acccessed on 13 July 2009).
Dibbern, J., Winkler, J. and Heinzl, A. (2008), "Explaining Variations in Client Extra Costs Between Software Projects Offshored to India," *MIS Quarterly*, 32(2): 333–366.

Dutta, A. and Roy, R. (2005), "Offshore Outsourcing: A Dynamic Causal Model of Counteracting Forces," *Journal of Management Information Systems,* 22 (2): 15–35.

Economic Daily (2007), "Second Batch of Chinese Service Outsourcing Cities," 1/7/2007.

Eisenhardt, K. M. (1989), "Building Theories from Case Study Research," *Academy of Management Review,* 14(4): 532–550.

Eisenhardt, K. and Martin, J. (2000), "Dynamic Capabilities: What Are They?" *Strategic Management Journal,* 21:1105–1121.

Ethiraj, S. K., Kale, P., Krishnan, M. S. and Singh, J. V. (2005), "Where Do Capabilities Come From and How Do They Matter? A Study in the Software Services Industry," *Strategic Management Journal,* 26: 25–45.

Feenstra, R. C. and Hanson, G. H. (2005), "Ownership and Control in Outsourcing to China: Estimating the Property-Rights Theory of the Firm," *Quarterly Journal of Economics,* May, 729–761.

Feeny, D. F. and Willcocks, L. P. (1998), "Core Is Capabilities for Exploiting Information Technology," *Sloan Management Review,* 39(3): 9–21.

Feeny, D., Lacity, M. and Willcocks, L. P. (2005), "Taking the Measure of Outsourcing Providers," *Sloan Management Review,* 46(3): 41–48.

Ferratt, T. W., Agarwal, R., Brown, C. V. and Moore, J. E. (2005), "IT Human Resource Management Configurations and IT Turnover: Theoretical Synthesis and Empirical Analysis," *Information Systems Research,* 16 (3): 237–255.

Friedman, T. (2005), *The World is Flat: A Brief History of the Twenty-First Century.*

Garud, R. and Kumaraswamy, A. (2005), "Vicious and Virtuous Circles in the Management of Knowledge: The Case of Infosys Technologies," *MIS Quarterly,* 29 (1): 9–33.

Gewald, H. and Dibbern, J. (2009), "Risks and Benefits of Business Process Outsourcing: A Study of Transaction Services in the German Banking Industry," *Information & Management,* 46: 249–257.

Goles, T. (2001), *The Impact of Client-Vendor Relationship on Outsourcing Success,* Unpublished Ph.D. Dissertation, University of Houston, Houston, TX 2001.

Gonzales, R., Gasco, J. and Llopis, J (2006), "Information Systems Outsourcing: A literature Analysis," *Information & Management,* 43(7): 821–834.

Gupta, U. and Raval, V. (1999), "Critical Success Factors for Anchoring Offshore Projects," *Information Strategy,* 15(2): 21–27.

Herbsleb, J., Zubrow, D., Goldenson, D., Hayes, W. and Paulk, M. (1997), "Software Quality and the Capability Maturity Model," *Communications of the ACM,* 40(6): 30–40.

Hitt, M. A., Bierman, L., Uhlenbruck, K. and Shimizu, K. (2006), "The Importance of Resources in the Internationalization of Professional Service Firms: The Good, the Bad, and the Ugly," *Academy of Management Journal,* 49(6): 1137–1157.

Hu, W., Chen, Y., Fan, Y. and Cao, K. (2007), "Software Outsourcing in Beijing: Fundamentals, Trends, and Implications," Working Paper, Renmin University of China, 2007.

Hsieh, C.-T. and Woo, K. T. (2005), "The Impact of Outsourcing to China on Hong Kong's Labor Market," *The American Economic Review,* December 1673–1687.

Iacono, C. S., Subramani, M. and Henderson, J. C. (1995), "Entrepreneur or Intermediary: The Nature of the Relationship Manager's Job," *International Conference on Information Systems,* 289–301.

Jarvenpaa, S. L. and Mao, J.-Y. (2008), "Operational Capabilities Development in Mediated Offshore Software Services Models," *Journal of Information Technology,* 23: 1–17.

Ju, D. (2001), "China's Budding Software Industry," *IEEE Software,* May–June, 92–95.

Kaiser, K. and Hawk, S. (2004), "Evolution of Offshore Software Development: From Outsourcing to Co-Sourcing," *MIS Quarterly Executive,* 3 (2): 69–81.

Kennedy, G. and Clark, G. (2006), "Outsourcing to China – Risks and Benefits," *The Computer Law and Security Report*, 22(3): 250–253.

Koh, C., Ang, S. and Straub, D.W. (2004), "IT Outsourcing Success: A Psychological Contract Perspective," *Information Systems Research*, 15(4): 356–373.

Krishnan, M. S., and Kellner, M. I. (1999), "Measuring Process Consistency: Implications for Reducing Software Defects," *IEEE Transactions on Software Engineering*, 25(6): 800–815.

Levina, N. (2006), "Collaborating Across Boundaries in a Global Economy: Do Organizational Boundaries and Country Contexts Matter?" *Twenty-Seventh International Conference on information Systems*, Milwaukee, 527–542.

Levina, N. and Ross, J. W. (2003), "From the Vendor's Perspective: Exploring the Value Proposition in Information Technology Outsourcing," *MIS Quarterly*, 27(3): 331–364.

Levina, N. and Su, N. (2008), "Global Multisourcing Strategy: The Emergence of a Supplier Portfolio in Services Outsourcing," *Decision Sciences*, 19(3): 541–569.

Levina, N. and Vaast, E. 2008 "Innovating or Doing as Told? Status Differences and Overlapping Boundaries in Offshore Collaboration," *MIS Quarterly*, 32(2): 307–322.

Luo, Y. (2002), "Capability Exploitation and Building in a Foreign Market: Implications for Multinational Enterprises," *Organization Science*, 13(1): 48–63.

Liker, J. K. and Choi, T. Y. (2004), "Building Deep Supplier Relationships," *Harvard Business Review*, 82(12): 104–113.

Mao, J.-Y., Lee, J.-N. and Deng, C.-P. (2008), "Vendors' Perspectives on Trust and Control in Offshore Information Systems Outsourcing," *Information & Management*, 45: 482–492.

Morstead, S. and Blount, G. (2003), *Offshore Ready: Strategies to Plan & Profit from Offshore IT-Enabled Services*, ISANI Press, USA.

Nicholson, B. and Sahay, S. (2001), "Some Political and Cultural Issues in the Globalization of Software Development: Case Experience from Britain and India," *Information and Organization*, 11: 25–43.

Organisation for Economic Co-operation and Development (OECD) (2007), "Is China the New Centre for Offshoring of IT and ICT-enabled Services?" 29 March 2007, JT03224696.

Oshri, I., Kotlarsky, J. and Willcocks, L. (2007), "Managing dispersed expertise in IT offshore outsourcing: Lessons from Tata Consultancy Services," *MIS Quarterly Executive*, 6(2): 53–65.

Pan, S., Pan, G. and Hsieh, M. J. (2005), "A dual-level analysis of the capability development Process: A case study of TT&T," *Journal of the American Society for Information Science and Technology*, 57(13): 1814–1829.

Penrose, E. T. (1959), *The Theory of the Growth of the Firm*, Wiley: New York.

Pries-Heje, J., Baskerville, R. and Hansen, G. I. (2005), "Strategy models for enabling offshore outsourcing: Russian short-cycle-time software development," *Information Technology for Development*, 11(1): 5–30.

Qu, Z. and Brocklehurst, M. (2003), "What will it take for China to become a competitive force in offshore outsourcing? An analysis of the role of transaction costs in supplier selection," *Journal of Information Technology*, 18(1): 53–67.

Rajkumar, T. M. and Mani, R. V. S. (2001), "Offshore software development: The view from indian suppliers," *Information Systems Management*, 18: 63–73.

Ross, J. W., Beath, C. M. and Goodhue, D. L. (1996), "Develop long-term competitiveness through IT assets," *Sloan Management Review*, 38(1) 31–42.

Rottman, J. W. and Lacity, M. C. (2006), "Proven Practice Effectively Offshoring IT Work," *Sloan Management Review*, 47(3): 56–63.

Sapienza, H. J., Autio, E., George, G. and Zahra, S. A. (2006), "A capabilities perspective on the effects of early internationalization of firm survival and growth," *Academy of Management Review*, 31(4): 914–933.

Su, N. (2008), "Internationalization strategies of IT vendors from emerging economies: The case of China," *Proceedings of Twenty Ninth International Conference on Information Systems*, Paris 2008.

Tanriverdi, H., Konana, P. and Ge, L. (2007), "The choice of sourcing mechanisms for business processes," *Information Systems Research*, 18(3): 280–299.

Vashistha, A. and Vashistha, A. (2006), *The Offshore Nation: Strategies for Success in Global Outsourcing and Offshoring*, McGraw-Hill, New York.

Wade, M. and Hulland, J. (2004), "The resource-based view and information systems research: Review, extension, and suggestions for future research," *MIS Quarterly*, 28 (1): 107–142.

Vestring, T., Rouse, T. and Reinert, U. (2005), "Hedge your offshoring bets," *Sloan Management Review*, 46(3): 27–29.

Willcocks, L. and Lacity, M. C. (2000), "Relationships in IT outsourcing: A stakeholder Perspective," in R. Zmud (ed), *Framing the Domains of IT Management*, Pinnaflex Inc. Cincinnati, OH, 2000, 355–384.

Willcocks, L. and Lacity, M. (2006), *Global Sourcing of Business and IT Services*, Palgrave, London.

Vlaar, P. W., Van Fenema, P. C. and Tiwari, V. (2008), "Cocreating understanding and value in distributed work: How members of onsite and offshore vendor teams give, make, demand, and break sense," *MIS Quarterly*, 32: 227–255.

Wu, L.-Y. (2006), "Resources, dynamic capabilities and performance in a dynamic environment: Perceptions in Taiwanese IT enterprises," *Information and Management*, 43: 447–454.

Wu, Q., Klincewicz, K. and Miyazaki, K. (2005), "Sectoral systems of innovation in Asia: Partnership networks of software companies in China and India" Working paper, Graduate School of Innovation Management, Tokyo Institute of Technology, 16 December 2005.

Zahra, S. A., Sapienza, H. J. and Davidsson, P. (2006), "Entrepreneurship and dynamic capabilities: A review, model, and research agenda," *Journal of Management Studies*, 43(4): 917–955.

Zollo, M. and Winter, S. G. (2002), "Deliberate learning and the evolution of dynamic capabilities," *Organization Science*, 13(3): 339–351.

Yin, R. K. (1989), *Case Study Research Design and Methods*, Sage Publications, Vol. 5, Newbury Park, CA.

Youndt, M. A., Snell, S. A., Dean, J. W. and Lepak, D. P. (1996), "Human resource management, manufacturing strategy, and firm performance," *Academy of Management Journal*, 39(4): 836–866.

6
Testing Alternative Perspectives of Governance in China: A Focus on Social Ties, Relational Governance and Contracts

Laura Poppo and Kevin Zheng Zhou

Introduction

Our understanding of the economic institutions that govern the exchange of products and services is rather well informed. Empirical work that emphasizes the comparative governance choice of "economic" institutions (contracts, market competition and vertical integration) largely validates the transaction cost framework (Shelanski and Klein, 1995), leading Williamson (1999: 1092) to claim that "transaction cost economics is an empirical success story". While we seem to know a fair amount about how institutions matter (North, 1990), we have little systematic evaluation, and thus knowledge, about an equally important process: the evolution of governance (Hamilton and Biggart, 1988; Hill, 1995; North, 1990; Peng, 2003: 277; Powell, 1996; Zhao et al., 2005 and 2008). This gap in knowledge is especially germane to emerging economies, which must "deinstitutionalize" (Oliver, 1992: 564) existing social, economic and political systems as economies privatize, secure property rights and develop legal institutions to enforce contract law (North, 1992). Theory is surprisingly sparse since no one knows how to create adaptively efficient institutional frameworks (North, 1990). The challenge is that managers may not choose the most efficient arrangements since they are predisposed to use their existing institutions (North 1990; Tolbert and Zucker, 1996: 178).

A central issue for emerging economies is whether governance evolves into a Western style, in particular, that endorsed by transaction cost economics (TCE). Consistent with TCE, some opinions advance that as economic trade grows in scope and complexity, governance shifts from personal, reciprocal social ties to more impersonal institutions such as market competition and contract law (North, 1990: 334–35; 1992: 6; Williamson, 1991). Peng (2003: 280), for example, argues that "as the economy expands, the scale, scope, and specificity of transactions rise exponentially, calling for the emergence of third-party enforcement through formal legal and regulatory regimes."

Interestingly, an alternative and potentially conflicting perspective argues that social ties continue to govern exchange relationships in emerging economies such as China. Social ties as a governance mechanism is not culturally unique to China; yet it is a deeply embedded institution with a history of more than 5000 years (Park and Luo, 2001). Boisot and Child (1996) suggest that social ties fundamentally distinguish governance in China from the Western practice: "It is therefore not the presence of networking that is distinctive about China's emerging economic order but, rather, the depth and nature of its social embeddedness" (1996: 623). They further argue that the Chinese system of network transactions does not fit with Western analyses and China's rapid economic development is not merely in transition to a Western model but being accomplished through a system of governance and transaction system that differs from Western experience. Xin and Pearce (1996) similarly argue that social ties as a 'personal trust-based' form of governance largely defines governance in China (see also Park and Luo, 2001).

Controversy thus exists as to the choice of institutions that will invariably define governance of markets in China. While Peng (2003) suggests, consistent with a transaction cost logic, that China is in an institutional transition toward more market governance, Boisot and Child (1996) beg to differ and endorse a reliance on social ties. To explore this controversy, we take a snapshot of governance in China in an effort to both document its evolution as well as examine the determinants of the governance choice. In particular, we examine alternative governance choices such as social ties, market competition, contracts, or relational governance in the face of exchange hazards, namely asset specificity, uncertainty and transaction frequency. As the first study of its kind, we aim to contribute to the literature in deepening our understanding of the choices of governance institutions in emerging economies and shed some light to inform the ongoing controversy.

Social ties, relational governance and contracts

Social ties as a governance mechanism coordinates exchange through repeat dealing, shared values and a lack of third-party enforcement (North, 1990). Long-standing social ties characterize economic activities in many emerging economies (North, 1990; for review see Peng, 2003: 284), and have been referred to the "lifeblood...of business conduct in Chinese society" (Park and Luo, 2001; Xin and Pearce, 1996; Zhao et al., 2005). While family members constitute the strongest type of ties, membership also extends to close friends and non-family members. A central feature of social ties is coordinating *renqing*, unpaid debts or favours that accrue over time through reciprocal offerings of gifts and favors (Chen, 2001). Interestingly, while *"renqing* obligations must always be repaid, ... there is no specified time frame for the return of favors": it is precisely the non-specific nature of the timeframe that makes *renqing* obligations so binding and social ties so enduring and pervasive (Chen, 2001: 39–50). In addition, favours do not have to be equitable. In fact it is preferred that favours do not balance each other since because favours are owed, relationships continue.

Empirical and case study work indicates that social ties are central to the governance of business transactions and also foster economic performance in China (Park and Luo, 2001; Xin and Pearce, 1996). Informal interpersonal relationships exist not only with managers at other firms but also with government officials: as such, the manager is a broker armed with useful ties and contacts (Peng and Heath, 1996). As Boisot and Child (1996) note, many business transactions are settled through negotiation within a system of networked interpersonal reciprocal obligations. Peng and Luo (2000) also find that ties with political officials as well as with other firms positively impact firm performance.

As compared to social ties, relational governance is a more specific social institution that has received great attention from researchers and practitioners alike in the past two decades. Whereas social ties reflect the "general" exchange of favours, relational governance refers to specific reciprocal practices that facilitate the business exchange: disclosure of proprietary information, joint planning and operations, and commitments to work closely and cooperatively (Anderson and Narus, 1990; MacNeil, 1980; Noordewier et al., 1990). Hence, compared to social ties, relational governance tends to be more calculative, with more codification and transparency (Peng, 2003: 292). A second distinction is that while the timeframe for social ties is non-specific, window for reciprocal action of relational governance can be quite small: price adjustments, for example, require immediate reciprocal disclosures of private information in production costs (Anderson and Narus, 1990; MacNeil, 1980). Similar to ties, however, relational governance requires shared norms and values that help extend exchange in the future: bilateralism, mutuality, favour exchange and trust. These norms enable relational governance to deter opportunism, enhance adaptation, and secure exchange-specific investments (Noordewier et al., 1990; Ring and Van de Ven, 1992; Zaheer and Venkatraman, 1995).

In contrast to social intuitions, some scholars suggest that economic institutions are more efficient and effective structures for governing complex exchanges in markets (Williamson, 1985, 1991). In particular, the transaction cost logic advances that for simple exchanges, markets efficiently coordinate adaptation since "price" serves as a sufficient mechanism (Williamson, 1996: 102). That is, the future is expected to conform to the present, such that price can reflect the change in demand or supply (Burczak, 2001). As exchanges are met with a high risk of opportunistic behaviour, managers develop more customized contracts (Williamson, 1991). Such neo-classical contracts invariably function as a "framework" by specifying processes and procedures to guide resolution to unexpected changes. As such, they offer a level of flexibility not found in classical contracts, which more simply focus on the terms of trade and imply no dependency between the buyer and supplier and no need for "identity" (e.g. a social relation) (Williamson, 1996: 95). Moreover, neo-classical contracts specify a "tolerance zone within which misalignments will be absorbed"; "information disclosure and substantiation if adaptation is proposed"; and, arbitration if adaptation fails (Williamson, 1996: 96).

The governance choice

In the sections below, we examine differing logics for the choice of alternative governance forms in the face of asset specificity, environmental uncertainty and transaction frequency – three exchange characteristics described by TCE. Figure 6.1 presents our conceptual framework.

Social ties or market governance

Asset specificity emerges when the product or service requires significant relationship-specific investments in physical and/or human assets (Williamson, 1985). According to TCE, market competition most efficiently coordinates relatively simple, standard products with low levels of asset specificity. Since the

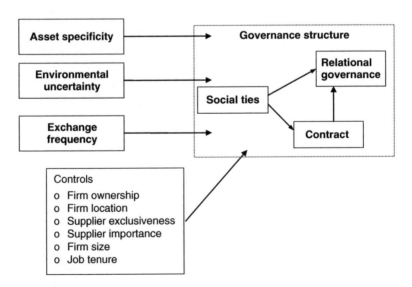

Figure 6.1 The conceptual model

assets are fully transferable to other businesses, price reflects the impact of changes in product demand or supply and is sufficient to coordinate exchange (Williamson, 1991). For market exchanges, parties do not have to know each other. As Granovetter (1985) explains, if traders encounter difficult relationships characterized by mistrust or malfeasance in market exchanges, they simply move on to others who are willing to do business on market terms; social relations thus become frictional matters.

When assets become specialized to the transaction, markets no longer effectively coordinate exchanges. Parties cannot simply resort to price to determine the adjustment – they may behave strategically by distorting information or disclosing it incompletely and selectively (Williamson, 1991). Because specialized assets cannot be redeployed without sacrifice, should contracts be interrupted or prematurely terminated, such investments are inherently risky (Williamson, 1985). In this case, a safeguarding problem arises, that is, the firm who deploys specific assets may fear that its partner may exploit these investments opportunistically (Rindfleisch and Heide, 1997). Thus, identity clearly matters when assets become more specialized, because the two parties must coordinate adaptation to unexpected changes.

According to this logic, market governance is superior to personal, social relationships for simple, non-specialized exchanges. Market-supporting institutions such as systems of weights and measures are intricately and completely standardized for simple exchanges; accordingly, parties can rely on market institutions to determine price and quantity (North, 1991). China, according to Peng (2003), is evolving toward market governance, and is replacing personal with more impersonal forms of governance. Based on this TCE logic, we expect that parties will forgo their reliance on social ties if assets are less specialized; price and quantity, not prior ties, are used to match buyers and suppliers. Therefore:

H1a: The lower the level of asset specificity, the less the reliance on long-standing social ties.

Others, however, counter that China "is moving not toward a market order, as it claims, but toward a form that can be labeled network capitalism" (Boisot and Child, 1996: 19; see also Biggart and Hamilton, 1992). For Boisot and Child (1996), a glaring inefficiency of network capitalism occurs when exchanges that could be efficiently coordinated through arm's-length transactions are instead managed through personal interactions. Parties rely on social ties for the most benign transactions, simply because of the long-standing history and reliance on this social institution. Boisot and Child (1996) explain: "The roots of networking as an institutionalized practice are ancient and extensively developed in China." Such social institutions are very resistant to change, and therefore pose the problem of inertia. While political laws can be turned overnight, social institutions persist, despite complementary changes in political, legal and market institutions (North, 1991). Based on this logic, reliance on long-standing social ties is independent of asset specificity. We do not formalize this alternative hypothesis. Instead, if we find no significant relationship in H1, we can infer that exchanges in China are still characterized by long-standing social ties and are resisting the impersonal mode of market governance.

Social ties and relational governance

An alternative logic is built on the benefits of trust that accrue from doing business with a long-standing partner. Information from a trusted informant is cheap, more detailed, and tends to be accurate (Granovetter, 1985). For continuing relations, parties also have an economic incentive to be trustworthy in order to maintain a long-term relationship. Aside from pure economic incentives, social content often overlays with ongoing economic relations in that it carries strong expectations of trust (Granovetter, 1985). Through ongoing interactions, exchange partners learn about each other and develop trust around norms of equity (Gulati, 1995). Because trust may supplant the vulnerability and investment risk of specialized assets, managers may strategically match investments in specialized assets with long-term trading partners. We do not formalize this hypothesis, since it is the reverse way of stating H1a.

The above logic also underlies the development of relational governance. As opportunism becomes probable in market exchanges, managers turn to relational governance to deter malfeasant behaviour (Artz and Brush, 2000; Bradach and Eccles, 1989; Noordewier et al., 1990). Trust enables partners to act as if the expected value of the exchange were stable, even in the presence of specific assets (Luhmann, 1979). Such stability is central to the functionality of relational governance since its business practices are aimed at projecting exchange into the future by joint planning and operations, information exchange and cooperation. Moreover, relational governance also serves as a requisite safeguard, since parties must commit sizeable investments to develop this social institution, thereby implying high termination costs (Zaheer and Venkatraman, 1995). Therefore:

H1b: The higher the level of asset specificity, the higher the level of relational governance.

Environmental uncertainty, the unanticipated changes in circumstances surrounding an exchange, is also likely to foster a greater reliance on long-standing trading partners and relational governance. Uncertainty challenges coordination by requiring the parties to adapt to problems that arise from unforeseeable changes by modifying their business agreement. In such conditions, adaptation can be problematic. For example,

A manufacturer that, because of competitive entry, must modify the design of its product also may need to modify the design of the purchased components that constitute the end product. Unless a comprehensive contract can be written with its supplier, which specifies in advance the required component designs and the associated terms of trade, the manufacturer may need to assume the considerable transaction costs associated with ongoing renegotiations. (Rindfleisch and Heide, 1997: 31)

Yet, because trust underlies long-standing ties and relational governance, adaptation to unexpected events is likely to be less problematic. With trust, parties can act with greater certainty, since they have expectations about how each party with behave in the future (Zaheer and Venkatraman, 1995). Managers, realizing this governance advantage, build social ties and relational governance in response to uncertainty.

> **H2a:** The higher the level of market uncertainty, the greater the reliance on long-standing social ties.
>
> **H2b:** The higher the level of market uncertainty, the higher the levels of relational governance.

A third factor that affects the choice of social ties is transaction frequency. According to North (1990: 34), governance through 'repeat dealing' is characteristic of small-scale regional transactions. Repeat dealing is critical to the development of norms that govern exchange behaviour. For example, personal relations emerging from past interaction in turn exert pressures for conformity to mutual expectations (Macaulay, 1963). Larson (1992) also argues that repeat interactions create mutual expectations and, over time, governance emerges from the network of social interactions, not from administrative controls. Ring and Van de Ven (1992) advance that repeated market transactions enable parties to affirm the observance of norms of equity; as a consequence, reliance on social ties will emerge. That is, through frequent transactions, parties become known to each other better and thus rely more on long-standing ties to facilitate exchange and safeguard against uncertainties. That is:

> **H3:** The higher the transaction frequency, the greater the reliance on long-standing social ties.

We extend this logic to understand the social origin of relational governance. Exchange frequency enables social ties, which in turn enables relational governance. Because social ties underlie the formation of interpersonal relations, sociologists believe that relational governance evolves from prior social ties. This logic advances that social ties enable reputations of trustworthiness to develop, and without confidence of another's nature, parties would not commit to costs and risks of developing joint business practices (Granovetter, 1985; Gulati, 1995; Uzzi, 1997). Relational governance is predicted on trust, and requires parties to adopt specialized business practices that directly facilitate ongoing adaptation through better coordination and planning. For example, relational business practices include the disclosure of private information, initiatives to work in close local to one another, and norms that focus on equitable outcomes to adjustments (Heide and John, 1992). Since trust initially emerges from long-standing social ties, such ties are likely to characterize the emergence of relational governance. Hence, we hypothesize:

> **H4**: The more long-standing the social ties, the higher the level of relational governance.

In China, however, it is not obvious that social ties will evolve toward greater levels of relational governance. While such ties are founded on norms of reciprocity and trust, parties may simply lack incentives and suffer from the adherence to the status quo, forestalling adoption of relational governance. North (1991: 102,) explains that incentives must exist for players to invest "their time, resources, and energy in knowledge and skills that will improve their material status". Tribal societies, for example, resist such evolution because a dense social network indicates a delicate balance of power and deviance and innovation from existing ties are viewed as a threat to group survival (North, 1991). Thus managers may not choose to evolve their social ties into joint business practices.

A second factor that might undermine the evolution of social ties to relational governance is that deeply embedded social ties are less likely to have access to new information or opportunities. Uzzi (1997: 58) explains, if "all the firms in a network are connected through embedded ties ... there are few or no links to outside members who can potentially contribute innovate ideas" (see also Burt, 1992). Such embeddedness forestalls creativity and novelty, which are believed to be essential to value creation. Consistent with this logic, Peng and Heath (1996) find that state-owned enterprises do not fuel growth by adopting new practices, such as internal expansion or acquisition. Instead, these firms rely on personal trust and informal agreements to coordinate exchanges. Thus, managers with deeply embedded ties may simply lack knowledge of the benefits of coordinated business practices through relational governance.

Contracts

Formal contracts represent promises or obligations to perform particular actions in the future (MacNeil, 1980). According to TCE, asset specificity and uncertainty trigger the use of more customized contracts, since clauses tailor the duration, expectations, processes and procedures aimed at preserving the cost, quality and service of the product (Williamson, 1985). In doing so, contracts narrow the domain of risk imposed by non-salvageable assets, since premature termination of the relationship imposes a capital loss (i.e., parties have not fully recovered the non-salvageable investments). Accordingly, managers generally rely on more complex contracts as asset specificity increases (Joskow, 1988). While contracts are not necessarily complete, and gap-filling occurs, they inevitably function as a framework for guiding adaptation due to unexpected events. Managers, therefore, craft contracts to provide a safeguard, albeit not perfect, from the uncoordinated, self-interested actions that may increase with uncertainty. Infrequent exchange is a third factor that increases the use of contracts. For exchanges that approximate a 'one-time' purchase, incentive effects from repeat purchases do not exist. Knowing that the potential for opportunistic behaviour exists, parties develop more customized contracts to safeguard their interests (Williamson, 1985). That is:

H5a: The higher the level of asset specificity, the higher the level of contract customization.

H5b: The higher the level of market uncertainty, the higher the levels of contract customization.

H5c: The lower the transaction frequency, the higher the level of contract customization.

Although firms may use contracts to coordinate exchanges (see Luo, 2002), there are several institutional factors that may undermine the legitimacy of this governance choice, thereby potentially hindering the use of contracts. First, despite the continued institutional reform since 1979, legal institutions still lack predictability in China owing to "high levels of inconsistency, arbitrariness, and corruption of the part of officials" (Child and Mollering, 2003: 72). In such conditions, firms cannot be certain that the courts will enforce the payment of accounts receivable by other companies or uphold sanctions against untrustworthy behaviour by employees (Child and Mollering, 2003). Because of the lack of consistency in its implementation, uncertainty still characterizes the legal system in China and may hinder the use of contracts.

A second factor that may deter the use of contracts is the lack of formal rules. In order for a decentralized market economy to function, information must necessarily be codified. In China, however, such codification has been problematic, primarily because of a preference towards 'interpersonal accommodation' – an orientation to particular individuals and relationships – rather than to impersonal rules (Boisot and Child, 1988). Without predictability and the systematic use of laws, China's traditional model of social organization persists (Gernet, 1982). Peng and Heath (1996) similarly suggest that uncertain economies, such as Eastern Europe, former Soviet republics, and China may utilize personal relations to compensate for the not fully developed political institutions (such as transparent laws and regulations). Given this context, it is difficult to predict at what time China will fully move to a more 'rule-based', contract law-driven system to govern complex and specialized commerce (Peng, 2003).

If contracts cannot reduce uncertainty by providing a reliable structure for business conduct, managers may not choose contracts in accordance with TCE logic. Given that crafting customized contracts is costly and enforcement is uncertain, managers may not bother with such an investment, resulting in a 'noisy' (that is, a non-significant) relationship between exchange hazards and contract customization (H5a~ H5c).

Contracts and relational governance

Recent literature also suggests that customized contracts may foster relational governance (Luo, 2002; Poppo and Zenger, 2002). Contracts alone serve simply to facilitate termination of an exchange as courts use it to review the broken aspects of the contract and then allocate assets between the parties on some basis deemed equitable (MacNeil, 1980). Knowing this, managers realize that to enhance commitment to the contract, they can invest in the social safeguard of relational governance. The stability and cooperation of relational governance complements the adaptive limits of customized contracts (Poppo and Zenger, 2002). In addition, the cooperation necessary to produce a contract mimics the cooperation necessary for relational governance, thereby setting routines in place for its development. That is:

> **H6**: The higher the level of contract customization, the higher the level of relational governance.

Research method

To test the hypothesis, we examined buyer–supplier relationships for manufacturing firms located in three major areas (Beijing, Guangzhou and Shanghai) in China, the largest emerging and fastest-growing economy. These three areas represent the most developed regions, and are still transitioning toward a market economy (Luo, 2002; Zhou et al., 2003). Hence, they offer a rich context to test our model of governance choices in an emerging economy. We collaborated with local researchers to have trained interviewers to carry out the survey through on-site personal interviews, as this is a key means of obtaining reliable and valid information in emerging economies (Hoskisson et al., 2000: 258).

We first developed an English version of the questionnaire and then had independent translators to translate it into Chinese with back translation to ensure conceptual equivalence (Hoskisson et al., 2000). To further ensure content and face validity of the measures, we conducted seven in-depth interviews with senior purchasing managers, in which each respondent was asked to check the relevance and completeness of the measures. Based on their responses, a small number of questionnaire items were revised to enhance their clarity. Then, we conducted a pilot study with 50 purchasing professionals, in which the respondents were requested not only to answer all the questionnaire items but to provide their feedback on the design and wording of the questionnaire. We then finalized the questionnaire based on the results of the pilot study.

A sample of 1,450 firms was randomly selected from a list of all manufacturing firms in four-digit standard industrial classification (SIC) codes 2011 ~ 3899 that were located in Beijing, Guangzhou and Shanghai. These firms spanned diversified industries (e.g., electronics, computer equipment, chemicals, transportation equipment, apparel, furniture, food and plastics), which increases the generalizability of our findings. In each firm, a senior manager (e.g., CEO, VP, or senior purchasing manager) was chosen as the key informant because our field interview revealed that these managers were heavily involved with major suppliers.

Managers were first contacted by telephone to solicit their cooperation. To motivate managers to participate, we informed them of the academic nature of this study and confidentiality of their responses, as well as offering an incentive in the form of a summary report. A total of 515 managers from different firms orally agreed to participate and we successfully interviewed 373 managers, representing a response rate of 25.7 per cent (373 out of 1,450 firms). Informants were first asked to select one of their firm's major suppliers, and they then answered the survey questions regarding their exchanges with the chosen supplier. After eliminating 12 surveys with excessive missing data, we obtained 361 complete responses. A comparison between the responding and non-responding firms using MANOVA indicated there were no significant differences in terms of key firm characteristics (i.e., industry type, firm ownership, location, the number of employees and annual sales revenues) (Wilks' $\Lambda = .946$; $F = 1.743$; $p = .632$), suggesting that non-response bias is not a concern in our study. After the fieldwork, one of the authors randomly called 30 respondents to confirm that the interviews had been conducted. No cheating in the fieldwork was found.

The final sample consisted of 361 firms across major SIC groups in the manufacturing sector, such as industrial and commercial machinery and computer equipment (28.6 per cent), electronic and other electrical equipment and components (13.0 per cent), chemicals and allied products (10.5 per cent), food and kindred products (5.3 per cent), fabricated metal products (4.2 per cent), apparel and other finished products made from fabrics and similar materials (3.9 per cent), and rubber and miscellaneous plastics products (3.9 per cent).

Nearly three quarters of the companies (74.8 per cent) had annual sales revenue of more than 3 million US dollars. The majority of the firms (68.4 per cent) had 100 to 500 employees. In addition, 61.2 per cent were Chinese firms (20.8 per cent were state-owned, 27.7 per cent were private, and 12.7 per cent were listed stock companies) and 38.8 per cent were foreign-owned firms or joint ventures.

Measures

The measures used in the survey were adapted from established studies. The measurement items and validity assessment are presented in Appendix 6.

> **Exchange hazards.** TCE identifies three characteristics that pose hazards to market transactions: asset specificity, environmental uncertainty and transaction frequency. *Asset specificity* refers to transaction-specific assets which are not redeployable to alternative uses (Williamson, 1985). It was measured with five items (five-point scale: 1 = not at all, 5 = very much) adapted from Hallén et al. (1991). These items capture buyers' specific investments in product features, personnel, inventory and distribution, marketing, as well as capital equipment and tools to accommodate the suppliers' needs. The measure of *environmental uncertainty* was adapted from John and Weitz (1989) and Noordewier et al. (1990), and consisted of four items (five-point scale: 1 = minor, 5 = major change) that assess the environmental changes in the supply market with respects to pricing, product feature and specification, vendor support services, and technology. Consistent with Anderson (1985) and Anderson and Schmittlein (1984), we measured *transaction frequency* by asking respondents to indicate how frequently their firms place purchasing orders with their suppliers.
>
> **Governance structures**. We measured three types of governance structures, that is, social ties, contract customization and relational governance. Luo and Park (2001: 148) suggest that because it takes time to cultivate social ties, the length of relationship is a good indicator of social ties. Uzzi (1999: 493) based on his extensive interviews with managers, also concludes that a good measure of embedded social ties is the duration of the relationship (see also Poppo and Zenger 2002: 717). Hence, we measured *social ties* by asking how long the firm has been doing business with its supplier. *Contract customization* was measured with three items (five-point scale: 1=strongly disagree, 5=strong agree) adapted from Lusch and Brown (1996). These items measure the specificity, formality, and details of contractual agreements between manufacturers and their suppliers.
>
> Relational governance is based on the use of shared norms to monitor and coordinate the behaviours of the exchange partners (MacNeil, 1980), and is a multidimensional construct consisting of both shared

norms and joint actions (e.g., Heide and John, 1992; Jap and Ganesan, 2000; Zaheer and Venkatraman, 1995). Consistent with Jap and Ganesan (2000), we measured relational governance as a higher-order factor consisting of cooperative norms, information sharing and joint operation. All three sub-dimensions were measured on a five-point scale (1 = strongly disagree, 5 = strong agree). The measure of cooperative norms has five items pertaining to a firm's willingness and belief to cooperate with its partner (Anderson and Narus, 1990). The measure of information sharing has four items regarding the extent to which two firms share their proprietary information, cost information, product development, and supply and demand forecasts (Mohr and Sohi, 1995). The measure of joint operation contains three items related to the degree to which the buyer and suppler have worked together to facilitate operations (Zaheer and Venkatraman, 1995).

Controls. We controlled three sets of variables. First, we controlled *firm size* and *job tenure* because firm size and manager's work experience may affect governance decisions (Poppo and Zenger, 2002). We used the number of employees in the company to indicate firm size, and the length of time the manager has worked for the firm to proxy job tenure (both are categorical variables). Second, a firm's dependence on the supplier may impact the way it builds a relationship with its supplier (Lusch and Brown, 1996). Hence, we included *supply exclusiveness* and *supply importance* as controls. The supply exclusiveness scale contains four items related to the availability of same or similar products and suppliers. The supply importance scale consists of three items concerning the importance, essentiality and priority of the product from the supplier compared to the purchases from other suppliers. Third, owing to the prevalent influence of institutional factors in emerging markets (Hoskisson et al., 2000), we controlled the effects of *state-owned buyer* and *supplier location* – two important institutional factors in China (Park and Luo, 2001: 460). State-owned buyer was coded as a dummy variable with 1 = state-owned and 0 = non-state-owned firms. Supplier location was also coded as a dummy variable where 1 = located in China and 0 = located overseas.

Common Method Assessment. Since we collected information on dependent and independent variables from the same respondent, a common method bias may occur. We checked this potential problem with the Harman one-factor test (Podsakoff and Organ, 1986). This technique loads all the variables into an exploratory factor analysis. If (a) a single factor emerges from the factor analysis, or (b) factor 1 accounts for the majority of the variances, then common method bias is a concern. In the test, a factor analysis of all the measurement items resulted in a solution which accounted for 64.80 per cent of the total variance; and factor 1 accounted for 19.01 per cent of the variance. Because a single factor did not emerge and factor 1 did not explain most of the variance, common method bias is unlikely to be a concern in our data.

Construct Validity. We refined the measures and assessed their construct validity following the guidelines suggested by Anderson and Gerbing (1988). First, exploratory factor analyses were run for all multiple-item variables and resulted in factor solutions as theoretically expected. Reliability analyses further showed that these measures possessed satisfactory coefficient reliability. Then, confirmatory factor analyses were run for each of the three sets of constructs (i.e., exchange hazards, governance structures and controls), as well as an overall 12-factor model with all the variables included. All the confirmatory models fit the data satisfactorily (e.g., the overall model: $\chi^2(264) = 696.76$, p <.001; GFI=. 90, CFI=. 91, IFI=. 91; RMSEA=. 067), indicating the uni-dimensionality of the measures (Anderson and Gerbing, 1988). Further, all factor loadings were highly significant (p <.001). The composite reliabilities of all constructs except one were greater than .70, and the reliability of uncertainty was .667, which was also above the usual .60 benchmark (Bagozzi and Yi, 1988: 80). Thus, these measures demonstrate adequate convergent validity.

The discriminant validity of the measures was assessed through chi-square difference test. The tests were run for all the multiple-item scales in pairs (15 tests altogether) to test if the restricted model (in which the correlation was fixed as one) was significantly worse than the freely-estimated model (in which the correlation was estimated freely). All the chi-square differences were highly significant (e.g., the test for supply importance and contract customization: $\Delta\chi^2(1) = 232.234$, p =.000), providing evidence for discriminant validity (Anderson and Gerbing, 1988). Overall, these results show that the measures in this study possess satisfactory reliability and validity.

The results of CFA (i.e. confirmatory factor analysis) such as goodness-of-fit index, factor loading and composite reliability are reported in the Appendix 6. Table 6.1 presents means, standard deviations and correlations for the constructs.

Analyses and results

To test the hypotheses, we employed structural equation modelling with maximum likelihood estimation method, using the model illustrated in Figure 6.1 as the base model. In the model, asset specificity, environmental uncertainty and transaction frequency are treated as important exogenous constructs, with social ties, contract customization and relational governance as the dependent variables. The six control variables are also included in the model and are linked

Table 6.1 Basic descriptive statistics of the constructs

Construct	1	2	3	4	5	6	7	8	9	10	11	12
1. Asset specificity	1.00											
2. Uncertainty	-.16**	1.00										
3. Transaction frequency	.07	-.09	1.00									
4. Social ties	.05	.10*	.26**	1.00								
5. Contract customization	-.07	.23**	-.10*	.10*	1.00							
6. Relational governance	.39**	.25**	-.02	.07	.28**	1.00						
7. Supply exclusiveness	.39**	-.20**	-.03	-.04	-.08	.33**	1.00					
8. Supply importance	.07	.22**	.06	.12*	.41**	.36**	.14*	1.00				
9. State-owned buyer	-.08	.04	-.01	.17**	-.08	-.16**	-.21**	-.08	1.00			
10. Supplier location	-.06	-.07	.09	-.11*	.00	-.13*	-.14*	-.02	.11*	1.00		
11. Firm size	.04	.00	.03	.26**	.00	-.01	-.13*	-.01	.31**	-.02	1.00	
12. Job tenure	-.03	.01	-.06	.20**	-.02	-.09	-.04	.00	.21**	-.06	.31**	1.00
Mean	2.07	3.66	4.46	3.00	3.99	3.18	2.07	3.94	.21	.77	3.84	2.60
S.D.	.80	.61	1.37	1.28	.82	.60	.86	.69	.41	.43	2.35	.93

Note: n = 361 ** p < .01 * p < .05 (2-tailed)

Table 6.2   Standardized structural equation parameter estimates (t-value)

	Social ties	Contract customization	Relational governance
Exogenous variables			
Asset specificity	**H1a:.044**	**H5a:.005**	**H1b:.349** ***
	(.720)	(.076)	(4.892)
Environmental uncertainty	**H2a:.092**	**H5b:.086**	**H2b:.464** ***
	(1.337)	(1.192)	(5.294)
Transaction frequency	**H3:.275** ***	**H5c: −.165** ***	−.014
	(5.607)	(−3.062)	(−.241)
Social ties	____	.097*	**H4: -.001**
		(1.731)	(−.023)
Contract customization	____	____	**H6:.172** **
			(2.372)
Controls			
State-owned buyer	.109*	−.103*	−.050
	(2.107)	(−1.879)	(−.882)
Supplier location	−.128**	.025	−.016
	(−2.595)	(.481)	(−.294)
Supplier exclusiveness	−.011	−.201**	.398***
	(−.148)	(−2.482)	(4.318)
Supplier importance	.098	.486***	.186*
	(1.584)	(6.876)	(2.323)
Firm size	.176***	.007	.088
	(3.330)	(.120)	(1.526)
Tenure	.131**	−.031	−.104+
	(2.605)	(−.576)	(−1.895)
R-Square	.201	.329	.711

Goodness-of-fit: (χ^2 (264) $= 696.76$, p $<.001$, GFI $=. 90$, CFI $=. 91$, IFI $=. 91$; RMSEA $=. 067$)

Note: ***p < 0.001 ** p < 0.01 *p < 0.05 +p $< .10$

directly to the dependent variables. The model fit the data satisfactorily (χ^2 (264) $= 696.76$, p $<.001$, GFI $=. 90$, CFI $=. 91$, IFI $=. 91$; RMSEA $=. 067$). The results are summarized in Table 6.2.

Our first set of hypotheses (H1a, H2a and H3) examines the origins of long-standing social ties. H1a examines the choice of market governance versus social ties. It tests if buyers rely on social ties less as the assets associated with the exchange decrease in specificity, and conversely, if buyers rely more on the use of social ties to safeguard their business interests as assets become more specialized. We find no support for this hypothesis (b$=. 044$, p $>. 10$): buyers do not appear to shift from a "personal" to "impersonal" model of governance as asset specificity decreases. We also examined additional determinants of social ties in H2a and H3. Contrary to H2a, we do not find that managers mitigate environmental uncertainty by selecting suppliers that they have done business with for a longer period of time (b=.092, p >.10). Consistent with H3, we find that more frequent exchanges are positively associated with supply relationships of a longer duration (b=.275, p <.001), suggesting that frequent interaction triggers the development of long-standing social ties.

We next test the determinants of relational governance (H1b, H2b, H4 and H6). We find support for our first two hypotheses (H1b and H2b): increasing levels of asset specificity (b=.349, p <.001) and environmental uncertainty (b =.464, p <.001) lead to greater levels of relational governance. Apparently, managers develop relational governance to safeguard their interests and investments from transactional risks. However, we find no support that relational governance emerges from prior social ties (H4): longer exchange histories are not associated with greater levels of relational governance (b = −.001, p >.10). Our analyses also show that the use of more customized contracts is associated with greater levels of relational governance (b=.172, p <.01), supporting H6.

H5 focuses on the determinants of contract customization. Contrary to H6a and H6b, managers do not appear to craft increasingly customized contracts in response to increasingly levels of asset specificity (b=.005, p >.10) and environmental uncertainty (b=.086, p >.10). Rather, infrequent exchanges trigger higher levels of contract customization (b = −.165, p <.001), supporting H6c. While not hypothesized, social ties positively impact on contract customization (b =.097, p <.05), suggesting that previous contacts enable managers to craft more customized contracts.

Additional results are evident. Institutional parameters, such as state-run enterprises (b=.109, p <.05), location of both buyer and supplier in China (b = −.128, p <.01), larger firms (b=.176, p <.001), and managers with longer job tenure (b=.131, p <.01), increase firms' reliance on long-standing trading partners. This illustrates sources of inertia that may well retard China's transition toward a more "market" economy. Interestingly, state-owned buyers are less likely to customize contracts than privately-held firms (b = −.103, p <.05). Finally, the level of the buyer's dependence on the supplier has a strong influence on governance choices. Increasing levels of supplier importance lead to greater contract customization (b=.486, p <.001) as well as deeper levels of relational governance (b=.186, p <.05). Increasing levels of supplier exclusiveness has mixed effects on governance: it decreases the use of customized contracts (b = −.201, p <.01), yet increases the development of relational governance (b=.398, p <.001).

Discussion

Our chapter contributes to the literature in deepening our understanding of an important, but relatively unexplored topic: the choices of governance institutions in emerging economies. Consistent with Boisot and Child (1996), we find that social ties appear to be prevalent and underlie exchanges in China: managers do not increase their use of 'impersonal markets' for relatively standard, certain exchanges. Instead, they rely on social ties for both hazardous and non-hazardous exchanges. Interestingly, managers largely resist using contracts when they should, at least according to the transaction cost logic. Managers embrace contracts for infrequent exchanges, but not for exchanges associated with greater levels of uncertainty and asset specificity.

Consistent with North (1990), however, we find that path dependencies of reliance on social ties can be altered through vehicles that dismiss or are not as easily bounded by tradition and customs, such as privatization, cooperation with non-Chinese partners, less-embedded (i.e. younger) firms and less tenured managers in their respective companies. We also find consistent with a transaction cost logic that companies build relational governance in response to increasing levels of asset specificity and environmental uncertainty. Moreover, contract customization fosters the development of relational governance. These results suggest that governance shifts are possible and it is premature to conclude that governance in China will necessarily be fundamentally different from the Western experience. Taken together, our findings suggest that governance choices in China are probably more complex than previously depicted.

The persistent yet evolving use of social ties

Our results show that social ties evolve from frequent transactions between buyers and suppliers. However, companies are not switching from a "personal" to a more "impersonal" model of governance as transactions become more certain and less specialized. That is, companies remain in "embedded" relationships with their suppliers regardless of exchange hazard levels. Consistent with the position of Boisot and Child (1996), we suspect that the historical and cultural institutions underlie the persistent use of social ties.

In particular, our findings of control variables show that several institutional factors endorse the use of the existing social order. First, state-owned firms are more likely to rely on social ties than privately held firms. Top managers of state-owned businesses may not be motivated to adopt new governance practices because, unlike top managers of privately held businesses, they are not owners, and therefore are not rewarded on a basis of governance (or performance) efficiency. Such incentive incompatibility would imply that managers lack the requisite market-based skill set (Peng and Heath, 1996). Moreover, since state-owned businesses tend to have much stronger ties with, and thus access, to government officials, should they run into trouble, they naturally turn to the government for assistance (Park and Luo, 2001). Thus, state-owned companies seem to rely more on long-term partners for exchange because they lack experience with and incentives to adopt market-based behaviour.

Second, we find that when both exchange partners are located within China, ties are of a longer duration than when the supplier is located outside of China. Chinese exchange partners may be more resistant to ending trade because both parties share expectations and norms for maintaining the existing social order. Alternatively, when trading partners are located outside China, they are removed from normative pressures to retain existing partners, and can select partners who can best supply the desired product. Third, the duration of buyer-supplier ties are significantly longer for large firms and for long-standing managers at the buying firm. We suspect that larger firms demonstrate greater inertia to convert to more impersonal models of exchange. Similarly, managers with longer job tenure may have a longer history of endorsing social ties, and are therefore more resistant to seeking new trade partners than managers with less job tenure.

While the above results are consistent with the institutional perspective that social customs are culturally embedded and therefore slow to change (DiMaggio and Powell, 1983; North, 1990), they also suggest strategies for facilitating the evolution of more impersonal (market) governance. First, they affirm that a critical strategy in China's reform (and also in other transitional economies) lies in its privatization of businesses that were previously state operated (Park and Luo, 2001). Second, business arrangements can disrupt tradition: joint ventures with non-Chinese firms, young start-ups, and "new" blood within the firm are less likely to be as committed to the existing social order of personal exchange. These results suggest a means through which "paths get reversed" (North, 1992: 6), despite the prevailing normative customs and beliefs.

The economic but not social origins of relational governance

Consistent with our predictions, we find that managers invest in greater levels of relational governance in response to increasing asset specialization and environmental uncertainty. It appears that managers find relational governance a requisite safeguard from the transactional risk associated with asset specialization and environmental uncertainty. It offers transaction efficiencies from perceptions of stability and from ease of ongoing coordination in the presence of exchange hazards.

Consistent with previous empirical work in China (Luo, 2002) and the USA (Poppo and Zenger, 2002), we find that managers develop increasing levels of relational governance to complement their use of increasingly customized contracts. Customized contracts are necessarily incomplete and, as such, function more as a framework for proceeding with adaptation than a static set of performance-oriented rules found in more standard contracts. Commitment to follow through on adaptation, however, is nowhere guaranteed in the contract;

rather, it stems from the stability and relational investments inherent in relational governance. Knowing this, managers build relational governance based on contract customization.

Somewhat striking is our finding that relational governance does not evolve from pre-existing social ties. Received theory generally argues that since trust evolves over time, long-standing partnerships are more trustworthy. Managers are, therefore, more likely to select such relationships to develop relational governance, as confirmed in empirical work in the USA (Poppo and Zenger, 2002). This, however, is not the case in our sample. Rather than concluding that "trust" does not exist in social relationships, we believe the fault is inertia: long-standing partners, while trusting, do not want to depart from favour-exchange norms. It is also entirely possible that they do not see the value of increased coordination in their business practices, given the costs of developing such practices. Alternatively, since they operate in a "closed" environment, they may lack access to information regarding the benefits or how to develop relational governance. Future empirical work is needed, however, to verify our inferences.

The institutionalism of contracts

In the presence of asset specificity and environmental uncertainty, managers do not craft increasingly customized contracts. This finding departs significantly from TCE, which predicts that managers use more customized contracts to reduce their risk of losses due to mal-adaptation. This finding is not surprising, given the uncertain enforcement of laws as well as the limited formal system of laws that exist in China.

We do find, however, that managers choose to customize contracts for infrequent exchanges, which is consistent with the logic of TCE. When exchange is less frequent, opportunism tends to occur; contracts, therefore, can help safeguard against opportunistic behaviour by specifying expectations, obligations and penalties for non-compliance. We further find long-standing social ties help develop more customized contracts. We infer that contracts gain legitimacy because they are socially sanctioned through social contact, and thus promote greater stability and clarity in the exchange relationship by formally specifying agreements (see also Luo, 2002). Taken as a whole, our findings suggest, consistent with received literature, that creating legitimate structures is critical to the evolution of formal institutions (DiMaggio and Powell, 1983).

Limitations and future research

Our study represents an initial effort to examine a complex phenomenon. Future research is necessary to overcome the limitations of this study and further investigate the phenomenon. For example, because our study was cross-sectional, we cannot test Peng's (2003) two-stage transitional model on the evolution of governance in emerging economies. Ideally, a study would follow a set of companies over time to observe if and how governance transitions from personal ties to a rule-based system of impersonal exchanges. Equally important, our model does not examine costs and benefits associated with different governance mechanisms, which is necessary to test if the costs of personal relationships outweigh their benefits. While our results suggest that the benefits of social ties seem to still outweigh their costs, the costs of social ties may be increasing due to the expanded transactions and legal enforcement. Thus, it would be worthwhile to expand our model by taking governance costs and benefits into consideration. In short, we propose that perhaps the best way to determine such knowledge is to continuously blend case study and systematic empirical work to document China's evolutionary course.

Acknowledgements

This study is supported by a research grant from the Research Grants Council, Hong Kong SAR Government (CERG HKU 7430/06H).

Appendix 6 Measurement items and validity assessment

Exchange Hazard
($\chi^2(33) = 81.12$, p < .001; GFI = .96, CFI = .96, IFI = .96; RMSEA = .06)

	SFL
Asset Specificity: composite reliability (CR) = .892	
1. just for this supplier, we significantly changed our product's features	.767
2. just for this supplier, we significantly changed our personnel	.781
3. just for this supplier, we significantly changed our inventory and distribution	.810
4. just for this supplier, we significantly changed our marketing	.751
5. just for this supplier, we significantly changed our capital equipment and tools	.832

Environmental Uncertainty: CR = .677
Please indicate the significance of changes in the supply market with respects to the following factors.

1. Pricing	.461
2. Product feature and specifications	.759
3. Vendor support services	.559
4. Technology	.554

(Continued)

Transaction Frequency
How frequently has your company been placing orders with this supplier? (reverse-coded)

1 = More than once a day	2 = Once a day	3 = Once a week	—
4 = 2–3 times a month	5 = Once a month	6 = 5–11 times a year	
7 = 2–4 times a year	8 = Once per year		

Governance Structure
($\chi^2(12) = 97.90$, p $< .001$; GFI $= .93$, CFI $= .92$, IFI $= .92$; RMSEA $= .09$)

Social Ties
How many years has your company been doing business with this supplier?
(a) 1~2 (b) 3~4 (c) 5~6 (d) 7~8 (e) 9~10 (f) 11~12 (g) 13~15 (h) 16~19 (i) 20 or   —
more

Contract Customization: CR = .861

1. We have specific, well-detailed agreements with this supplier.	.741
2. We have formal agreements that detail the obligations of both parties.	.911
3. We have detailed contractual agreements with this supplier.	.805

Relational Governance: second-order indicator, CR = .791

Cooperative Norms: first-order indicator, CR = .702   SFL   969

1. No matter who is at fault, problems are joint responsibilities.	.453
2. No party will take advantage of a strong bargaining position.	.531
3. Both sides are willing to make cooperative changes.	.704
4. We must work together to be successful.	.656
5. We do not mind owing each other favors.	.473

Information Sharing: first-order indicator, CR = .814,   .598

1. Proprietary information is shared with each other.	.807
2. We will both share relevant cost information.	.811
3. We include each other in product development meetings.	.704
4. We always share supply and demand forecasts.	.552
1. Our business activities are closely linked with this vendor.	.688
2. This supplier's systems are essential to our operations.	.776
3. Some of our operations are closely connected with this supplier.	.664

Controls
($\chi^2(24) = 32.78$, p $> .10$; GFI $= .98$, CFI $= .99$, IFI $= .99$; RMSEA $= .03$)

Supply Exclusiveness: Composite Reliability = .745

1. This supplier almost has a monopoly for what it sells	.737
2. This is really the only supplier we could use for this product	.699
3. No other vendor has this supplier's capabilities	.671
4. Other vendors could provide what we get from the firm (reverse-coded)	*

Supply Importance: Composite Reliability = .771

Compared to other purchases your firm makes, the product from   .777
this supplier is

A. important	1	2	3	4	5	unimportant (reverse-coded)	.769
B. nonessential	1	2	3	4	5	essential	.631
C. high priority	1	2	3	4	5	low priority (reverse-coded)	

State-owned Buyer: 1 = State-owned; 0 = non-state-owned

Supplier Location: 1 = China; 0 = otherwise

Firm Size: Number of employees of the firm(categorical variable)

Job Tenure: how long have you been working in this firm (categorical variable)

Overall Model Fit:

$\chi^2(264) = 696.76$, p < .001; GFI = .90, CFI = .91, IFI = .91; RMSEA = .067

Note: CR = composite reliability; SFL = standardized factor loading
* Items deleted from further analysis due to low factor loading.

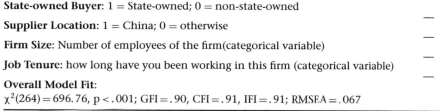

References

Anderson, E. (1985), "The salesperson as outside agent or employee: A transaction cost analysis," *Marketing Science*, 4: 234–254.

Anderson, E. and Schmittlein, D. (1984), "Integration of the sales force: An empirical examination," *Rand Journal of Economics*, 15 (3): 385–395.

Anderson, J. C. and Gerbing, D. W. (1988), "Structural equation modeling in practice: A review and recommended two-step approach," *Psychological Bulletin*, 103: 411–423.

Anderson, J. C. and Narus, J. A. (1990), "A model of distributor firm and manufacturer firm working partnerships," *Journal of Marketing*, 54 (1): January: 42–58.

Artz, K. and Brush, T. H. (2000), "A transaction cost examination of performance in collaborative strategic alliances," *Journal of Economic Behavior and Organization*, 41: 337–362.

Bagozzi, R. P. and Yi, Y. (1988), "On the evaluation of structural equation models," *Journal of the Academy of Marketing Science*, 16 (Spring): 74–94.

Biggart, N. W. and Hamilton, G. G. (1992), "On the limits of a firm-based theory to explain business networks: The Western bias of neoclassical economics," in N. Nohria and R. G. Eccles (eds), *Networks and Organizations: Structure, Form and Action*: 471–490. Boston: Harvard Business School Press.

Boisot, M. and Child, J. (1988), "The iron law of fiefs: Bureaucratic failure and the problem of governance in the Chinese economic reforms," *Administrative Science Quarterly*, 33: 507–527.

Boisot, M. and Child, J. (1996), "From fiefs to clans and network capitalism: Explaining China's emerging economic order," *Administrative Science Quarterly*, 41: 600–628.

Bradachm J. L. and Eccles, R. G. (1989), "Price, authority and trust: From ideal types to plural forms," *Annual Review of Sociology*, 15: 97–118.

Burczak, T. (2001), "The labor theory of property and the injustice of capitalist exploitation," *Review of Social Economy*, 59 (2): 161–183.

Burt, R S. (1992), *Structural Holes*. Cambridge, MA: Harvard University Press.

Chen, M. J. (2001), *Inside Chinese Business: A Guide for Managers Worldwide*. Boston, MA: Harvard Business School Press.

Child, J. and Mollering, G. (2003), "Contextual confidence and active trust development in the Chinese business context," *Organization Science*, 14 (1): 69–80.

DiMaggio, P. J. and Powell, W. W. (1983), "The iron cage revisited: institutional isomorphism and collective rationality in organizational fields," *American Sociological Review*, 48 (April): 147–160.

Gernet, J. (1982), *A History of Chinese Civilization*, Cambridge: Cambridge University Press.

Granovetter, M. (1985), "Economic action and social structure: The problem of embeddedness," *American Journal of Sociology*, 91: 481–510.

Gulati, R. (1995), "Does familiarity breed trust? The implications of repeated ties for contractual choice in alliances," *Academy of Management Journal*, 38 (1): 85–112.

Hallén, L., Johanson, J. and Seyed-Mohamed, N. (1991), "Interfirm adaptation in business relationships," *Journal of Marketing*, 55 (2) April: 29–37.

Hamilton, G. G. and Biggart, N. W. (1988), "Market, culture and authority: A comparative analysis of management in the far east," *American Journal of Sociology*, 94: S52–S94.

Heide, J. B. and John, G. (1992), "Do norms matter in marketing relationships?" *Journal of Marketing*, 56 (2) April: 32–44.

Hill, C. W. L. (1995), "National institutional structures, transaction cost economizing and competitive advantage: The case of Japan," *Organization Science*, 6 (1): 119–131.

Hoskisson, R. E., Eden, L., Lau, C. M. and Wright, M. (2000), "Strategy in emerging economics," *Academy of Management Journal*, 43 (3): 249–267.

Jap, S. D. and Ganesan, S. (2000), "Control mechanisms and the relationship life cycle: Implications for safeguarding specific investments and developing commitment," *Journal of Marketing Research*, 37 (May): 227–245.

John, G. and Weitz, B. (1989), "Salesforce compensation: An empirical investigation of factors related to use of salary versus incentive compensation," *Journal of Marketing Research*, 26 (February): 1–14.

Joskow, P. L. (1988), "Asset specificity and the structure of vertical relationships: Empirical evidence," *Journal of Law, Economics and Organization*, 4: 95–117.

Joskow, P. L. (1991), "The role of transaction cost economics in antitrust and public utility regulatory policies," *Journal of Law, Economics, and Organization*, 7: 53–83.

Larson, A. (1992), "Network dyads in entrepreneurial settings: A study of the governance of exchange relationships," *Administrative Science Quarterly*, 37: 76–104.

Lubman, S. (1995), "Introduction: The future of Chinese law," *China Quarterly*, No. 141 (Special Issue on China's Legal Reform): 1–21.

Luhmann, N (1979), *Trust and Power*, Chichester: John Wiley & Sons.

Luo, Y. (2002), "Contract, cooperation, and performance in international joint ventures," *Strategic Management Journal*, 33 (1): 169–181.

Luo, Y. and Park, S. H. (2001), "Strategic alignment and performance of market-seeking MNCs in China," *Strategic Management Journal*, 22 (2): 141–155.

Lusch, R. F. and Brown, H. R. (1996), "Interdependency, contracting, and relational behavior in marketing channels," *Journal of Marketing*, 60 (4): 19–38.

Macaulay, S. (1963), "Non-contractual relations in business," *American Sociological Review*, 28: 57–66.

MacNeil, I. R (1980), *The New Social Contract, An Inquiry Into Modern Contractual Relations*, New Haven, CT: Yale University Press.

Mohr, J. J. and Sohi, R. S. (1995), "Communication flows in distribution channels: Impact on assessments of communication quality and satisfaction," *Journal of Retailing*, 71 (4): 393–416.

Noordewier, T. G., John, G. and Nevin, J. R. (1990), "Performance outcomes of purchasing arrangements in industrial buyer-vendor relationships," *Journal of Marketing*, 54 (4) October: 80–93.

North, D. C. (1990), *Institutions, Institutional Change, and Economic Performance*, Cambridge: Cambridge University Press.

North, D. C. (1991), "Institutions," *Journal of Economic Perspectives*, 5(1): 97–112.

North, D. C. (1992), "Institutions and economic theory," *The American Economist*, 36(1): 3–6.

Oliver, C. (1992), "The antecedents to deinstitutionalization," *Organization Science*, 13: 563–588.

Park, S. H. and Luo, Y. (2001), "Guanxi and organizational dynamics: Organizational networking in Chinese firms," *Strategic Management Journal*, 22: 455–477.

Peng, M. W. (2003), "Institutional transitions and strategic choices," *Academy of Management Review*, 28 (2): 275–296.

Peng, M. W. and Heath, P. S. (1996), "The growth of the firm in planned economies in transition: Institutions, organizations, and strategic choice," *Academy of Management Review*, 21 (2): 492–528.

Peng, M. W. and Luo, Y. (2000), "Managerial ties and firm performance in a transition economy: The nature of a micro-macro link," *Academy of Management Journal*, 43 (3): 486–501.

Podsakoff, P. M. and Organ, D. W. (1986), "Self-reports in organizational research: Problems and prospects," *Journal of Management*, 12 (Winter): 531–543.

Poppo, L. and Zenger, T. (1998), "Testing alternative theories of the firm: Transaction cost, knowledge-based, and measurement explanations for make-or-buy decisions in information services," *Strategic Management Journal*, 19: 853–877.

Poppo, L. and Zenger, T. (2002), "Do formal contracts and relational governance function as substitutes or complements?" *Strategic Management Journal*, 23 (8): 707–725.

Powell, W. (1996), "On the nature of institutional embeddedness: Labels vs. explanation," in *Advances in Strategic Management*, 13: 292–300.

Rindfleisch, A. and Heide, J. B. (1997), "Transaction cost analysis: Past, present, and future applications," *Journal of marketing*, 61 (October): 30–54.

Ring, P. S. and Van de Ven, A. H. (1992), "Structuring cooperative relationships between organizations," *Strategic Management Journal*, 13: 483–498.

Shelanski, H.A. and Klein, P. G. (1995), "Empirical research in transaction cost economics," *Journal of Law, Economics, and Organization*, 11 (2): 335–361.

Tolbert, P. S. and Zucker, L. G. (1996), "The institutionalization of institutional theory," in S. Clegg, C. Hardy and W. R. Nord (eds.), *Handbook of Organization Studies*. London and Thousand Oaks: Sage Publications.

Uzzi, B. (1997), "Social structure and competition in interfirm networks: The paradox of embeddedness," *Administrative Science Quarterly*, 42: 35–67.

Uzzi, B. (1999), "Embeddedness in the making of financial capital: How social relations and networks benefit firms seeking financing," *American Sociological Review*, 64 (4): 481–505.

Williamson, O. E. (1985), *The Economic Institutions of Capitalism: Firms, Markets, and Relational Contracting*, New York: Free Press.

Williamson, O. E. (1991), "Comparative economic organization: The analysis of discrete structural alternatives," *Administrative Science Quarterly*, 36 (2) June: 269–296.

Williamson, O. E. (1996), *The Mechanisms of Governance*, Oxford: Oxford University Press.

Williamson, O. E. (1999), "Strategy research: Governance and Competence Perspectives," *Strategic Management Journal*, 20: 1087–1108.

Xin, K. R. and Pearce, (1996), "Guanxi: Connections as substitutes for formal institutional support," *Academy of Management Journal*, 39 (6): 1641–1658.

Zaheer, A. and Venkatraman, N. (1995), "Relational governance as an interorganizational strategy: An empirical test of the role of trust in economic exchange," *Strategic Management Journal*, 16: 373–393.

Zhao, Z., Anand, J. and Mitchell, W. (2005), "A dual networks perspective on inter-organizational transfer of R&D capabilities: International joint ventures in the Chinese Automotive industry," *Journal of Management Studies*, 42 (1): 127–160.

Zhou, X., Zhao, W., Li, Q. and Qiang, H. (2003), "Embeddedness and contractual relationships in China's transitional economy," *American Sociological Review*, 68: 75–102.

Zhou, K, Poppo, L. and Yang, Z. (2008), "Relational ties or customized contracts? An examination of alternative governance choices in China," *Journal of International Business Studies*: 39: 526–534.

7
Knowledge Sharing in Professional Services Firms in China

Robert M. Davison, Maris G. Martinsons and Carol X. J. Ou

Introduction

In times of economic turbulence, the pressure on organizations to compete effectively is intense. This is true for industrial giants as well as for small and medium-sized enterprizes (SMEs). It is also true not only for manufacturers, where capital and physical resources predominate, but also for professional services firms, where knowledge is a central resource. In order to thrive, these knowledge-intensive firms are increasingly seeking to leverage the knowledge of their employees. Leveraged knowledge has been found to not only improve the productivity of individuals and teams (cf. Fuller et al., 2006) but also to enhance the agility of the organization (cf. Sambamurthy et al., 2003). Indeed, employees who not only create knowledge, but also archive, harvest, disseminate and recontextualize it, contribute significantly towards personal productivity, team performance and organizational agility.

As the value of employee knowledge sharing is increasingly recognized, we have witnessed a greater emphasis on knowledge management (KM) in terms of both the increasing investment of money and energy by businesses and page space devoted to the topic in various academic and practitioner books, journals, magazines and websites. The recent emphasis on KM has yielded some significant advances in our understanding of how to manage knowledge. However, the associated technology, commonly known as IT-driven KM systems (KMS), still represents a large and often risky investment. The costs can be exorbitant, the benefits unclear and the return on investment, at best, unpredictable. Indeed, it is commonly reported that KMS are abandoned or underutilized after an initial honeymoon period (Akhavan et al., 2005; DeSouza and Awazu, 2005).

In this chapter, we examine the knowledge sharing practices of the Chinese professional services industry, focusing on the experiences of two SME firms in the public relations (PR) sector: Eastwei (www.eastwei.com) and SoftFocus (a pseudonym). The background to each of these companies follows before we briefly review the literature on knowledge sharing and its key motivators in the Chinese context. A comparative analysis of the two firms' knowledge sharing strategies and practices then follows, leading to a discussion where we consider the future of knowledge sharing in the Chinese context and present our conclusions.

Since November 2006, the authors have been engaged in a longitudinal investigation of knowledge sharing practices and strategies, firstly in Eastwei and more recently in SoftFocus. This investigation is structured as a Canonical Action Research (Davison et al., 2004) project. The authors are engaging with the clients in such a way as to initiate and follow through on significant organizational change.

Following an extensive series of conversations and interviews with the management and employees of the client organizations, we have collected data through surveys (to test structural research models) and ethnographic techniques (so as to understand the nature of day-to-day work in the firms). We are also in the process of independently helping both firms to develop a knowledge focused strategy. This gives us a unique and intimate perspective on both the similarities and the differences in knowledge sharing practices and strategies present in these two firms, which we treat as a microcosm of the broader PR industry in China.

Eastwei is headquartered in Beijing, with offices in Shanghai, Chengdu and Guangzhou. SoftFocus' Chinese operations are likewise headquartered in Beijing, with offices in Shanghai, Guangzhou and Hong Kong. Both firms deliver a range of PR services to their clients, which are a mix of domestic and international corporations that aim to develop and maintain a sustained presence in the Chinese market. Employees liaise with journalists and other members of the mass media so as to ensure that news and infomercial stories reflect client's products and press releases. They analyse market reactions to recent product and press releases and continuously update their awareness of journalists' expectations while building and maintaining strong interpersonal relationships. They also interact with a variety of client employees such as PR managers and media event organizers to ensure that all related products and services are delivered at an appropriate standard. Given the nature of this work, the employees of both Eastwei and SoftFocus spend much of their time communicating with various interlocutors, both formally and informally.

The two companies differ significantly in several respects, including their attitude to us, the researchers. Eastwei's chairman (Johan Björkstén) agreed that we should openly identify his firm by name (rather than using a pseudonym) in all our research publications. SoftFocus has been more cautious to date, asking that we not reveal the company's real name in our publications. Nevertheless, its Asia-Pacific CEO and many of his subordinates have participated actively in the project.

Literature review

Prior research on knowledge sharing has tended to focus on large companies in either North America or, to a lesser extent, Western Europe. The tone of these studies is generally positive, and most scholars agree that KM has at least potential value for an organization. While these studies are important, not all firms are large and other parts of the world should not be ignored. China is an example, given its economic and social transformation (Martinsons, 2005) and important role as "factory to the world" (Haddad, 2007). However, there has been very little serious investigation of knowledge sharing in the Chinese context to date. This is particularly true if we exclude studies involving captive populations such as MBA students. Prominent real-world research of KM in China includes Voelpel and Han's (2005) study of Siemens' ShareNet project in China, Martinsons et al.'s (2009) case-based analysis of KM failure in two Chinese firms, Lu et al.'s (2005) study of managerial knowledge sharing in China, and Hutchings and Michailova's (2004) comparison of knowledge sharing practices in Chinese and Russian subsidiaries.

It has been suggested that Chinese firms lag behind their Western counterparts in the formal implementation of KM initiatives. Wang (2002) suggests a number of primary causes, including: poor planning and resource allocation, ineffective KM initiative to core business alignment, and the absence of qualified KM experts. These reasons may also in part explain the lack of detailed research attention to the topic. A related issue is that most studies of KM in Chinese firms are informed by etic, Western theories and assumptions (Tsui, 2006), instead of reporting empirically on Chinese experiences and developing the type of indigenous theory that Martinsons (2008) has done for e-commerce in China.

The lack of indigenous KM theory is problematic because Western theories and assumptions are unlikely to capture the full richness of the Chinese context as well as its very different social and organizational culture. In our current research, we deliberately attempt to balance this etic (i.e., external) perspective with an emic (i.e., internal) one, investigating the socio-psychological constructs that are significant to Chinese employees who engage in knowledge sharing. One of these constructs is *guanxi*. A second is the in-group. Each of these is briefly reviewed below.

Guanxi describes "the existence of direct particularistic ties between two or more individuals" (Tsui and Farh, 1997, cited in Fu et al., 2006) and is both critical to, and ubiquitous in, Chinese societies (see also Chapter 6). Conceptually, *guanxi* is comparable to relationships and connections, but it also includes social network-based favours, mutual reciprocity and long-term benefits (Xin and Pearce, 1996). As such, *guanxi* is a core component of knowledge sharing behaviour, since reliable knowledge is a scarce resource in China (Burrows et al.,

2005). Consequently, it is entirely reasonable that the exchange of information and knowledge should be accompanied by the development of *guanxi*.

Although interpersonal *guanxi* may spill over so as to have an impact on the organization (Björkstén et al., 2008), *guanxi* is nevertheless an individual level construct, at least in the context of knowledge sharing. Individual employees must therefore develop their own *guanxi* networks if they are to secure knowledge resources. The quality of knowledge that can be received is also *guanxi* dependent: stronger *guanxi* will assure the recipient of the knowledge's reliability, richness and trustworthiness (Luo, 1997). With strong *guanxi* networks, knowledge searching costs can be reduced, individual productivity can be enhanced and better informed decisions realized (Ramasamy et al., 2006). Notwithstanding these benefits, both the *guanxi* system and knowledge sharing practices are highly informal in China, so informal methods of knowledge transfer are more common (ibid.).

A notable feature of peer-colleague *guanxi* in China is the "in-group". Understanding the psychology of in-groups is critical to an appreciation of how the Chinese share knowledge in organizational contexts. An in-group comprises a small group of people (usually fewer than 6), who are psychologically and communicationally proximate, with whom one has mutual and reciprocal obligations (Chow et al., 2000). It is psychologically easier to share knowledge within the in-group (Triandis, 1989) not only because it enhances one's personal reputation (Voelpel and Han, 2005) but also because such communication tends to be informal and implicit (Martinsons and Westwood, 1997), with a reliance on "interpersonal contact, rather than through formal and/or written means" (Burrows et al., 2005).

Leadership style is potentially critical for knowledge sharing in organizations. Two such styles are often referred to – transactional and transformational – and it is agreed (Bass et al., 2003; Yukl, 2005) that they are conceptually distinct. In the knowledge sharing context, transformational leadership is most effective if it can motivate employees' intrinsic interest to share their knowledge, even to the extent of this being seen as either a form of self-sacrifice or a potential loss of knowledge power. On the other hand, transactional leadership focuses on extrinsic motivation and so incorporates a management style built around employee monitoring and the provision of tangible incentives and rewards, as well as punishments. A transactional leadership style is comparable with the extrinsic motivational perspective seen in recent KM research (e.g. Bock et al., 2005; Kankanhalli et al., 2005). The research literature is split on the relative efficacy of the two styles, each of which is culturally bound to a certain extent. In Western cultures, an empowering leadership style tends to be emphasized to a greater extent (e.g. Kulkarni et al., 2006; Srivastava et al., 2006), but in the Chinese context, the transactional style is more appropriate (Hempel and Martinsons, 2009; Huang et al., 2008).

IT is often assumed to be a prerequisite for effective KM in organizations (McDermott and O'Dell, 2001), given its ability to enable "collaboration among different units and individuals unconstrained by the boundaries of geography and time" (Lu et al., 2005, p. 27). However, formal IT applications rarely fulfil this role in the Chinese context. This is largely because even "in the digital era, there is still no perfect substitute for the motivational effects of human bonding and social connectedness" (Lu et al., 2005). Consequently, it is not surprising that Voelpel and Han (2005) found in-groups to be salient for the employees of Siemens in China despite organizational pressures embodying German values and promoting a public-good form of knowledge that should be shared across in-group boundaries (cf. Lu et al., 2005). Indeed, even though knowledge sharing in-groups may not make extensive use of formal IT applications, instead preferring a more socially facilitated set of processes, the knowledge that is shared may still be sufficiently explicit to be reused by the recipient. One way in which this is regularly achieved involves instant messaging (IM).

Instant messaging tools such as MSN Messenger, QQ and WangWang, facilitate near-synchronous communication by interlocutors (Handel and Herbsleb, 2002; Ou et al., 2008). Although IM tools were originally developed for the social context, they have now found a new role in the workplace, particularly for unscheduled, unstructured and interactive tasks such as coordination and knowledge sharing where several exchanges may be needed to reach closure or agreement (cf. Kraut et al., 1990). Nardi et al. (2000) demonstrated the importance of IM tools for both collocated and distributed workers, although the evidence remains inconclusive as to the disruptiveness of the technology (cf. Cameron and Webster, 2005). Some knowledge workers have grown highly dependent on IM tools: not only are they dyadic communication devices but they are amenable to information and knowledge harvesting, in polychronic combination with other tools, for future recall (Cameron and Webster, 2005; Halverson, 2004).

Research method

Following this brief review of the academic literature on *guanxi*, in-groups and the instant messenger, we now describe our research methods in more detail. In blending academic research and practical investigation, we have relied on canonical action research (CAR) (Davison and Martinsons, 2007; Davison et al., 2004), which has served as an overarching framework for our project.

CAR is premised on three key elements, which identify it as the canonical form (after Susman and Evered, 1978): iteration, rigour and collaboration. Iteration means that researchers and clients must expect to cycle through a number of iterations of actions (seldom only one) before they can reach a satisfactory state of closure. Rigour here refers to the correct application of methods so as to achieve the desired outcome (cf. Benbasat and Zmud, 1999). CAR's own specific methods are detailed in Davison et al. (2004) and briefly reviewed below. Collaboration means that researchers and clients must act together: neither researcher nor client should significantly gain an upper hand in the process, though each will have a different role to play. CAR is also unique when compared to other forms of action research, given its focus on both organizational change and development and the generation of scholarly knowledge.

CAR typically involves a sequence of five activities in each cycle: diagnosis, planning, action taking, action evaluating and reflecting. The rigour of the method ensures the validity and relevance of the findings for the organization. In order to understand the nature of the problem as experienced by employees of Eastwei and SoftFocus, we have undertaken extensive interviews with them. Employees at all levels were asked about their knowledge management practices, including the processes and technologies used currently in their knowledge acquisition and sharing as well as the opportunities for future development.

We have also surveyed all the employees in both firms on the critical influences of knowledge sharing behaviour. More intensively, we have engaged in an ethnographic observation of employees at work in order to go beyond the perceptual and reflective data typical of interview and survey methods and so learn precisely how employees work. These observations have been paralleled by strategic discussions with senior management (team leaders, account directors, general managers and vice-presidents) on the development of a knowledge-focused strategic position for the firm and the implementation of pilot projects that test new ways of engaging employees in knowledge sharing behaviours.

Findings and analysis

A number of findings have emerged from our investigations. First, there is considerable evidence to demonstrate that, as the research literature predicts, *guanxi*-lubricated in-groups are critical contexts for knowledge sharing activity. Second, both email and instant messenger applications are widely used for communication. Third, while both firms are characterized by well developed knowledge sharing cultures, the actual intention to share knowledge is influenced by both transactional and transformational leadership styles, while the knowledge itself is perceived to have a significant impact on both organizational agility and team productivity. Measuring the actual impact of knowledge sharing is more problematic, however, and requires a multifaceted approach. In the following sections, we present and discuss each of these findings in more detail.

Guanxi, in-groups and knowledge sharing

The basic unit of work organization in Eastwei and SoftFocus is the client team. The responsibility of a client team is to handle all issues associated with one client. This is unlikely to be restricted to a single project, since over time clients require work on a variety of projects, such as new product launches. The size of a client team varies from 2–3 people at the small end to 40 at the large end, although large teams tend to be split into smaller sub-teams. Teams may be located in one physical office or they may be distributed across offices. All teams have a team leader, who is normally associated with a single office. This means that each team essentially has a home location, and may have one or more satellite locations where remote team members are located.

Knowledge sharing within these teams is generally both frequent and beneficial. It may take place in face-to-face or online mode, with tools such as IM and email frequently used. Such knowledge sharing is especially prevalent in teams (or parts of teams) that are located in the same office, since interpersonal trust tends to be higher in these contexts. Indeed, these relatively small team contexts form one of the basic structures for in-groups – small groups of people who work closely together and who trust each other – facilitated by interpersonal, dyadic *guanxi*.

However, not all in-groups are restricted to people located in the same office. We found examples of two other kinds of in-group. First among these are in-groups spread across two or more offices within the same company. These generally comprise people who work closely together, who rely on each other, and who need to share information and knowledge with one another in order to get their work done. Second are in-groups whose members are not all located within the same company. Indeed, in some cases only one member of these in-groups may be located within Eastwei or SoftFocus, with all other members located elsewhere, often in competing companies.

Individual employees at both firms have up to 500 individual people on their IM contact lists. This is far more than the numbers who work for either Eastwei or SoftFocus. Most of the people on the contact lists were working for other firms in public relations or related industries. Others were simply friends who are part of the employee's social in-groups. We noticed that the Eastwei and SoftFocus employees would regularly use their *guanxi* so as to call in favours from remote in-group colleagues (i.e. people working in other companies), and to be called upon in turn. The *guanxi* network of each individual employee is thus much wider than the immediate confines of the employer and knowledge sharing takes place with a wide variety of inside and outside people. We queried this behaviour of Eastwei's CEO, who was neither surprised nor alarmed by the situation. In his view, nothing that could be shared online was worth stealing. The one critical resource, *guanxi*, was dependent on interpersonal relationships and as such was not stealable.

Tools for communication and sharing

A wide variety of tools are used by the employees of Eastwei and SoftFocus, including: telephones (fixed line, mobile, VoIP), traditional email (both from company email systems and private providers), instant messengers (MSN/WLM and QQ are the most common), Web 2.0 applications like blogs, wikis, Facebook, KaiXin001 and del.icio.us.

In Eastwei, the instant messenger (IM) is the communication tool of choice – almost all employees use it to some extent, from the CEO downwards, and some are so utterly dependent on it that they seem to have forged an almost symbiotic relationship. For instance, we observed one Shanghai employee with 17 simultaneously open IM chats – she was searching widely for information from local and remote colleagues, as well as helping others with their searches. In another example, two people sitting on opposite sides of the same room used an IM to discuss a common team problem for ten minutes. When they were unable to solve the problem online, they adjourned to an adjacent breakout room for a face-to-face discussion. In other cases, colleagues sitting next to each other would use IM to communicate, instead of simply turning to each other and talking. As a result, the office was sometimes strangely quiet, except for keyboard noise.

Most of this instant messaging is done in Chinese, with most employees preferring Microsoft's Messenger (MSN) or Windows Live Messenger (WLM) tools. Younger employees may also use QQ, a social chat tool developed by Tencent, a Chinese IT firm. Email is used much less regularly, though more formal communications with clients are an exception. We analysed the chat logs (3069 messages over two months) of one prominent IM user (with this user's explicit permission) in order to understand the frequency of occurrence of different types of chat content. This revealed that the most frequently occurring chat type was 'coordination' (45.45 percent of chats), including the coordination of meetings, projects and events. The second most frequently occurring type was social (chats with friends, invitations, jokes, etc.), at 20.1 percent. Surprisingly, information and knowledge sharing only accounted for 10.56 percent of chats, brainstorming constituted 5.28 percent, relationship building and maintaining 2.25 percent and decision making 0.33 percent. Even though these figures cannot be generalized widely, they are indicative of how IM tools may be used and highlight future research directions.

The data collected from the chat logs also helped to rebut a concern that IM tools are only used for social chatting, at the cost of work productivity. As one senior manager at Eastwei remarked "people should talk on the phone", suggesting that IM tools are too disruptive to be useful. By contrast, an Eastwei consultant said, "MSN saves me lots of time by allowing me to keep in regular contact with hundreds of journalists on my account." Unlike Eastwei, SoftFocus employees use email as the communication tool of choice in most situations, with IM used relatively infrequently, and only between colleagues who are not physically proximate. People in the same office tend to walk to each other and talk, occasionally using the telephone. Distributed teams rely heavily on conference calls (either with fixed line or VoIP technology). The telephone is widely used for contacting clients, though some clients are moving to smart phones and PDAs with IM-capability.

Knowledge sharing practices and influences

Knowledge sharing behaviour in Eastwei and SoftFocus appears to be widespread. In both firms there is an active and healthy knowledge sharing culture and all employees espoused a willingness to share knowledge, either on demand or on their own initiative. This culture is significantly mitigated, however, by physical distance. Most active sharing takes place between people who are near each other. Much less sharing takes place when people are geographically remote and this situation has prompted some of the current research as we attempt to foster more effective cross-office knowledge sharing behaviour. Knowledge sharing is currently practiced informally, using the technology applications discussed above, since there is no formal knowledge management system (KMS).

In order to understand the extent to which leadership style influences knowledge sharing practices, we surveyed all employees on the relative importance of transactional and transformational leadership on their intention to share knowledge. According to our interview data and observations, leadership style appears to be a strong motivator for knowledge sharing practice in both Eastwei and SoftFocus. In Eastwei, both the CEO and team leaders share their project experiences and personal reflections in the company's blog (www.eastvoice.com). The weekly Monday morning meeting, usually facilitated by a team leader, constitutes a physical place for sharing knowledge. The contribution of leadership to knowledge sharing behaviour was also highlighted by one Eastwei interviewee:

> The first time I became a small team leader and needed to train new staff, my boss reminded me that I need to share my experience, not just let my subordinates learn by themselves. My method is to tell people my personal lessons and experiences when I know others meet the similar situation. My aim is to prevent people from repeating my mistakes . . . Eastwei encourages people to make mistakes, but not to repeat mistakes.

In addition, our survey of employees in Eastwei and SoftFocus indicates that while a transactional style of leadership significantly enhances in-group knowledge sharing, an empowering style of leadership does not. This finding is consistent for both firms. This finding is in line with the literature (Hempel and Martinsons, 2009; Huang et al., 2008) on the role of leadership in Chinese organizations, in which the researchers found that a transactional leadership style is more appropriate than a transformational leadership style in promoting KM practice. Thus, we suggest that tangible incentives and rewards, as well as explicit monitoring of performance, tends to be more effective in promoting knowledge sharing in China.

Measuring the impact of knowledge sharing

As we have already noted, while knowledge sharing practices appear to be widespread in Eastwei and SoftFocus, it is rather more difficult to gauge the organizational impact of such knowledge sharing. We have attempted to measure the impact theoretically by examining the extent to which *guanxi*-lubricated knowledge sharing practices are associated with a perceived increase in teamwork quality and organizational agility. These are vicarious measures of impact for two reasons. First, they can only reflect the perceptions of survey respondents. Second, they cannot readily be converted into more formal financial values or used as measures of productivity. In principle, it might be possible to construct an evidence-based scenario so as to illustrate how a particular shared piece of knowledge contributed to a specific organizational outcome.

Such an evidence-based approach was taken by Siemens in China and elsewhere (Voelpel and Han, 2005; Voelpel et al., 2005). Siemens asserted that their formal KMS 'ShareNet' had not only saved the corporation a total of €5,000,000 from 1992 to 2001, but that it had also been crucial in enabling the organization to gain 27 new projects totalling €120 million in revenue. In reviewing these assertions, we note that the comparison should be to a do-nothing alternative that would have essentially saved Siemens the unknown amount of resources that it invested in developing ShareNet.

Notwithstanding our concerns with the method of evaluation used by Siemens and the general challenges of identifying the direct and indirect benefits of KM, we have tried to assess the relative impact of knowledge sharing practices on the perceived quality of teamwork and organizational agility. Our analysis of data from a large-scale employee survey suggests that knowledge sharing has significantly contributed to both teamwork quality and organizational agility in Eastwei and SoftFocus. Consistent with this finding, our interviews and on-site observations in these two companies also indicate that knowledge sharing is embedded in daily work practices, implying the critical role of knowledge and knowledge sharing in organizations' ability to thrive and survive. In considering how we can measure productivity more directly, we have developed a balanced scorecard for Eastwei, which we describe in the next section.

Developing a knowledge strategy using a balanced scorecard

A significant component of our CAR intervention at Eastwei and SoftFocus has been to develop a strategic knowledge focus within each firm. At Eastwei, this has been formalized in a balanced scorecard (BSC) structure (Kaplan and Norton, 1992; 1996; Martinsons et al., 1999). The BSC is a strategic management system designed to address all measures that are critical to an organization. Unlike traditional accounting measures of performance, the conventional BSC does not focus exclusively on financial measures but also includes internal processes, customer satisfaction, and being prepared for the future. These four perspectives are logically connected to each other as shown in Figure 7.1.

For each of the four BSC perspectives, it is necessary to identify

a) objectives;
b) targets (including a timeframe);
c) measures that pertain to those targets; and
d) specific initiatives that should result in the objectives being achieved.

If a BSC is designed diligently, with due attention to organizational realities, then it should assist managers in planning for future organizational success. Indeed, a formal identification of strategic objectives, as well as the organization's strategic destination, is highly desirable if the BSC is to be appropriately aligned to both strategic position and organizational reality. It is also possible

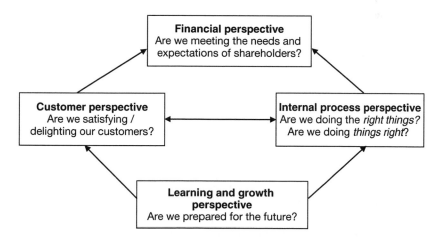

Figure 7.1 Relationships between the four perspectives in the balanced scorecard based on Kaplan and Norton (1992) and Martinsons et al. (1999)

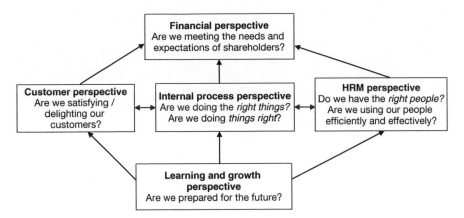

Figure 7.2   The balanced scorecard at Eastwei

to construct a BSC that is tailored to specific organizational functions (cf. Martinsons et al., 1999), in this case a knowledge management strategy.

As we engaged in strategic planning with Eastwei, we developed a prototype BSC that incorporates five perspectives: organizational competitiveness and profitability; internal process; HR management; client satisfaction; and learning and growth (see Figure 7.2). These five perspectives were finalized as a result of strategic discussions between members of the research team and Eastwei's CEO, who decided to separate people-related activities from work-related activities. Through a series of cause-and-effect relationships, from initiatives to objectives, so the rigour of the BSC is ensured.

As indicated above, the targets and measures in a BSC should be quantifiable and the data should be easy to collect. It is in this numerical data that we get closest to identifying how a knowledge sharing initiative engenders productivity enhancements. This is most clearly seen in the internal process perspective (see Table 7.1). Six linked initiatives can be identified:

  (a) 'providing advanced KM tools';
  (b) 'directors involved in coaching';
  (c) 'getting two teams to pilot the new knowledge sharing concepts';
  (d) 'identifying current process inefficiencies';
  (e) 'identifying opportunities for sharing routine and ad hoc information'; and
  (f) 'identifying IT levers/enablers'.

These initiatives are intended to enable the achievement of two initiatives: 'improved internal process efficiency', and 'develop a knowledge creation culture so as to facilitate the creation of value for clients'.

Table 7.1 The internal process perspective of Eastwei's prototype BSC

Perspective	Objective	Target	Measure	Initiative
Internal Process	• Improved internal process efficiency so as to provide value to clients	• 30% improvement by mid-2009	• Revenue per Consultant	• Advanced KM tools, e.g. wiki. • Coaching by directors • Weekly time tracking follow-up with project group leaders and team leaders
	• Develop a knowledge creation culture to facilitate the creation of value for clients	• Progressive with effect from early 2009	• Number of people engaged in a new model of work • Volume and quality of knowledge created, accessed, shared, reused	• Two teams (centres of excellence) to pilot the concept • Identify current process inefficiencies • Identify opportunities for sharing what may seem routine and ad hoc • Identify IT levers/enablers

Quantitative measures are needed in order to assess whether the objectives that make up the balanced scorecard have been achieved. The most appropriate measure of internal process efficiency was found to be 'revenue per consultant' – that is, how much revenue each consultant brings into the firm. The target is an increase of 30 percent by a specific deadline (in this case, mid-2009). The measure of the achievement of a knowledge creation culture is twofold – the number of people engaged in the new work style and the quantity and quality of knowledge created, accessed, shared and reused.

Initiatives need to be specific, if they are to be measured as having an impact on an objective. Targets need to be precise for the same reason – we need to know if the target has been achieved. The measures, however, are the most tricky, and here we see some problems with Eastwei's prototype. Counting the number of people involved in a new style of work is fine, and it should be possible to count how much knowledge they create, how frequently they access knowledge, and how often they share. Reuse is a more difficult measure, because it depends on the employee reporting the reuse.

Quality, however, is something quite different. Subjective measures of quality are possible, though not necessarily useful – we can ask one or more individuals to rate the quality of the knowledge, and somehow calculate a quality index. But this is a very time intensive activity, and as organizational slack in SME PR firms is close to zero, it is hardly viable. Objective measures of knowledge quality are very hard to come by – indeed, it may only be possible to offer proxy measures. Arguably, a piece of knowledge that is frequently accessed and reused (if we can measure reuse) is of higher quality than a piece of knowledge that is never accessed and reused. For these reasons, measuring the extent to which a knowledge culture has been developed is extremely difficult in objective terms. Revenue per consultant, on the other hand, is much easier to measure. Like the Siemens example referred to above, it is also financially linked – did the knowledge sharing initiative produce measurable financial benefits over and above the costs of developing the KMS in the first place? Siemens was able to make the argument that it did. Eastwei hopes to follow in Siemens' footsteps.

Discussion and implications for practice

Our action research at Eastwei and SoftFocus clearly shows that the adoption of a systematic approach to knowledge sharing can improve the organizational performance of professional services firms in China. By applying the balanced scorecard concept to directly link knowledge management initiatives and, more generally, IT applications to specific performance objectives, we ensured that the focus of our action research projects during both the diagnosis and planning stages was on improving the organizational performance. Instead of restricting our investigation to how knowledge and information were managed, we adopted a strategic management perspective to identify, plan and implement changes that could improve the organization as a whole, as represented by key performance indicators (KPIs) such as revenues, profits, customer satisfaction and employee satisfaction.

Our research highlights the relative importance of efficiency and flexibility for SMEs that are providing professional services in the Chinese context. The dynamic nature of the business environment in China, together with the varying (and often unpredictable) demands of clients, requires those offering professional services (such as public relations expertise) to adapt quickly to the circumstances and deliver customized solutions. It is less important to have the highest level of efficiency, especially if achieving that efficiency compromises the flexibility and creativity of the organization and its employees.

The rapid development of the Chinese economy has provided many growth opportunities for businesses. Both Eastwei and SoftFocus are among many professional services firms in China that have grown rapidly in recent years. Their expanding scale of operations has undeniably created a knowledge management challenge. In particular, the continued reliance on human memory indexing of knowledge has become increasingly ineffective. In consequence, to ensure their future success, professional services providers in China need to consider introducing IT-supported KM systems. Such systems need not be either large in scale or expensive. They may run on open source platforms such as wikis and make use of informal Web 2.0 applications like IM tools and even Facebook or KaiXin001, Facebook's Chinese equivalent. Furthermore, the implementation of these systems does not need to be accompanied by rigid business process models, such as those prescribed in the business process re-engineering literature. The entrenchment of specific ways of doing work such as unmodifiable best practices in elaborate IT-enabled systems is likely to be counterproductive in a dynamic environment where flexibility is more important than certainty and business transactions are still based primarily on the leveraging of personal relationships rather than systematic rules (Martinsons, 2008).

Instead, we suggest that the management of both knowledge and client work in China will be enhanced when IT applications are used to support, but not determine, human-centric work processes. Indeed, an important lesson reinforced by our action research cases is that technology should never be unilaterally imposed on human-centric work processes, but rather that it should be adapted to the prevailing societal and organizational cultures.

The influence of the societal culture in China on information systems and IT-enabled change has been investigated thoroughly (cf. Burrows et al., 2005; Martinsons and Westwood, 1997). However, the influence of the organizational culture on the application of IT in China is less well understood. Our research suggests that the use of IT to support knowledge sharing in Chinese SMEs must recognize their distinctive organizational culture. We found the prevailing cultures of both Eastwei and SoftFocus to be very organic and humane rather than mechanistic (machine-like) or materialistic (money oriented). Formality and transparency were not among the primary objectives in these organizations. IM was found to be an effective tool for communicating rich but implicit knowledge, linking interlocutors through informal relationships, that is, *guanxi*, in social networks. The current choice of knowledge sharing tools (such as IM, blogs and wiki) provides evidence of the organization's fit with the *guanxi*-oriented Chinese circumstances. Information and knowledge were shared informally while business planning was based largely on reviewing historical data rather than projecting the future or developing alternative scenarios and considering their implications. Consequently, the introduction of a BSC, together with an IT-enabled KMS, represented a major step forward in terms of providing an integrated platform for business planning and knowledge sharing, respectively. This is the type of major step that professional services firms in China need to take in order to remain successful as they grow beyond the paternalistic small business model where a single "big boss" informally plans, directs and controls the organization. Remarkably, the focus of our efforts in planning and implementing these "systematic" solutions to enable business growth has been on the people rather than the technology. In China, we may say that success will be driven by people and their relationships with each other, rather than by technology alone.

References

Akhavan, P., Jafari, M. and Fathian, M. (2005), "Exploring failure-factors of implementing knowledge management systems in organizations," *Journal of Knowledge Management Practice*, 6 www.tlainc.com/articl85.htm. (accessed 28 May 2009).

Bass, B. M., Avolio, B.J., Jung, D.I. and Berson, Y. (2003), "Predicting unit performance by assessing transformational and transactional leadership," *Journal of Applied Psychology*, 88(2): 207–218.

Benbasat, I. and Zmud, R. (1999), "Empirical research in information systems: The practice of relevance," *MIS Quarterly*, 23(1): 3–16.

Björkstén, J., Wang, L.S. and Yin, T. (2008), *Chinese Public Relations* (中国式公关: Zhong Guo Shi Gong Guan), CITIC Press: Beijing, China.

Bock, G.W., Zmud, R.W. and Kim, Y.G. (2005), "Behavioral intention formation in knowledge sharing: Examining the roles of extrinsic motivators, social-psychological forces, and organizational climate," *MIS Quarterly*, 29(1): 87–111.

Burrows, G.R., Drummond, D.L. and Martinsons, M.G. (2005), "Knowledge management in China," *Communications of the ACM*, 48(4): 73–76.

Cameron, A. and Webster, J. (2005), "Unintended consequences of emerging communication technologies: Instant messaging in the workplace," *Computers in Human Behavior*, 21(1): 85–103.

Chow, C.W., Deng, F.J. and Ho, J.L. (2000), "The openness of knowledge sharing within organizations: A comparative study of the United States and the People's Republic of China," *Journal of Management Accounting Research*, 12: 65–95.

Davison, R.M. and Martinsons, M.G. (2007), "Action research and consulting: Hellish partnership or heavenly marriage?" in N.F. Kock (ed.) *Information Systems Action Research: An Applied View of Emerging Concepts and Methods*, Berlin, Springer, pp. 377–394.

Davison, R.M., Martinsons, M.G. and Kock, N. (2004), "Principles of canonical action research," *Information Systems Journal*, 14(1): 65–86.

DeSouza, K.C. and Awazu, Y. (2005), "Maintaining knowledge management systems: A strategic imperative," *Journal of the American Society for Information Science and Technology*, 56(7): 765–768.

Fu, P.P., Tsui, A.S. and Dess, G.G. (2006), "The dynamics of guanxi in Chinese high-tech firms: Implications for knowledge management and decision making," *Management International Review*, 46(3): 277–305.

Fuller, M.A., Hardin, A.M. and Davison, R.M. (2006), "Efficacy in technology-mediated distributed teams," *Journal of Management Information Systems*, 23(3): 209–235.

Haddad, M. (2007), "Trade integration in East Asia: The role of China and production networks," World Bank Policy Research Working Paper No. 4160, http://papers.ssrn.com/sol3/papers.cfm?abstract_id=969237 (Accessed 28 May 2009).

Halverson, C.A. (2004), "The value of persistence: A study of the creation, ordering and use of conversation archives by a knowledge worker," *Proceedings of the 37th Hawaii International Conference on System Sciences*, Waikaloa, Hawaii, pp. 40108.1, http://portal.acm.org/citation.cfm?id=962752.962971&coll=GUIDE&dl=GUIDE&CFID=36731944&CFTOKEN=39603263 (Accessed 28 May 2009).

Handel, M. and Herbsleb, J.D. (2002), "What is Chat Doing in the Workplace?" in the *Proceedings of the 2002 ACM Conference on Computer Supported Cooperative Work*, New Orleans, LA, pp. 1–10. http://portal.acm.org/citation.cfm?id=587080 (Accessed 28 May 2009).

Hempel, P.S., and Martinsons, M.G. (2009), "Developing international organizational change theory using cases from China," *Human Relations*, 62(4): 459–499.

Huang, Q.V., Davison, R.M., Liu, H.F. and Gu, J.B. (2008), "The impact of leadership style on knowledge sharing intentions in China," *Journal of Global Information Management*, 16(4): 67–91.

Hutchings, K. and Michailova, S. (2004), "Facilitating knowledge sharing in Chinese and Russian subsidiaries: The role of personal networks and group membership," *Journal of Knowledge Management*, 8(2): 84–94.

Kankanhalli, A., Tan, B.C.Y. and Wei, K.K. (2005), "Contributing knowledge to electronic knowledge repositories: An empirical investigation," *MIS Quarterly*, 29(1): 113–143.

Kaplan, R. and Norton, D. (1992), "The balanced scorecard: Measures that drive performance," *Harvard Business Review*, 70(1): 71–79.

Kaplan, R. and Norton, D. (1996), "Using the balanced scorecard as a strategic management system," *Harvard Business Review*, 74(1): 75–85.

Kraut, R.E., Fish, R.S., Root, R.W. and Chalfonte, B.L. (1990), "Information communication in organizations: Form, function and technology," in S. Oskamp and S. Spacapan (eds), Human Reactions to Technology: The Claremont Symposium on Applied Social Psychology. Beverly Hills, CA: Sage Publications. Newbury Park, Sage, pp. 145–199.

Kulkarni, U.R., Ravindran, S. and Freeze, R. (2006), "A knowledge management success model: Theoretical development and empirical validation," *Journal of Management Information Systems*, 23(3): 309–347.

Lu, L., Leung, K. and Koch, P.T. (2005), "Managerial knowledge sharing: The role of individual, interpersonal and organizational factors," *Management and Organization Review*, 2(1): 15–41.

Luo, Y. (1997), "Guanxi: Principles, philosophies and implications," *Human Systems Management*, 16(1): 43–51.

Martinsons, M.G. (2005), "Transforming China," *Communications of the ACM*, 48(4): 44–48.

Martinsons, M.G. (2008), "Relationship-based E-commerce: Theory and evidence from China," *Information Systems Journal*, 18(4): 331–356.

Martinsons, M.G. and Westwood, R.I. (1997), "Management information systems in the Chinese business culture: An explanatory theory," *Information & Management*, 32(5): 215–228.

Martinsons, M.G., Davison, R.M. and Huang, Q.V. (2009), "Knowledge management challenges in small professional services firms: Action research in China", in the *69th Academy of Management Conference*, Chicago, August 6–11.

Martinsons, M.G., Davison, R.M. and Tse, D.S.K. (1999), "The balanced scorecard: A foundation for the strategic management of information systems," *Decision Support Systems*, 25(1): 71–88.

McDermott, R. and O'Dell, C. (2001), "Overcoming cultural barriers to sharing knowledge," *Journal of Knowledge Management*, 5(1): 76-85.

Nardi, B.A., Whittaker, S. and Bradner, E. (2000), "Interaction and outeraction: Instant messaging in action," in *proceedings of the ACM conference on Computer Supported Cooperative Work*, 79–88, http://portal.acm.org/citation.cfm?id=358975 (accessed 28 May 2009).

Ou, C.X.J., Davison, R.M., Pavlou, P.A. and Li, Y. (2008), "Leveraging rich communication tools: Evidence from online trust and guanxi in China," in *29th International Conference on Information Systems*, Paris, December 14–17.

Ramasamy, B., Goh, K.W. and Yeung, M.C.H. (2006), "Is Guanxi (relationship) a bridge to knowledge transfer?" *Journal of Business Research*, 59(1): 130–139.

Sambamurthy, V., Bharadwaj, A. and Grover, V. (2003), "Shaping agility through digital options: Reconceptualizing the role of information technology in contemporary firms," *MIS Quarterly*, 27(2): 237–263.

Srivastava, A., Bartol, K.M. and Locke, E.A. (2006), "Empowering leadership in management teams: Effects on knowledge sharing, efficacy, and performance," *Academy of Management Journal*, 49(6): 1239–1251.

Susman, G.L. and Evered, R.D. (1978), "An Assessment of the scientific merits of action research," *Administrative Sciences Quarterly*, 23(4): 582–603.

Triandis, H.C. (1989), "The self and social behavior in differing cultural contexts," *Psychological Review*, 96(3): 506–520.

Tsui, A.S. and Farh, J.L. (1997), "Where guanxi matters," *Work and Occupations*, 24(1): 56–79.

Tsui, A.S. (2006), "Contextualization in Chinese Management Research," *Management and Organization Review*, 2(1): 1–13.

Voelpel, S.C. and Han, Z. (2005), "Managing Knowledge Sharing in China: The case of Siemens ShareNet," *Journal of Knowledge Management*, 9(3): 51–63.

Voelpel, S.C., Dous, M. and Davenport, T.H. (2005), "Five steps to creating a global knowledge-sharing system: Siemens' shareNet," *Academy of Management Executive*, 19(2): 9–23.

Wang, J. (2002), "Chinese enterprises need knowledge management," *Automobile Technology*, 6: 44–46.

Xin, K.R. and Pearce, J.L. (1996), "Guanxi: Connections as substitutes for formal institutional support," *Academy of Management Journal*, 39(6): 1641–1658.

Yukl, G.A. (2005) *Leadership in Organizations*, 6th edn. Upper Saddle River, NJ: Prentice Hall.

8
The Role of Trust and Control in IS Offshoring from Vendors' Perspectives

Ji-Ye Mao, Jae-Nam Lee and Chun-Ping Deng

Introduction

Offshore information systems (IS) outsourcing has been the most talked about phenomenon in IS management in recent years (e.g., Smith et al., 1996). The extent of offshoring IS-related services has been significant and the trend seems likely to continue in the foreseeable future. According to an International Data Group report, the global information technology outsourcing market was expected to have grown to US$17 billion by 2008 (Tapper et al., 2005). The clients are concentrated in North America, Western Europe and Japan, with the USA accounting for 40 percent of the market, followed by Japan at 10 percent. Whereas India has been the leading destination for offshoring, China has emerged as having both a huge potential destination for offshoring and an internal market, which has been largely neglected by research.

Offshore IS outsourcing refers to the migration of all or part of an organization's IS assets, people, and/or activities to vendors located in a country different from that of the organization. Such arrangements can take many forms ranging from transferring IS personnel from the client country to the vendor one and vice versa, to work being done in the vendor country for lower labour costs and access to specialized personnel (Hirschheim et al., 2005). Offshore outsourcing often leads to partnership relationships between clients and their vendors in the forms of joint ventures and foreign subsidiaries established in the vendor country (Steensma and Corley, 2001).

As in traditional outsourcing, relationship management is considered a key factor for successful offshore outsourcing. On the one hand, according to the transaction-cost theory, tightening control through a well-designed contract that shapes the relationship between outsourcing partners is viewed as a centrepiece in reducing production and transaction costs (Williamson, 1979). However, control in outsourcing contract is inherently more complicated than in other business contracts (Choudhury and Sabherwal, 2003). The reason is that offshore outsourcing is much riskier compared to traditional outsourcing, as offshore vendors come from different parts of the world with different cultures (Dutta and Roy, 2005). On the other hand, as in any relationship, interactions between offshore partners often go beyond the rules, agreements and exceptions specified in the contract. There is an element of trust, commitment and mutual interests that are intangible and not easily captured in the contract. The vendor-client relationship rooted in mutual trust gives rise to a strong bond between the client and its service provider. There is also evidence from an increasing number of outsourcing projects that shift from contract-based to trust-based relationship (Lacity and Willcocks, 2001). In this sense, having a certain level of trust between the client and its service provider is indispensable in reaping greater outsourcing benefits.

Whereas trust and control are essential to successful outsourcing relationship, it is particularly important for clients to exert control over their offshore vendor and to create trust in their relationship in order to ensure quality and delivery. Therefore, this research investigates the following research questions from a vendor's viewpoint:

(1) What kinds of client behaviour contribute to a vendor's trust in the client and a client's control over the vendor?
(2) What are the impacts of a vendor's trust in the client and a client's control over the vendor on project performance?

In other words, this research investigates what kinds of client behaviour influence a vendor's perceptions of trust and control and ultimately the vendor's performance. To answer the research questions, a survey was conducted from outsourcers in China working with Japanese clients.

This research addresses three gaps in the extant literature. First, very limited research has been done on the outsourcing relationship from the vendor's viewpoint, as critiqued by Koh, Ang and Straub (2004) and Levina and Ross (2003) in general and the vendor's perspective on offshore outsourcing in particular (see Swinarski et al., 2006, for exception). One of the main reasons is the difficulty with conducting cross-cultural studies and generating culturally unbiased findings. An understanding of the vendor in an offshore outsourcing relationship is important because a successful outcome is determined not by the outsourcing client alone but by both. Second, although there has been a great deal of interest in trust and control in outsourcing research, prior studies reported conflicting results with no integrated study in the offshore outsourcing setting. This deficiency needs to be rectified with a stronger theoretical base and empirical evidence. Third, the existing literature tends to focus on India-bound offshoring from the USA, overlooking a rapid growth in Japan to China offshoring (China Economic Net, 2007). Valuable lessons can be learned from this unique context, which could benefit theory development and practice of global offshore outsourcing.

The remainder of this chapter is organized as follows. The first section introduces the theoretical background and research model of this research. The next two sections give a description of the research method, and the results of data analyses. These sections are followed by a presentation of the key findings, and discussion on the contributions, implications and limitations of this work. The final section briefly presents some concluding remarks.

Theoretical framework

Prior literature in transaction cost and social exchange theories suggest two different avenues to maximize the value of outsourcing: trust and control. According to the extant literature on outsourcing, there are two different ways to enhance the value of outsourcing and to increase the possibility of outsourcing success: tightening the control through well-designed contracts (e.g., Kirsch, 2004) and improving the relationship quality based on mutual trust.

In organizational settings, trust is the degree of a firm's belief that its partner company will perform actions that will result in positive outcomes for the firm (Gulati, 1995). Following this definition, trust in this study refers to one's expectations about a partner's goodwill and reliability in working together (Boon and Holmes, 1991). In this study, we are concerned with a vendor's trust in the client and a client's control over the vendor. Control is considered "a regulatory process by which the elements of a system are made more predictable through the establishment of standards in the pursuit of some desired objective or state" (Leifer and Mills, 1996: 117).

The difference between a successful and failed outsourcing project may be dictated by the level of control through well-designed contracts. In order to have an appropriate level of control over partners, the contract clauses should be well specified under the name of service level agreement so that unexpected contingencies, possible cost increases and opportunistic behaviours between the client and its vendor can be reduced. In offshore outsourcing, given the cultural differences, communication barriers, greater physical distance and lack of personal contact, the need for control is stronger than in traditional outsourcing, thus it is particularly important to study the role of control in vendor performance. Prior literature related to the social exchange theory has identified trust as the most important contributing factor to outsourcing success (Mayer and Davis, 1999). In many cases, organizations seek a flexible relationship based on trust with their partners after they identify the limitations of the legal contracts. Because any forms of the partnership relationships in offshore outsourcing involve coordinating two parties to achieve shared objectives, satisfactory cooperation is critical to the success of offshore outsourcing. Against such a backdrop, this study singles out trust and control as key contributors to offshore outsourcing success from the vendor's viewpoint.

Trust-building behaviours in offshore outsourcing

To investigate factors influencing vendors' trust in the client and client control over the vendor, this research draws on prior literature on outsourcing and a conceptual framework by Das and Teng (1998). The framework identified various means for developing trust and control in partner cooperation. Trust-building behaviours are organizational arrangements designed to determine and affect the degree of trust between parties. Key methods to build trust include communication quality, and inter-firm adaptation, among others, whereas prior research on IS outsourcing suggests that information sharing is also important (Konsynski and McFarlan, 1990). Therefore, in this study, three types of vendor behaviours: information sharing, communication quality, and inter-firm adaptation, have been identified as essential for influencing vendors' trust in the client.

Information sharing

Information sharing refers to the range and depth of information exchanged between collaborating partners. The effectiveness of information sharing is associated with the willingness for both parties to be open with each other. Many researchers reported that trust results from more frequent and relevant information exchanges among partners (Henderson, 1990). Nelson and Cooprider (1996) argued that it is the shared information between organizational groups that determine the degree of trust. That is, repeated intergroup exchanges of information generate trust, and eventually facilitate more effective interactions and better relationships (Anderson and Narus, 1990).

In Japan–China offshore outsourcing, Chinese vendors depend on their client for providing not only domain knowledge but also process management know-how, to a lesser degree (Li et al., 2008). However, the Japanese culture is considered a high-context one (Hall, 1976), which heavily relies upon non-language cues and subtle context hints in communication. It values indirect and holistic communication styles (Tan and Tian, 2006), which hinder the free flow of task and process know-how to the vendors. It takes extra goodwill and sincerity from the client side to overcome the cross-cultural barriers. Therefore, the perceived willingness of the client to be open and forthcoming in sharing domain and process information is expected to have a strong impact on the vendor's trust in the client in a true partnership:

H1: The client's willingness to share information with the vendor will have a positive impact on the vendor's trust in the client of an offshored project.

Communication quality

Compared to information sharing, communication quality focuses on the process and means of communication. According to the social exchange literature, effective communication between collaborating partners is essential to achieving the intended objectives (Mohr and Spekman, 1994). Intensive communication keeps the partners better informed, which in turn should make each party more confident in the relationship and more willing to keep it alive (Anderson and Weitz, 1989). Prior research emphasizes the need for effective communication to achieve and monitor integrative agreements, and for preventing misunderstanding from arising. Communication quality was treated as an antecedent of trust, and found positively related to trust in organizational relationship (Morgan and Hunt, 1994). Landera et al. (2004) also found that communication quality was an important trust-building mechanism in outsourced IS development projects.

In this research context, a wide range of communication patterns exist between the vendors and their clients. Usually, the client sends their experts to introduce the project to the vendor team but the follow-up communication involves a wide variety of channels ranging from emails and phone calls to personnel exchange. The quality of communication also depends on the client's other project commitments and the level of importance attached to the given project, which influences the vendors' perception of their relationship. The vendor team may receive reliable and prompt response or be left alone for weeks without feedback, and this can be seen by the vendor team as reflecting the presence or absence of goodwill and reliability of the client. Thus, higher quality of communication is expected to enhance the level of vendor's trust in the client:

> *H2: Communication quality will have a positive impact on a vendor's trust in the client of an offshored project.*

Inter-firm adaptation

An effective way to develop trust between partners is to make adaptations in accordance with the needs of the relationship. Inter-firm adaptation is defined as the extent to which there exists an effort of joint adjustment and cooperation between organizations (Bensaou and Venkatraman, 1995). It is necessary because environmental changes require modifications in the way that partners collaborate (Sanker et al., 1995). Inter-firm adaptation provides a mechanism for negotiating and agreeing upon mutual benefits, and for creating a common goal for the relationship. Therefore, as the extent and scope of inter-firm adaptation increase, more trust is earned between offshore partners.

In the context of Japan–China offshoring, inter-firm adaptation is particularly pertinent, as a successful relationship usually involves extensive inter-firm adaptation with regard to project schedule, processes and scope. This is partly due to the evolving requirements and style of communication of the Japanese clients discussed earlier (Hall, 1976; Tan and Tian, 2006). Moreover, the client's effort in adapting to the vendor's constraints could also send a strong signal of goodwill, and commitment to the relationship with the vendor. Therefore, we hypothesized that:

H3: Inter-firm adaptation will have a positive impact on a vendor's trust in the client of an offshored project.

Control mechanisms in offshore outsourcing

Control, as an important concept in management, refers to an organizational set-up, a process of regulating behaviours, and an organizational outcome (Feenstra and Hanson, 2005; Lui and Ngo, 2004). The level of control is a direct outcome of the controlling process, whereas control mechanisms are the organizational arrangements designed to influence what organization members will do. Das and Teng outlined three important control mechanisms, goal setting, structural specifications and cultural blending, which are relevant for partnership relationships (1998). Based on the specific context of this study and prior literature on IS outsourcing (e.g., Kirsch et al., 2002), this research focuses on goal setting and cultural blending for determining client control over the vendor.

Goal setting

One of the difficult and pervasive problems in any social relationship is misunderstanding of the partner's objective. Understanding the partner's intention is essential to establishing specific and challenging goals between participants (Rai et al., 1996). Through the establishment of specific goals, partners can have common beliefs about what behaviours and policies are important or unimportant, appropriate or inappropriate, and right or wrong (Benson, 1975). That is, clear goals between participants help set the direction of their relationship and also facilitate the establishment of specific rules and regulations which are required to efficiently manage and control their relationship. Therefore, common goals between participants are crucial for formal control.

In offshore IS outsourcing, goal setting is particularly important because the success of IS projects hinges heavily on the quality of requirements (Li et al., 2008), which are difficult to define clearly and completely at the outset; and sometimes requirements evolve. The clarity of goal setting is expected to exert a strong influence on the vendor. One of the distinct issues in Japan–China offshoring is the frequently evolving client requirements, which is partly due to the largely service nature of the offshored projects and the Japanese clients' relentless pursuit of service excellence to their own clients. The extent to which the client can clearly establish project objectives is critical, and can significantly affect client control over the vendor. Accordingly, we hypothesized:

> *H4: Goal setting will have a positive impact on a client's control over the vendor of an offshored project.*

Cultural blending

Much research has reported the importance of cultural blending for social relationship (Bates et al., 1995). Differing assumptions on relationship can spark potentially damaging conflicts and dampen the spirit of cooperation. Because organizations are guided by their shared values and beliefs, they are likely to behave in a manner that is desired by other organizations. Consequently, the existence of cultural blending between participants is considered a critical element of control mechanisms, similar to the notion of clan control (Kirsch, 1997), which is a form of informal control. Cultural blending is defined as the degree of effort to create shared values, norms, and beliefs between organizations (Martinsons, 1993).

Naturally, the need for cultural blending is greater in the context of offshore outsourcing (Krishna et al., 2004). In the case of Japan–China outsourcing, successful projects tend to involve extensive personnel exchange, cultural immersion, Japanese language training, bridging engineers on the client site, and client personnel visits to the vendors (Jarvenpaa and Mao, 2008). All of these activities have an element of cultural blending, which is expected to increase the social influence of the client culture on the vendor. For example, a vendor executive in the industry commented that even a dining experience in Japan could help his employees appreciate the Japanese customer service culture, which could lead to willingness to accommodate evolving requirements from the client.

Moreover, the Japanese culture is categorized as collectivist as opposed to individualist, with a propensity to take actions that avoid high uncertainty (Hofstede, 1983). It emphasizes group harmony and higher priorities to group goals, calling for rules and regulations. Within a team, the manager is expected to issue clear instructions, and initiatives from subordinates are tightly controlled. In contrast with the high process formality of the Japanese clients, the Chinese development teams tend to be less observant of rules and regulations, exhibiting a more individualist and idiosyncratic style (Mao, 2005). Therefore,

cultural blending can facilitate the Chinese project teams to be more collectivist, group goal-oriented, and strict about conformance to formal processes
required by the Japanese client. In essence, cultural blending constitutes a
form of control. Following this line of reasoning, the following hypothesis was
developed:

*H5: Cultural blending will have a positive impact on a client's control over the
vendor of an offshored project.*

Trust and control as contributors to vendor's performance

Trust has been studied widely in the social exchange literature, as one of the
most desired qualities in any close relationship (Moorman et al., 1993). Since it
is not possible to monitor and control every detail in most exchanges, building
a minimum level of trust between partners is a must. Previous studies have identified a wide range of benefits of trust in traditional outsourcing relationships,
including lower transaction and monitoring costs, reduction in opportunistic
behaviours, and promotion of desirable behaviours (e.g., Diromualdo and
Gurbaxani, 1998). Consequently, building a certain level of trust might be a
key predictor of outsourcing success. In offshore outsourcing, greater benefits
of trust can be expected, given the more complex environment and higher
risks. Many of the practices for mitigating risks (Rottman and Lacity, 2004) and
a beneficial relationship between trust and vendor performance (Sabherwal,
1999) were found in the practice of offshoring Japanese clients and the Chinese
vendors.

There is much anecdotal evidence on the relationship between trust and vendor performance. For example, the president of one of the largest and most
successful Chinese outsourcers to Japan indicated, "It is all about trust. When
I sign a contract with my client, I don't need to look at the numbers and I can
do it with my eyes closed, 'cause I know they will treat me fairly." Therefore,
he could just focus on doing his best to get the job done, in the belief that
all of his extra effort would be compensated sooner or later. In such cases,
vendors would put in more and better resources, and take more initiatives
to deal with requirements and quality enhancement. Aside from the benefits
accrued from lower transaction costs, which contribute to vendor productivity
and performance in terms of cost management, trust may also contribute to
project quality because of the extra effort driven by the expectation of a long-
term relationship and the strong motivation for high quality work (Klein and
Nooteboom, 2002).

Vendor performance is a concept derived from the three critical objectives
of project management, quality, budget and schedule (Gopal et al., 2002).

However, since schedule is usually fixed by the client without much flexibility, it is more meaningful to focus on quality and cost control in terms of vendor performance. To the outsourcing vendor, good quality and cost management means future, and bigger, projects from the client, and budget control in terms of labour input affects its own viability and profitability. Therefore, vendor performance has both a quality dimension based on a vendor's perception of project quality and a cost control dimension that reflects the vendor's budget management. Therefore, the following two hypotheses were proposed:

> *H6: A vendor's trust in the client will have a positive impact on the quality of the offshored project.*

> *H7: A vendor's trust in the client will have a positive impact on the cost management of the offshored project.*

Control is a critical notion in inter-firm relationships because organizations are likely to have more confidence about their partners' cooperation when they feel they have an adequate level of control over those partners (Sohn, 1994). The ultimate purpose of having control in an outsourcing relationship is to be able to fashion activities in accordance with expectations and make the outsourcing goals attainable. In this sense, it is truism that effective control over the vendor in offshoring relationships helps ensure more desirable outcomes.

The need for control over the vendor in offshore outsourcing could be stronger than in traditional outsourcing for the following two reasons. First, the vendors are further removed from the real requirements along with the physical and psychological distance. Second, in the current context of offshoring to Japan, Chinese outsourcers in general possess lower maturity levels in project and process management (Jarvenpaa and Mao, 2008), and are not as experienced as their clients, who are typically IS outsourcers to their own Japanese clients (Qu and Brocklehurst, 2003). The consensus in the industry is that there is a huge differential in the sophistication of project management between Chinese vendors and Japanese clients. Therefore, in the offshore context, strong influence from the client is likely to have greater benefits, that is, in project quality and cost management, for the vendor's performance. Based on the above reasoning, the following two hypotheses were formulated, along with other hypotheses depicted in Figure 8.1:

> *H8: A client's control over the vendor will have a positive impact on the quality of the offshored project.*

> *H9: A client's control over the vendor will have a positive impact on the cost management of the offshored project.*

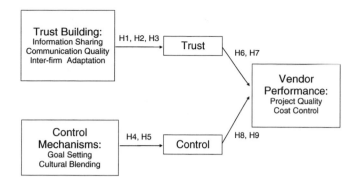

Figure 8.1 The research model

Research method

A survey was conducted to test the research hypotheses. Our unit of analysis was offshored IS project, and in each case the project manager was the informant. The scale development went through three stages:

(1) The scale generation was based on prior literature and extensive interviews conducted in seven companies to understand the industry and the general practice of offshore outsourcing in China.
(2) Prior to the pilot test, the scales were pre-tested by two executives from different firms and one project manager.
(3) A pilot test was conducted involving 31 project managers from two IS offshore outsourcing firms, which further refined the scales.

Interviews for scale generation

Interviews were arranged through a senior executive of each target firm, and senior management including the CEO or president usually participated in the study. The interviews in each firm were scheduled in a top-down sequence, and this way assured open and active participation of lower-level personnel. The interviews lasted from 45 to 90 minutes. The interviewees included executives, project managers and developers from seven Chinese vendors, and three of the companies participated in the survey later.

The interviews revealed that Japan–China offshoring has several unique characteristics, which needed to be considered in our research design. First, in most cases the client was not the end-user organization but a Japanese IS outsourcer, which was the source of both domain knowledge and process management expertise. Moreover, most of the offshored IS projects from Japan were tailor-made projects as services rather than software package development.

As such they involved changing and gradually-developed requirements. There-fore, it was important to study control and influence of the Japanese clients. Second, Japan and China had very different customer service cultures, which were further complicated by the vague Japanese style of communication. Third, the market structure was one of the buyers', featuring numerous Chinese ven-dors vying for a limited number of offshored projects. As a result, there was a huge asymmetry of bargaining power, favouring the clients. This finding fur-ther reinforced the need to study client control over vendors. Fourth, in the relationship between the Chinese vendor and Japanese client, there was a heav-ier emphasis on trust and mutual adaptation than on formal contract, to the extent that a project could be launched without a formal contract. Lastly, the vendor's revenue and profit had a near linear relationship with contract size calculated based on man-month. Therefore, it was critical for the vendor to control the cost by completing projects on time and within budget.

The interviews also helped us generate the measures for vendor performance (see Appendix 8a for examples), and other scales. Since most existing measures dealt with clients' outsourcing success, we took an exploratory approach to vendors' performance, based on the interviews with senior management, to identify key indicators of project success in terms of project quality and cost control. The project quality aspect of vendor performance was operationalized as client satisfaction with the offshored project, the fit between the com-pleted project and client standards, and the overall assessment of the project output. In contrast, cost control included budget control, overtime work and the percentage of financial compensation for extra labour input, which are key concerns for vendors in offshored IS outsourcing.

The initial measurements and pretest

Most of the measures were based on previously validated instruments, whereas the others were developed based on relevant prior research, with considera-tion to the context of this research and findings from the interviews. More specifically, trust, as one of the central constructs in this research, was opera-tionalized as the vendor's perception of the client's goodwill and reliability in a working relationship. An instrument by Lee and Kim (1999) was adopted and revised based on the context of this study. Control was operationalized as the degree to which the client has adequate influence to ensure the vendor does its best to complete the project and to make the project predictable through the establishment of standards and processes.

With regard to the three determinants of trust, information sharing was operationalized first as the degree to which useful or critical information is communicated from the client to the vendor. Second, communication quality was measured from several dimensions, including adequacy, timeliness, frequency and methods of communication between the vendor and client. Lastly, inter-firm adaptation, as a key trusting-building behaviour, was operationalized mostly in terms of "contractual flexibility", for example, "The client gives us flexibility in adjusting our schedule, work procedures, and process standards."

The two theorized determinants of control were measured similarly. First, goal setting was concerned with the degree of congruence and specificity of project objectives between the client and vendor. A five-item measure was developed for this construct, which mainly drew from our interview data. Second, the construct of cultural blending drew from both prior studies (e.g. Lasher et al., 1991) and our interview data.

To account for extraneous sources of variation in vendor performance, we incorporated task type, relationship type, and age of relationship as control variables in our model. Depending on the project task type (i.e., coding, unit test, analysis, design, system integration and integration test), that Japanese clients outsource, the complexity and importance of the project might differ and so can influence the degree of the vendor performance in offshored IS outsourcing. We also controlled for relationship type, which consisted of two different categories, that is, direct outsourcing (a Japanese client as the direct user of the system) and indirect outsourcing (a Japanese IS firm working on the project for another company). The number of layers between the development team and the end-user organization is likely to affect the flow of task domain knowledge, client relationship and project outcome. In addition, since the duration of prior relationship might influence vendor performance (Ethiraj et al., 2005), we decided to control the duration of the relationship with a client to eliminate the potential spurious effect of time on vendor performance.

A seven-point Likert-style questionnaire was developed, including 40 items to measure vendors' trust and client control, along with clients' behaviours that influence the constructs. In addition, there were three items to measure the cost control aspect of vendor performance in terms of budget adherence, and four items for project quality.

The questionnaire was initially developed in English. We then translated it into Chinese, and made an effort to maximize the consistency in sentence structure and terminology use. A bilingual IS professor, who was not related to this research, translated the Chinese version back to English. Next, we compared the back translation with the original version, and found that they were highly consistent.

A pre-test was conducted involving two executives and one project manager who had significant expertise in the area of offshore outsourcing. As a result, among the 47 items in total, three items from trust, control and their determinants and one item from project quality were removed to improve the survey's face validity based on comments gathered from interviews.

Pilot testing

The pilot test, which focused on the questionnaire's internal validity, involved 31 project managers in two companies in China, in keeping with our investigation of the vendor's perspective. The project managers had managed at least one offshoring project. In their capacity as project managers, they had dealt with clients and were familiar with the key parameters of projects. This role could be easily identified with relatively homogeneous responsibilities in a comparable pool.

The responses from 31 project managers were analysed for the discriminant and convergent validity of the target constructs through factor analysis and item-to-total correlation. The levels of internal consistency were all acceptable, ranged from 0.73 to 0.94. Items, whose item-to-total correlation scores and factor loading values were lower than 0.5, were dropped from further analysis. A factor analysis was performed on the 37 items that measured all variables except for vendor performance. Thirteen items with factor loading values lower than 0.5 were dropped. Internal consistency (Cronbach's alpha) was also measured in order to assess the reliability of the measurement. The final questionnaire used in this study consisted of 30 items for nine constructs, including two dependent variables measured with project quality and cost control, as shown in Appendix 8b.

The two phases of instrument validation resulted in a significant degree of refinement to the survey instrument, and the establishment of initial face validity and internal validity of the measures.

Sample and data collection

For the main survey, a convenience sample was used, through the researchers' personal networks and referrals. Effort was made to include companies of various backgrounds, in terms of their businesses, ownership structures and sizes (see Appendix 8c for the profile of the Chinese outsourcers). Usually an executive in a company was contacted first. A meeting was requested to explain the purpose and significance of the study, and then a request was made for permission to distribute questionnaires to the project managers. Participating companies and managers were assured that the questionnaire collected no trade secrets or confidential information. It was thought that such a top-down approach was an effective way of getting access to the busy project managers. In one case, after the meeting with the CEO of a company, all project managers were called into a conference room where they filled out the questionnaire on the spot, which took about 10–15 minutes.

Project managers were asked to focus on their most recently completed project as the focal point for answering the questionnaire, which began with three background questions on the project, breakdown of tasks, project types and client type, to get them focused on a particular project. Nine companies participated in this study including one of the largest and most successful Chinese outsourcers to Japan, resulting in 110 valid questionnaires. In all but one case, hard copies of the questionnaire with a sequential number and company code were used. In the one exception, a manager requested and returned an electronic copy of the questionnaire.

In light of the lack of prior studies of Japan-to-China offshoring, a comprehensive profile of the Chinese vendors and projects, respectively, is presented in Appendices C and D, along with the nature of the projects in our sample, to illustrate some of the unique features of this business. On average, the companies had been in business for 7.6 years, and had been outsourcers to Japan for 5.6 years. Most of the companies had a high percentage of income from Japan with the median being 90 percent. The median number of employees was 110, reflecting the fact that most of the Chinese outsourcers were small.

Seventy-eight percent of the projects surveyed were between long-term partners, and only 22 percent were for new clients. In other words, in most cases, there was an existing and stable relationship. Only about 30 percent of the project managers reported the primary approach to resolving major problem was to negotiate based on contract, and the rest were through creating consensus and mutual compromise, which were mostly likely due to well-established partner relationships.

Furthermore, about 60 percent of the tasks performed by the Chinese vendors were coding (32 percent) and unit test (28 percent), which were the low value-adding work (see Appendix 8d). Only 19 percent of the work dealt with detailed design, and virtually no conceptual design and analysis work. Moreover, consistent with the common belief in the industry, a high percentage of the projects was customized implementation of IS projects; fewer than 13 percent of the clients were end-user companies in Japan, but 84 percent of the Japanese clients were in fact IS outsourcers. With respect to the respondents, three quarters of the project managers had worked in Japan for at least three months, and 45 percent of them had studied in Japan for at least a year. This could be a result of the combination of the vendors' human resources strategy and frequent travel of the lead developers to the client's site if the budget would allow.

Prior to the model testing, we conducted two separate tests to assess data quality. First, we performed the following procedure to detect the possibility of multiple responses from the same project. No multiple respondents from the same project were found by comparing the breakdown of task details reported by the project managers. In addition, since only project managers were invited to participate in the study and normally there was only one project manager for an offshored outsourcing project, the chance of having multiple responses from the same project was minimal. Second, we performed a Harman's one-factor test for common method variance by running a principal component factor analysis on all of the questionnaire items, except items related to cost control and the control variables. The results of the confirmatory factor analysis indicates that a single factor model did not fit the data well, whereas the eight-factor model shows significantly better fitness (RMSEA $= 0.07$, $\chi^2/\mathrm{df} < 2$, $\geq \chi^2$ (28 df) $= 915.42$, $p < 0.001$). This result suggests that no general factor exists, indicating that the common method bias is not a serious concern in this study.

Analysis and results

The Partial Least Squares (PLS) method was chosen to examine the proposed model and its hypotheses for of the following reasons. First, PLS is suitable for assessing theories in the early stages of development (Chin, 1998), and this study may be a first attempt to advance a theoretical model by considering trust and control together from the vendor perspective. Second, PLS imposes minimal demands on sample size in order to validate a model compared to other structural equation model (SEM) techniques (Fornell and Bookstein, 1982). Owing to the onerous process of eliciting the participation of Chinese outsourcers, the size of the sample for the final analysis seems acceptable at the minimum level. This makes PLS appropriate for testing the proposed model using the gathered data. This study used PLS-Graph version 3.00 for analysing measurement and structural models.

Measurement model

Following the recommended two-stage analytical procedures (Anderson and Gerbing, 1988), a confirmatory factor analysis was conducted to assess the measurement model, and then the structural relationship was examined. The rationale for this approach was to ensure that our results on the structural relationship came from accurate and desirable representation of the reliability of the indicators in the measurement model.

To validate our measurement model, three types of validity were assessed: content validity, convergent validity and discriminant validity of the instrument. First, content validity refers to the representativeness and comprehensiveness of the items used to create a scale. It is assessed by examining the process by which scale items were generated. Content validity was established by ensuring the consistency between the measurement items and extant literature, by interviewing practitioners and pilot testing the instrument.

Second, convergent validity was assessed by looking at the composite reliability and the average variance extracted from the measures (Hair et al., 1995). Although many studies employing PLS use 0.5 as the threshold reliability of the measures, 0.7 is the recommended value for a reliable construct. As shown in Table 8.1, our composite reliability values of the measures range from 0.711 to

Table 8.1 Weights and loadings of the measures

Constructs	Items	Loading	T-value	Composite Reliability	Average Variance Extracted
Trust (TRST)	TRST1	0.772	17.485		
	TRST2	0.788	25.038	0.886	0.662
	TRST3	0.876	28.074		
	TRST4	0.814	21.800		
Control (COTL)	COTL1	0.861	24.194	0.862	0.676
	COTL2	0.774	12.102		
	COTL3	0.828	18.733		
Information sharing (INSH)	INSH1	0.835	18.728	0.889	0.729
	INSH2	0.916	49.620		
	INSH3	0.806	12.332		
Communication quality (COMM)	COMM1	0.877	30.210	0.911	0.773
	COMM2	0.886	22.676		
	COMM3	0.875	41.790		
Inter-firm adaptation (INAD)	INAD1	0.731	6.102	0.901	0.696
	INAD2	0.873	30.516		
	INAD3	0.869	14.489		
	INAD4	0.857	14.639		
Goal setting (GOSE)	GOSE1	0.863	26.168	0.927	0.760
	GOSE2	0.892	31.560		
	GOSE3	0.845	16.027		
	GOSE4	0.887	35.311		
Cultural blending (CUBL)	CUBL1	0.873	15.124	0.921	0.795
	CUBL2	0.936	43.286		
	CUBL3	0.865	18.580		
Project quality (QUAL)	QUAL1	0.932	42.397	0.900	0.752
	QUAL2	0.775	14.592		
	QUAL3	0.887	27.172		
Cost control (COST)	COST1	0.622	2.623	0.711	0.552
	COST2	0.742	3.756		
	COST3	0.682	2.765		

0.927. For the average variance extracted by a measure, a score of 0.5 indicates its acceptable level. Table 8.1 shows that the average variances extracted by our measures were satisfactory at 0.552 or above. Table 8.1 also exhibits the loadings and t-values of the measures in our research model. All measures are significant on their path loadings at the level of 0.01, as expected.

Lastly, the discriminant validity of our instrument was verified by looking at the square root of the average variance extracted, as recommended by Fornell and Larcker (1981). As shown in Table 8.1, the result revealed that the square root of the average variance extracted for each construct on our model is greater

Table 8.2   Results of confirmatory factor analysis

Constructs	Items	1	2	3	4	5	6	7	8	9
Trust (TRST)	TRST1	.777	−.010	.220	.072	.015	.081	−.058	.174	.098
	TRST2	.479	.126	.392	.087	.145	.142	.067	.259	.365
	TRST3	.788	.117	.018	−.055	.232	.093	.304	.170	.019
	TRST4	.681	.228	.085	−.180	.206	.212	.233	.132	.003
Control (COTL)	COTL1	.083	.756	.122	.110	.036	.103	.217	.102	−.098
	COTL2	.149	.821	−.080	.079	−.045	.289	.093	.034	.028
	COTL3	.047	.708	.340	−.039	−.012	.179	−.041	.082	.049
Information	INSH1	−.024	.202	.687	.046	.262	.176	.330	.214	−.088
sharing (INSH)	INSH2	.143	.143	.813	.088	.102	.150	.279	.106	−.059
	INSH3	.326	.038	.684	.007	.132	.217	−.028	.052	.157
Communication	COMM1	.356	.251	.064	.635	−.048	.355	.118	.260	−.016
quality (COMM)	COMM2	.303	.205	.191	.607	−.042	.243	.313	.379	−.081
	COMM3	.420	.162	.359	.617	.184	.191	.170	.209	−.154
Inter-firm	INAD1	−.002	−.038	.235	.139	.796	−.193	−.017	−.084	−.004
adaptation	INAD2	.153	−.011	.028	−.064	.814	.200	.048	.129	.082
(INAD)	INAD3	.128	−.004	.125	.004	.856	.089	.100	.025	−.027
	INAD4	.094	.035	−.004	.037	.771	−.031	.339	.110	.186
Goal setting	GOSE1	.058	.109	.219	.023	.023	.762	.270	.142	.047
(GOSE)	GOSE2	.178	.147	.240	.080	.112	.780	.147	.133	.072
	GOSE3	.017	.163	−.025	.116	−.034	.864	−.036	.096	.073
	GOSE4	.156	.148	.141	.105	.047	.850	.058	.073	−.006
Cultural	CUBL1	.225	.147	.123	.007	.360	.137	.692	−.064	.037
blending (CUBL)	CUBL2	.182	.179	.140	.142	.202	.060	.809	.041	.101
	CUBL3	.085	.145	.182	.027	.015	.118	.814	.037	.170
Project quality	QUAL1	.233	.154	.235	.065	.059	.112	.051	.809	.087
(QUAL)	QUAL2	.146	.005	−.081	−.080	.050	.143	.123	.739	.168
	QUAL3	.123	.080	.186	.071	.056	.119	.003	.861	−.102
Cost control	COST1	−.242	−.009	−.015	.057	.062	.099	−.047	−.128	.752
(QUAN)	COST2	.074	.247	.003	.087	.008	−.103	−.188	−.356	.655
	COST3	.090	−.044	.005	−.011	.134	.109	.126	.072	.898

than the correlations between it and all other constructs. Also, the results of the inter-construct correlations exhibited that each construct shared a larger variance with its own measures than with other measures. Since we included new measures derived from interviews in our study, we considered both loadings and cross-loadings to establish the discriminant validity; these are shown in Table 8.2. Overall, these results suggest that the measurement model is strongly supported by the gathered data and ready for further analysis.

In addition to the validity assessment, we planned to check multicollinearity of the measurement model since multicollinearity may potentially exist among the independent variables. However, as shown in Table 8.3 with the correlations among all variables, the highest correlation is only 0.543 between goal setting and communication quality. The remaining correlations among constructs ranged from −0.315 to 0.524 in the measurement model, which indicate that multicollinearity is not a serious problem for the proposed model.

Table 8.3 Correlation between constructs

	1	2	3	4	5	6	7	8	9
1.TRST	*0.814*								
2.COTL	0.353	*0.822*							
3.INSH	0.490	0.366	*0.854*						
4.COMM	0.524	0.455	0.520	*0.879*					
5.INAD	0.375	0.066	0.339	0.209	*0.834*				
6.GOSE	0.388	0.436	0.427	0.543	0.160	*0.872*			
7.CUBL	0.409	0.313	0.449	0.427	0.391	0.326	*0.891*		
8.QUAL	0.460	0.239	0.366	0.484	0.182	0.337	0.228	*0.867*	
9.COST	−0.315	0.124	−0.149	−0.038	−0.222	−0.126	−0.306	−0.258	*0.743*

Note: TRST: Trust; COTL: Control; INSH: Information sharing;
COMM: Communication quality; INAD: Inter-firm adaptation;
GOSE: Goal setting; CUBL: Cultural blending;
QUAL: Project quality; COST: Cost control
*The italicized numbers in the diagonal row are square roots of the average variance extracted.

Structural model

With an adequate measurement model and an acceptable level of multi-collinearity, the proposed hypotheses were tested with PLS. The results of the analysis of the structural model are depicted with the path coefficients and t-values in Figure 8.2 and summarized in Table 8.4. A test of significance of all

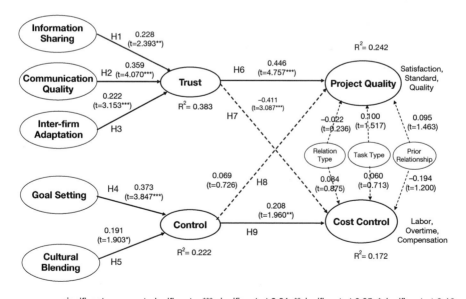

Figure 8.2 Results of data analysis

Table 8.4   Results of hypothesis testing

Hypotheses	Results
H1: The client's willingness to share information with the vendor will have a positive impact on the vendor's trust in the client of an offshored project.	**Supported**
H2: Communication quality will have a positive impact on a vendor's trust in the client of an offshored project.	**Supported**
H3: Inter-firm adaptation will have a positive impact on a vendor's trust in the client of an offshored project.	**Supported**
H4: Goal setting will have a positive impact on a client's control over the vendor of an offshored project.	**Supported**
H5: Cultural blending will have a positive impact on a client's control over the vendor of an offshored project.	**Supported**
H6: A vendor's trust in the client will have a positive impact on the quality of the offshored project.	**Supported**
H7: A vendor's trust in the client will have a positive impact on the cost management of the offshored project.	**Not supported** (significant but in opposite direction)
H8: A client's control over the vendor will have a positive impact on the quality of the offshored project.	**Not supported**
H9: A client's control over the vendor will have a positive impact on the cost management of the offshored project.	**Supported**

paths in the structural model was performed using the bootstrap resampling procedure.

Figure 8.2 shows the results of the PLS analysis, including the path loadings, t-values of the paths, and R-squares. Among the nine hypothesized paths, six are found significant at the 0.01 and 0.05 levels, and one at 0.10 level, while the two paths between trust and cost control and between control and project quality are insignificant.

Regarding the three determinants of trust, information sharing ($\beta = 0.228$; $t = 2.393$; $p < 0.05$), communication quality ($\beta = 0.359$; $t = 4.070$; $p < 0.01$), and inter-firm adaptation ($\beta = 0.222$; $t = 3.153$; $p < 0.01$) were significantly associated with trust, as expected, That is, the higher the degree of information sharing, communication quality and inter-firm adaptation between a client and its vendor, the greater the perception of trust felt by the vendor. Thus, the results support Hypotheses 1, 2 and 3. The three determinants of trust account for about 38 percent of the variance in trust.

As proposed in Hypotheses 4 and 5, goal setting ($\beta = 0.373$; $t = 3.847$; $p < 0.01$) and cultural blending ($\beta = 0.191$; $t = 1.903$; $p < 0.10$) between the Japanese client and the Chinese outsourcer had significant impacts on the degree of control in offshore IS outsourcing. The results suggest that establishing common goals and shared values and beliefs between outsourcing partners increased the degree of control by the client, which could facilitate desirable behaviours and discourage opportunistic behaviours by the client. Goal setting and cultural blending account for around 22 percent of the variance in control.

Lastly, trust was found to be significantly related to project quality ($\beta = 0.446$; $t = 4.757$; $p < 0.01$), but had an insignificant relationship with cost control (actually significant but in the opposite direction). Hence, Hypothesis 6 was supported, whereas Hypothesis 7 was not. In contrast, control had a significant impact on cost control ($\beta = 0.208$; $t = 1.960$; $p < 0.100.05$), as proposed in Hypothesis 9, but an insignificant relationship with project quality, providing no support for Hypothesis 8. The two constructs, trust and control explain about 24 percent and 17 percent of the variance in project quality and budget adherence, respectively.

None of the three control variables showed any significant relationship with project quality or cost control. The R-square values of project quality and cost control are 0.242 and 0.172, which are acceptable, as vendor performance in the offshore outsourcing project can be influenced by many more critical internal and external factors. This result indicates that trust and control have significant influence on vendor performance in offshore IS outsourcing, thus they should receive more attention in further studies.

Findings and discussion

This research has resulted in some interesting findings. First, this research has offered a new perspective to understanding the contributors to trust and control in the offshore outsourcing setting. With respect to trust, the client's effort in information sharing, communication quality and inter-firm adaptation appear to be useful mechanisms. Moreover, once trust is developed, the focuses are not only on specific actions or behaviours but also on the motives and intentions of the exchange partner (Rempel et al., 1985). As a result, trust increases the confidence which the collaborating partners have for one another in performing the tasks and achieving outsourcing objectives. Regarding control, both goal setting and cultural blending contributed to control by the client. It means that a higher degree of congruence in the project objective between outsourcing partners and harmony of shared values and belief are instrumental for creating client control.

Second, trust in the offshore clients is positively correlated with project quality, but negatively correlated with cost management, contrary to our expectation. It appears that a higher level of trust in the client is associated with higher quality standards and a higher level of effort, which could potentially hurt cost control. Although it was expected that lower transaction cost accrued from increased trust would contribute to efficiency, the potential gains in efficiency seemed either not to materialize, or inadequate to offset additional effort for a trusted client. A plausible explanation is that, although cost control is important in the competitive outsourcing business, vendors are willing to invest extra resources if they trust their client, and anticipate a continuing relationship. Moreover, the contract practice of outsourcing between Japan and China is that quality and the delivery schedule are explicit and strictly followed, for example, in terms of bug rates, but labour input is implicit and managed by the vendor. It is important to note that most of the vendor–client relationships in our sample were between long-term repetitive partners, as opposed to strictly contract-based relationships.

Lastly, as expected, client control over the vendor has a significant impact on cost control. However, it does not have any significant impact on project quality. It seems to suggest that vendor performance in budget adherence is under the influence of certain client behaviours, aside from the formal contract and normal project management. That is, a client's control actually helps the vendor prevent cost overrun. However, client control is not a significant factor influencing project quality, whereas creating trust by the vendor is.

Contributions and implications

The results of this study have several contributions and implications of both academic and practical importance. First, our study suggests that there are several things that a client can do to increase the vendor's trust, which would benefit not only customer relationship but also the quality of the project. The practical implications for clients are to ensure effective communication, and to increase the range and depth of information transfer to the vendor. Clients' effort to maintain some degree of flexibility and adaptability toward the vendor could help in gaining the vendor's trust.

Second, to offshore outsourcing clients, goal setting and cultural blending can be instrumental for the client to gain influence over the vendor, and client control can help the vendor's budget adherence. In light of the relatively low software process maturity of Chinese vendors, strong client influence is beneficial for the vendors' success in budget control, which ultimately affects vendors' profitability. The practical implications for offshore clients are the options for increasing their control over the vendor through cultural blending and goal-setting. The former can be achieved through providing the vendor project team with access to the client culture, social opportunities and language training. The latter entails clear specification of goals and deliverables and, more importantly, shared understandings that go beyond the contract.

Third, clients can influence outsourced IS project quality via trust nurturing behaviours. In other words, certain client behaviours have a significant effect on the vendor's trust in the client, which can help project quality. With trust in the client, the vendor works harder and becomes less concerned about cost, aiming for client satisfaction and a long-term relationship. The rationale is rooted in prior literature on the benefits of trust in inter-firm relationships, and confirmed by evidence from this research. This finding is a potential theoretical contribution to research on the effect of trust, which is not reported in the literature. From a practical point of view, clients in offshore outsourcing relationships can benefit from this finding.

Fourth, this research developed a preliminary measure of vendor performance based on interviews with the practitioners, encompassing both subjective measures and perceptions. The measure of vendor performance could be useful and further refined for future research for the offshore outsourcing context.

Fifth, given our focus on Japan-to-China outsourcing, which lacks prior research despite its significant market size, knowledge gained from this research could be potentially useful for research on offshore outsourcing global-wise. The exploratory data reported in this study, as a snapshot of the industry, could be useful for follow-up research.

Lastly, this study considered and tested the impact of both trust and control on two different dependent variables, that is, project quality and cost management. Prior studies have tried to investigate whether trust and control operate as complement or substitute, but reported conflicting results with no clear explanation. The main reason could be that they generally considered one dependent variable, in spite of the fact that there exists more than one outcome variable in outsourcing. To overcome the problem, this study considered two major dependent variables from the project management perspective, and found that trust has a significant impact on project quality while control is significantly associated with cost management. In other words, trust and control have different roles in improving outsourcing performance and operate as complement.

It may be useful to benchmark our findings with studies conducted in other offshoring relationships, and two studies were found. A study of Vietnamese vendors engaged in offshoring software outsourcing identified that vendors' understanding of the client culture, creditability, capabilities and personal visits are important factors in gaining the initial trust of a client, whereas, in maintaining that trust, vital factors include cultural understanding, communication strategies, contract conformance and timely delivery (Oza et al., 2006). However, a study of Indian vendors found that critical factors for maintaining trust in offshoring software outsourcing relationships include transparency, demonstrability, honesty, process followed and commitment (Babar et al., 2007). These studies are conducted with different perspectives from ours, and the factors are different.

However, a closer inspection reveals that they are related to ours, for example, cultural understanding and communication strategies appear to overlap with cultural blending and communication quality in our model. This comparison provides indirect support to our findings. It also adds to the significance of this research, and calls for the development of stronger theoretical models on trust in outsourcing, to facilitate cumulative research in the field.

Limitations and future directions

Findings of this research need to be interpreted with the limitations in mind, and understood as a starting point for future research. First, the survey was based on a convenience sample, and our sample was relatively small despite our effort. This was due to challenges in accessing project managers. In fact, in several cases, our requests based on referrals for access were turned down due to heavy workload. As a result, the use of a convenience sample poses a threat to the external validity of the results, whereas the small sample size has limited some of the data analysis options and reduced the statistical power of the analyses. Moreover, in our sample there were several projects from the same company, and the projects might come from the same client, thus the trust and control aspects were quite similar, which reduced variances. Second, this research studies Japan–China offshore outsourcing, which involves some unique cultural and cross-cultural influences. As a result, the generalizability of the results to other cultural contexts might be limited.

As to future research directions, it is necessary to continue enhancing the research model and measures, and increase the sample size so that we can compare and test variations of the model and competing models. It is also important to replicate the research in other cultural and cross-cultural settings to find out what is unique to this particular research setting and what is generalizable.

Conclusions

This exploratory research has filled some of the gaps in the current literature on offshore outsourcing, and offers the potential to start a new line of research on trust and control from the vendors' perspective. A model of trust-control in offshore outsourcing relationship was proposed, and it received empirical support to a large extent: Several trust building mechanisms have been identified, including the client's effort in information sharing, communication quality and inter-firm adaptation. Meanwhile, the client can also focus on goal setting and cultural blending with the vendors for its influence and control on the project. Furthermore, the vendor's trust in the client really stood out as a key factor for project quality, and vendor control actually helped prevent cost overrun. These results could be useful for global outsourcing practice and future research.

Appendix 8a   Sample interview transcripts

Concepts	Corresponding transcripts	
	Items in questionnaire	*Sample transcripts*
Interviews used for scales development	Control 1: Our client arranged process control to achieve its objectives.	"Our client has their own specifications and methods for project management, and these must be strictly followed."
	Trust 2: Our client was willing to provide assistance to us without exception.	"Some clients are more responsive, providing additional information to our questions, along with what they think you should know. When they make a suggestion, they send us relevant materials."
	Quality 1: To your knowledge, to what extent was the client satisfied with the project quality?	"After project delivery, we'd send a survey of client satisfaction to be filled in by their project manager, and other staff on-site, including quality, schedule and delivery punctuality."
Gap in customer service mentality	"Japanese projects are notoriously rigorous, as the clients are very rigid detail oriented. Those of us who went to the client office to participate in design have an acute feeling of this. The Japanese clients are careful with their end users. For example, their attention goes to the level of the exact position of a control on the desktop, which is confirmed by the client. Once the project is delivered and the end user changes his mind and requests the control to be placed in a different location, our client would agree unconditionally. They consider their client as God."	
Differences in project management	"The large Japanese firms have their mature processes, not only for systems development and project management, but also for supplier management, which is worth learning." "Many of the clients' norms in systems development have reference values for the Chinese side. In software development, our side lags behind in formal methods, whereas the Japanese is much more advanced."	
Cultural blending	"Capability development is important for working on Japanese outsourcing.... Our experience in on-site working in Japanese firms for design has a major impact on our development work, as well as on our daily life, on following procedures step by step. One gains capability in multiple aspects, Japanese language, execution power and ways of thinking."	
	"Client influence filters through to us subconsciously and consciously, probably subconsciously. Regardless of whether you understand it, you must follow the process, which is not negotiable. The subconscious influence made you accept their rules and processes. To a certain extent, this raises the competence of the Chinese team."	

(Continued)

Concepts	Corresponding transcripts
Vagueness of Japanese communication	"People talk about the vagueness of Japanese, which is true even in their emails, words are carefully chosen, very meticulous. They talk courteously with subtle meanings." "In their talk, very vague, he'd use multiple negations, leaving it to you to make sense of it."
Cultural differences	"Although there are many Chinese characters in Japanese, but their culture is much different (from ours). The way of getting things done, it is difficult for them to understand the behaviour of Chinese, and vice versa. I only understand a small portion of Japanese behaviour." "Speaking of their mentality, Japanese follow procedures rigidly. In contrast, every Chinese has a different idea. This causes a big headache for Japanese offshore projects, as each Chinese programmer does it in his own way, which causes major difficulty for maintenance. In a project done by the Japanese, it does not matter to replace developers, as everybody can still understand the work. The key is to follow procedures rigidly."

Appendix 8b Questionnaire items

Constructs	Origin	Operational Definitions	Question items
Trust	Boon and Holmes (1991); Gulati (1995); Lui and Ngo (2004); Mayer and Davis (1999)	The degree of the client's expectations about goodwill and reliability in working with the vendor	1. Our client was honest when it tried to resolve differences of opinion with us. 2. Our client was willing to provide assistance to us without exception. 3. Our client reliably provided support pre-specified in the contract. 4. Our client was sincere in dealing with us at all times.
Control	Leifer and Mills (1996)	The degree of adequate influence to ensure the vendor does its best and regulatory process installed to make the project more predictable	1. Our client arranged process control to achieve its objectives. 2. Our client tried to routinize our work procedures. 3. Our client emphasized process management.

Information sharing	Mohr and Spekman (1994); Morgan and Hunt (1994)	The degree to which task information and know-how is transferred	1. Our client shared project management experience with us. 2. Our client shared with us business domain knowledge. 3. Our client shared with us background information related to the project.
Communication quality	Anderson and Narus (1990)	The degree of timeliness, adequacy, effectiveness and quality of communication	1. With this client, the manner and methods of communication were timely. 2. With this client, the manner and methods of communication were effective. 3. With this client, the manner and methods of communication were complete and thorough.
Inter-firm adaptation	Bensaou and Venkatraman (1995)	The degree of flexibility in adjusting schedule, work procedures, and process standards	1. Our client modified its work procedures while working with us. 2. Our client modified its project schedules in order to suit our delivery capability. 3. Our client modified its process standards in order to suit our situation. 4. Our client modified our contract to accommodate our situation.
Goal setting	Benson (1975); Rai et al. (1996)	The degree of congruence and specificity of the project objective between partners	1. Our client and we reached consensus on the goals. 2. Our client took measures to make sure our two parties had a common understanding of the goals. 3. There was no ambiguity in our mind about the deliverables of the each stage of the project. 4. There was no inconsistency in our two parties' understanding of the deliverables.

(Continued)

Constructs	Origin	Operational Definitions	Question items
Cultural blending	Bates et al (1995); Martinsons (1993)	The amount of effort to create shared values, norms and beliefs between partners	1. Our client and we organized activities for our employees to socialize or train together. 2. Our client and we created opportunities to learn each other's culture, e.g., manner of communication. 3. Our client encouraged and facilitated our employees to learn their language and culture.
	N.A.	Perception of project quality	1. To your knowledge, to what extent was the client satisfied with the project quality? (1 – not at all ~ 7 – extremely) 2. According to the client specific quality standard for the project, this project is: (1 – far below; 2 – a bit below; 3 – close; 4 – reached standard; 5 – slightly exceeded; 6 – exceeded substantially; 7 – exceeded a great deal) 3. What is your overall assessment of the project quality? (1 – total failure ~ 7 – complete success)
		Management of cost and labour input to the project	1. What was the initial labour input set by the client____ (man-months), jointly planned labour input after discussion____ (man-months), and actual labour input ____ (man-months)? 2. What was the percentage of overtime work by the project team in the overall labour input to the project? _____% 3. Is the labour input beyond what was initially set by the client, what percentage of it was financially compensated by the client? _____%

Appendix 8c Profile of Chinese outsourcers

Firm	Industry	% of Equity held by Japanese clients	Outsourcing to Japanese (years)	No. of Japanese clients	Sales (million of RMB, 1US$ ~ 7 RMB)	No. of staff	% of sales from Japan
A	Serving clients in education and transportation	60	2.5	12	12	100	90
B	Finance, insurance, and e-commerce	4 – 4.5	10	9	2550	1800	92.5
C	Finance, telecomm, Transportation, etc.	100	8	1	5.72	270	100
D	Manufacturing, finance, etc.	51	14	6	19	170	100
E	Vendors of system software, middleware, and application development	0	8	3	10	100	90
F	Life sciences, healthcare, construction, entertainment	0	1.5	4	16	120	10
G	Transportation, trade, machinery, and e-government	25	2	2	2	22	100
H	Manufacturing and logistics	25	1	8	2	20	70
I	Manufacturing, finance, medical care, telecomm	0	3.5	15	10	110	100
Mean		29.5	5.6	6.7	291.9	301.3	73.3
S. D.		34.7	4.6	4.7	846.8	567.0	40.0
Median		25	3.5	6	10	110	90

Appendix 8d   Breakdown of the nature of tasks in each project

Tasks	Mean (%)	S.D. (%)
Coding	31.52	15.19
Unit test	27.77	12.89
Detailed design	19.18	12.35
Conceptual design	5.33	7.50
System integration	1.44	3.44
Integration test	7.67	11.37
Systems analysis	1.63	4.75
All other work	5.45	8.85
Total (n = 110)	100	–

Note: Percentage of breakdown of all tasks should add up to 100 percent for each project, otherwise not included in the calculation.

References

Anderson, J.C. and Gerbing, D.W. (1988), "Structural equation modeling in practice: A review and recommended two-step approach," *Psychological Bulletin*, 103(3): 411–423.

Anderson, J.C. and Narus, J.A. (1990), "A model of distributor firm and manufacturer firm working partnerships," *Journal of Marketing*, 54(1): 42–59.

Anderson, J.C. and Weitz, B. (1989), "Determinants of continuity in conventional industrial Channel Dyads," *Marketing Science*, 8(4): 310–323.

Babar, M.A., Verner, J.M. and Nguyen, P.T. (2007), "Establishing and maintaining trust in software outsourcing relationships: An empirical investigation," *Journal of Systems and Software*, 80(9): 1438–1449.

Bates, K.A., Amundson, S.D., Schroeder, R.G. and Morris, W.T. (1995), "The crucial inter-relationship between manufacturing strategy and organizational culture," *Management Science*, 41(10): 1565–1580.

Bensaou, M. and Venkatraman, N. (1995), "Configurations of interorganizational relationships: A comparison between U.S. and Japanese automakers," *Management Science*, 41(9): 1471–1492.

Benson, J.K. (1975), "The interorganizational network as a political economy," *Administrative Science Quarterly*, 20(2): 229–249.

Boon, S.D. and Holmes, J.G. (1991), "The dynamics of interpersonal trust: Resolving uncertainty in the face of risk," in Robert A. Hinde and Jo Groebel, (eds) *Cooperation and Prosocial Behaviour*, Cambridge: Cambridge University Press, pp. 190–211.

Chin, W.W. (1998), "The partial least squares approach to structural equation modeling in modern methods for business research," in G.A. Marcoulides (ed.) *Modern Methods for Business Research*, New Jersey: Lawrence Erlbaum Associates, pp. 295–336.

China Economic Net (2007), "China becomes Japan's biggest software outsourcing base." http://en.ce.cn/National/Politics/200704/13/t20070413_11025663.shtml (accessed 13 April 2007).

Choudhury, V. and Sabherwal, R. (2003), "Portfolios of Control in Outsourced Software Development Projects," *Information Systems Research*, 14(3): 291–314.

Das, T.K. and Teng, B.S. (1998), "Between trust and control: Developing confidence in partner cooperation in alliances," *Academy of Management Review*, 23(3): 491–512.

Diromualdo, A. and Gurbaxani, V. (1998), "Strategic intent for IT outsourcing," *Sloan Management Review*, 39(4): 67–80.

Dutta, A. and Roy R. (2005), "Offshore outsourcing: A dynamic causal model of counteracting forces," *Journal of Management Information Systems*, 22(2): 15–35.

Ethiraj, S.K., Kale, P., Krishnan, M.S. and Singh, J.V. (2005), "Where do capabilities come from and how do they matter? A study in the software services industry," *Strategic Management Journal*, 26(1): 25–45.

Feenstra, R.C. and Hanson, G.H. (2005), "Ownership and control in outsourcing to China: Estimating the property-rights theory of the firm," *The Quarterly Journal of Economics*, 120(2): 729–761.

Fornell, C. and Bookstein, F.L. (1982), "Two structural equation models: LISREL and PLS applied to customer exit-voice theory," *Journal of Marketing Research*, 19(4): 440–452.

Fornell, C. and Larcker, D.F. (1981), "Structural equation models with unobservable variables and measurement errors," *Journal of Marketing Research*, 18(2): 39–50.

Gopal, A., Mukhopadhyay, T. and Krishnan, M.S. (2002), "The role of software processes and communication in offshore software development," *Communications of the ACM*, 45(4): 193–199.

Gulati, R. (1995), "Does familiarity breed trust? The implications of repeated ties for contractual choice in alliances?" *Academy of Management Journal*, 38(1): 85–112.

Hair, J.F., Anderson, R.E., Tatham, R.L. and Black, W.C. (1995), *Multivariate Data Analysis with Readings* (4th edn), New York: Prentice Hall.

Hall, E.T. (1976), *Beyond Culture*, New York: Doubleday & Company.

Henderson, J.C. (1990), "Plugging into strategic partnerships: The critical IS connection," *Sloan Management Review*, 30(3): 7–18.

Hirschheim, R., Loebbecke, C., Newman, M. and Valor, J. (2005), "Offshoring and its Implications for the Information Systems Discipline," in the *Proceedings of twenty-sixth International Conference on Information Systems* (Las Vegas, Nevada, USA, 2005); 11–14 December: 1003–1018.

Hofstede, G. (1983), "The Cultural Relativity of Organizational Practices and Theories," *Journal of International Business Studies*, 14 (2): 75–89.

Jarvenpaa, S.L. and Mao, J.-Y. (2008), "Operational capabilities development in mediated offshore software services models," *Journal of Information Technology*, 23(1): 3–17.

Kirsch, L.J. (1997), "Portfolios of control modes and IS project management," *Information Systems Research*, 8(3): 215–239.

Kirsch, L.J. (2004), "Deploying common systems globally: The dynamics of control," *Information Systems Research*, 15(4): 374–395.

Kirsch, L.J., Sambamurthy, V., Ko, D.G. and Purvis, R.L. (2002), "Controlling Information Systems Development Projects: The view from the client," *Management Science*, 48(4): 484–498.

Klein, R.W. and Nooteboom, B. (2002), "Trust and Formal Control in Interorganizational Relationships," Erasmus Research Institute of Management, RSM Erasmus University.

Koh, C., Ang, S. and Straub, D.W. (2004), "IT outsourcing success: A psychological contract perspective," *Information Systems Research*, 15(4): 356–373.

Konsynski, B.R. and McFarlan, F.W. (1990), "Information Partnerships-shared Data, Shared Scale," *Harvard Business Review*, 68(5): 114–120.

Krishna, S., Sahay, S. and Walsham, G. (2004), "Managing cross-cultural issues in global software outsourcing," *Communications of the ACM*, 47(4): 62–66.

Lacity, M.C. and Willcocks, L.P. (2001), *Global Information Technology Outsourcing: In Search of Business Advantage*, Chichester, UK: John Wiley & Sons.

Landera, M.C., Purvisb, R.L., McCrayc, G.E. and Leighd, W. (2004), "Trust-building mechanisms utilized in outsourced IS development projects: A case study," *Information and Management*, 41(4): 509–528.

Lasher, D.R., Ives, B. and Jarvenpaa, S.L. (1991), "USAA-IBM partnerships in information technology: Managing the image project," *MIS Quarterly*, 15(4): 551–565.

Lee, J.N. and Kim, Y.G. (1999), "Effect of partnership quality on IS outsourcing success: Conceptual framework and empirical validation," *Journal of Management Information Systems*, 15(4): 29–61.

Leifer, R. and Mills, P.K. (1996), "An information processing approach for deciding upon control strategies and reducing control loss in emerging organizations," *Journal of Management*, 22(1): 113–137.

Levina, N. and Ross, J.W. (2003), "From the vendor's perspective: Exploring the value proposition in information technology outsourcing," *MIS Quarterly*, 27(3): 331–364.

Li, Y., Liu, Y., Li, M. and Wu, H. (2008), "Transformational offshore outsourcing: Empirical evidence from alliances in China," *Journal of Operations Management*, 26(2): 257–274.

Lui, S.S. and Ngo, H.Y. (2004), "The role of trust and contractual safeguards on cooperation in non-equity alliances," *Journal of Management*, 30(4): 471–485.

Mao, H.D. (2005), *A Research on Quality Management Based on Software Outsourcing from Japan (in Chinese)*, unpublished Master's thesis, East China Normal University, Shanghai, China.

Martinsons, M.G. (1993), "Outsourcing information systems: A strategic partnership with risks," *Long Range Planning*, 26(3): 18–25.

Mayer, R.C. and Davis, J.H. (1999), "The effect of the performance appraisal system on trust in management: A field quasi-experiment," *Journal of Applied Psychology*, 84(1): 123–136.

Mohr, J. and Spekman, R. (1994), "Characteristics of partnership success: Partnership attributes, communication, behavior, and conflict resolution techniques," *Strategic Management Journal*, 15(2): 135–152.

Moorman, C., Deshpande, R. and Zaltman, G. (1993), "Factors affecting trust in market research relationships," *Journal of Marketing*, 57(1): 81–101.

Morgan, R.M. and Hunt, S.D. (1994), "The Commitment-trust theory of relationship marketing," *Journal of Marketing*, 58(3): 20–38.

Nelson, K.M. and Cooprider, J.G. (1996), "The contribution of shared knowledge to IS group performance," *MIS Quarterly*, 20(4): 409–432.

Oza, N.V., Hall, T., Rainer, A. and Grey, S. (2006), "Trust in software outsourcing relationships: An empirical investigation of Indian software companies," *Information and Software Technology*, 48(5): 345–354.

Qu, Z.H. and Brocklehurst, M. (2003), "What will it take for China to become a competitive force in offshore outsourcing? An analysis of the role of transaction costs in supplier selection," *Journal of Information Technology*, 18(1): 53–67.

Rai, A., Borah, S. and Ramaprasad, A. (1996), "Critical success factors for strategic alliances in the information technology industry: An empirical study," *Decision Sciences*, 27(1): 141–155.

Rempel, J., Holmes, K. and Zanna, M. (1985), "Trust in close relationships," *Journal of Personality and Social Psychology*, 49(1): 95–112.

Rottman, J. and Lacity, M. (2004), "Twenty practices for offshore sourcing," *MIS Quarterly Executive*, 3(3): 117–130.

Sabherwal, R. (1999), "The role of trust in outsourced IS development projects," *Communications of the ACM*, 42(2): 80–86.

Sanker, C.S., Boulton, W.R., Davidson, N.W., Snyder, C.A. and Ussery, R.W. (1995), "Building a world-class alliance: The universal card – TSYS case," *Academy of Management Executive*, 9(2): 20–29.

Smith, M.A., Mitra, S. and Narasimhan, S. (1996), "Offshore outsourcing of software development and maintenance: A framework for issues," *Information & Management*, 31(3): 165–175.

Sohn, J.H.D. (1994), "Social knowledge as a control system: A proposition and evidence from the Japanese FDI behavior," *Journal of International Business Studies*, 25(2): 295–324.

Steensma, H.K. and Corley, K.G. (2001), "Organizational context as a moderator of theories on firm boundaries for technology sourcing," *Academy of Management Journal*, 44(2): 271–291.

Swinarski, M., Kishore, R. and Rao, H.R. (2006), "Impact of IT service provider process capabilities on service provider performance: An empirical study," *Thirty-ninth Hawaii International Conference on System Sciences* (Hawaii, USA, 2006); Chicago: IEEE Computer Society Press. 1–10.

Tapper, D., Motsenigos, A., Ravi, R. and Zhang, X.F. (2005), "IDC's top worldwide outsourcing deals of 2004," IDC, Doc#34024, November 2005.

Tan, L. and Tian, B. (2006), "A comparative research on U.S.-Japanese-European offshore service outsourcing models and revelations (in Chinese)," *China Soft Science*, 5: 128–134.

Williamson, O.E. (1979), "Transaction cost economics: The governance of contractual relations," *Journal of Law and Economics*, 22(2): 233–261.

9
Drivers and Obstacles of Outsourcing Practices in China

Kwok Hung Lau and Jianmei Zhang

Introduction

Outsourcing is a fast growing aspect of the world economy, which amounted to a worldwide spending of about US$3.7 trillion in 2001 (Clott, 2004). According to the latest survey jointly conducted by Capgemini, Georgia Institute of Technology, SAP and DHL, the use of third-party logistics (3PL) services continues to increase in Latin America, North America, South Africa, Western Europe and Asia-Pacific. For the years 2002–2005, the average percentage usage in the five regions studied range from 67 to 84 per cent (Capgemini et al., 2006). Another survey conducted by Lieb and Bentz (2004) reveals that 83 per cent of the Fortune 500 manufacturers use 3PL services. Driven by globalization and rapid advance in information technology (IT), organizations strive to improve competitiveness and responsiveness to customer and market demands (Razzaque and Sheng, 1998). Outsourcing has increasingly become an important strategy that can significantly assist organizations to leverage their skills and resources to achieve greater competitiveness (Quinn and Hilmer, 1994; Welson, 1996).

As a fast developing country, China has long been recognized as a popular place to outsource (Matteo, 2003). Low-cost labour and high-technology manufacturing have made China the leading destination for outsourcing (Brown, 2005). With its accession to the World Trade Organization (WTO), China has more favourable conditions to implement its economic reform and industrial restructuring. This has stimulated the development of its logistics industry and fostered a growing demand for outsourcing (Agarwal and Wu, 2004). Nevertheless, the 3PL industry in China is still regarded as being in its infancy (Trunick, 2003). Although much has been written about outsourcing to China (Brown, 2005; Forrest, 2005; Hannon, 2005; Matteo, 2003), limited studies have been conducted to thoroughly investigate the key outsourcing drivers and problems that organizations in China have considered and encountered.

216

Objectives of the Study

Owing to the differences in economic and infrastructure development between developed and developing countries, it is likely that there will be different reasons for outsourcing in China that have yet to be determined. This study attempts to fill the gap in the literature by exploring the key factors that motivate organizations in China to outsource and the obstacles they are facing. Six case studies involving companies of different types of ownership are discussed to examine the strategic reasons of organizations in China for outsourcing and the problems they have encountered. A comparison is also presented between China and Western developed countries on the drivers and challenges of outsourcing.

Literature Survey

A large number of studies have analysed the drivers of outsourcing from both a theoretical perspective (Jennings, 2002; Kakabadse and Kakabadse, 2000; Lankford and Parsa, 1999; Lynch, 2004; Quinn and Hilmer, 1994; Razzaque and Sheng, 1998; Trunick, 1989) and a practical point of view using case studies and surveys in developed countries such as USA, UK, Australia and New Zealand (Al-Qirim, 2003; Beaumont and Sohal, 2004; Bolumole, 2001; Corbett, 1998; Fan, 2000; Kakabadse and Kakabadse, 2005; McIvor, 2003). While many drivers are unique to specific organizations and industries, there are some common key factors that motivate organizations of all industries to make outsourcing decisions. These factors can broadly be categorized as economic, strategic and environmental ones as summarized in Table 9.1. By making use of outsourcing, organizations can gain a competitive advantage through cost reduction and improved responsiveness to changing business environment and market demand.

Although there are good reasons to outsource, a number of potential obstacles and problems associated with outsourcing are also recognized. There is evidence that outsourcing does not reduce costs as expected in some cases (Beaumont and Sohal, 2004; Gonzalez et al., 2005). As summarized in Table 9.2, loss of control (Blumberg, 1998; Claver et al., 2002; Kakabadse and Kakabadse, 2000; Lankford and Parsa, 1999; Lynch, 2004; Razzaque and Sheng, 1998), loss of critical skills (Beaumont and Sohal, 2004; Jennings, 2002; Quinn and Hilmer, 1994), inadequate capabilities of service providers (Al-Qirim, 2003; Razzaque and Sheng, 1998), loss of flexibility (Beaumont and Sohal, 2004; Embleton and Wright, 1998), failure to realize the hidden costs generated by the contract (Gonzalez et al., 2005; Kakabadse and Kakabadse, 2000; Palvia, 1995), difficulty in obtaining organizational support (Razzaque and Sheng, 1998), indecisiveness about which activities to outsource (Lankford and Parsa, 1999), inadequacy of

Table 9.1   Drivers of outsourcing

	Objectives or anticipated outcomes	**Authors**
Economic factors		
Cost reduction	To improve profitability To improve operating efficiency To add value to product	Trunick (1989), Richardson (1990), Gonzales *et al.* (2005)
Cost saving	To improve cash flow To increase efficiency	Embleton and Wright (1998), Claver *et al.* (2002)
Capital investment reduction	To make capital funds more available for core areas To improve return on assets	Corbett (1998), Razzaque and Sheng (1998), Trunick (1998), Lynch (2004)
Strategic factors		
Acceleration of business process re-engineering	To improve performance To achieve competitive advantage	Corbett (1998), Embleton and Wright (1998), Clott (2004)
Focus on core competence	To improve business focus To increase competitiveness To leverage the firm's skills and resources To enhance customer satisfaction	Prahalad and Hamel (1990), Quinn and Hilmer (1994), Weerakkody *et al.* (2003)
Flexibility enhancement	To reduce constraints of organization's own production capacity To convert fixed costs to variable costs To increase responsiveness to market change To reduce risks	Quinn and Hilmer (1994), Corbett (1998), Embleton and Wright (1998), Razzaque and Sheng (1998), Kakabadse and Kakabadse (2000), Jennings (2002), Lynch (2004)
Environmental factors		
IT development	To meet increasing demand for new information systems and resources more efficiently and economically	Lynch (2004)
Globalization	To help companies gain global competitive advantage	Clott (2004)
Capability of supplier	To enable partnering to improve service quality and customer service and increase competitive advantage	Jennings (2002)

cost and benefit analysis systems (McIvor and Humphreys, 2000), fear of job loss (Razzaque and Sheng, 1998), and damage to morale of existing workers (Embleton and Wright, 1998), are among the commonly cited inhibitors to outsourcing.

In recent years, the Chinese government has designated logistics as a strategic industry and invested heavily in improving infrastructure such as nationwide

Table 9.2 Main obstacles and problems of outsourcing

Obstacles and problems	Impacts	Authors
Loss of control	Loss of core competence Risks of alienating customers	Blumberg (1998), Lonsdale and Cox (2000)
Loss of critical skills	Loss of competitive advantage Increased number of competitors	Quinn and Hilmer (1994), Jennings (2002), Beaumont and Sohal (2004)
Inadequate capabilities of service provider	Loss of competitive advantage Loss of market share	Jennings (2002)
Loss of flexibility	Reduced responsiveness Risks of alienating customers	Embleton and Wright (1998), Beaumont and Sohal (2004)
Failure to realize hidden costs of contract	Increased operating cost	Palvia (1995), Kakabadse and Kakabadse (2000), Gonzalez *et al.* (2005)
Difficulty in obtaining organizational support	Increased chances of failure	Razzaque and Sheng (1998)
Indecisiveness on which activities to outsource	Increased chances of failure	Lankford and Parsa (1999)
Inadequate cost and benefit analysis systems	Lower return on investment Loss of competitive advantage	McIvor and Humphreys (2000)
Fear of job loss	Increased resistance to change Lower staff morale	Razzaque and Sheng (1998), Embleton and Wright (1998)

multi-modal transportation networks and large-scale modernized logistics and distribution centres (Trunick, 2003). The accession of China to the WTO has opened up several of her transportation and logistics sectors to direct foreign participation (Hertzell, 2001). Consequently, more intensive competition is expected between Chinese and foreign companies, both inside and outside China (Agarwal and Wu, 2004). Meanwhile, the pattern of ownership of Chinese enterprises has gradually shifted from absolute dominancy of the state-owned enterprises to the coexistence of ownership in hybrid forms (Chen and Huang, 2005). The increase in competition and growing awareness of the role of logistics lead more companies to exploit the potential of outsourcing.

Table 9.3   Key factors stimulating the growth of outsourcing in China

Key factors	Descriptions	Results
Government initiatives	Investment in logistics infrastructure	Has encouraged domestic companies to outsource a greater percentage of their logistics needs
Entry to WTO	High-quality foreign 3PL providers entering Chinese logistics market	Has enabled companies to outsource more functions
	Relaxation of regulations	Has encouraged more companies to exploit outsourcing potential
	Increased competition	
Economic reform and development	Enlargement of consumer market	Has increased demand for logistics solution
Consolidation in industries and emergence of national chains	Creation of large and more complex players	Has increased need for transportation and logistics solutions

Manufacturers are increasingly looking for logistics solutions to move their goods to the fast-expanding consumer markets. Further, the trend towards consolidation in many of the industries and the emergence of national chains are also creating demand for outsourcing (Hertzell, 2001). Table 9.3 summarizes the key factors that are expected to stimulate the growth of outsourcing in China.

Despite these favourable factors, China's 3PL industry is still in the early stage of development. Compared to an overall transportation and logistics expenditures of US$230 billion in 2001, outsourced logistics was estimated to be just under US$4.8 billion or about 2 per cent (Kadar and Huang, 2002). Poor infrastructure and entrenched regulatory environment are among the obstacles that hinder the development of 3PL. Although the Chinese government has made significant investments in the logistics sector in recent years, there is little integration of transportation networks, information technology, warehousing and distribution facilities. Meanwhile, regulations exert tight controls on business activities at provincial level, which hinder the creation of national networks (Kerr, 2005). Therefore, it is difficult for 3PLs in China to fully meet the requirements of their clients. Table 9.4 summarizes the key challenges for the Chinese logistics industry.

Table 9.4 Key challenges for the Chinese logistics industry

Challenges	Problems	Impacts
Poor Infrastructure	Lack of effective transportation networks	Higher transportation costs
	Lack of IT infrastructure	Lack of reliability in pick-up and delivery time
	Little integration of transportation networks, IT, warehousing, and distribution facilities	
Regulation issues	Local protection	Has restrained the development of national service networks
		Has made it difficult for 3PLs in China to fully meet the requirements of their clients
Finding qualified staff	Lack of logistics training programs	Shippers have little confidence in the service levels of 3PLs
	Lack of high-quality providers with the scope and scale to fully meet customers' requirements	Difficult to find good providers that can deliver high quality and consistent services across geographical regions

Methodology

This research uses a case study approach, which means in-depth investigation of a contemporary phenomenon within its real-life context (Yin, 2003). The case study approach lends itself to a concentrated focus on the topic and allows a combination of multiple sources of evidence, enabling the researcher to capture and place the complex reality under scrutiny (Saunders et al., 2003; Yin, 2003). Despite its ability to explore the complexity of an issue, however, the case study approach does have its limitation in the generalization of results. This is mainly because case studies are usually based on small samples for in-depth study. Inherent to most interview surveys, variations in position, knowledge level, experience of the participants, and so on, in structured interviews also render generalization of survey results difficult.

Nevertheless, case study research is a commonly adopted strategy in the study of outsourcing decision (Benson and Leronimo, 1996; Bolumole, 2001;

Fill and Visser, 2000; McIvor, 2003). The use of the case study approach in this study ensures an in-depth exploration of the research question and enables the researchers to gain an insight into the real motivations behind the companies engaged in outsourcing, the obstacles and problems in the outsourcing process, and their impacts on the organization performance. In order to make the findings representative, companies chosen for this study were selected across a wide range of industries and from those which are currently involved in outsourcing.

Six in-depth, semi-structured face-to-face interviews, each lasting for about two hours, were carried out to collect primary data for this research. Judgement sampling was employed to select sampling units for this study (Boyce, 2003; Zikmund, 2003). Survey respondents were selected from companies of three major ownership types in China, namely, state-, private-, and foreign-owned (The Institute of World Economics and Politics, 2005). Six persons, one from each of the six companies, including departmental and senior managers, directly participated in or responsible for making outsourcing decision, were interviewed. Secondary data such as company documents, reports and websites were also gathered to better understand the background of the responding organizations and their outsourcing performance. Tables 9.5 and 9.6 summarize the profiles of the six companies studied and their outsourced activities, respectively. The name of each responding company has been coded to preserve anonymity.

Content analysis, which categorizes responses from individual respondents into categories of themes or patterns, was used to facilitate within- and cross-case comparisons (Carson et al., 2001; Lukas et al., 2004). The within-case analysis identified issues, some are unique to the individual case and some are common to all six companies. Focusing on the more significant issues, the cross-case analysis compared and contrasted the findings across the six cases studied. Also, a comparison with the observations in Western developed countries was made to identify similarities and differences in the key drivers and obstacles of outsourcing between developed countries and China.

Results

The findings elicited from the six case studies indicate that the common drivers of outsourcing can be broadly grouped into three categories: economic, strategic and environmental. Successful outsourcing helps the six companies to achieve various objectives resulting in cost saving or efficiency improvement, which ultimately leads to a competitive advantage. The case studies also reveal that there are various obstacles and problems with outsourcing in China, such

Table 9.5 Profiles of the six companies studied

Company	Ownership type	Industry type	Establishment	Location	Annual company revenue	No. of employees	Position of interviewee
A	State-owned	Textile import and export company	1951	Beijing	US$1.45 billion in 2004	700	General manager of a strategic business unit
B	State-owned	Agricultural product and food import and export company	1952	Beijing	US$2.7 billion in 2004	1,000	IT department manager
C	Privately-owned	Electronics and home appliance retailer	1982	Beijing	Eight billion Yuan in 2004	15,000	General manager of a chain store
D	Privately-owned	Cultural business company	2000	Beijing	Ten million Yuan in 2004	10	General manager of the company
E	Foreign-owned	Measurement product manufacturer	1985 (entered China)	Beijing	US$1 billion in 2004	2,000	Logistics department manager
F	Foreign-owned	Soft drink manufacturer	1979 (entered China)	Shanghai	US$343 million in 2004	600	Human resource (HR) department manager

Table 9.6   Outsourced activities of the six companies studied

Company	Main activities outsourced	Starting time
A	100 per cent transportation 100 per cent warehousing 100 per cent freight and charge settlement, customs declaration, inspection, and insurance IT outsourcing under planning in 2005	1983
B	100 per cent transportation 100 per cent warehousing 10 per cent IT support There are plans to outsource more IT functions	1982
C	90 per cent transportation and warehousing 100 per cent deployment of seasonal workforce 90 per cent customer services including returns handling, installation, and maintenance work 100 per cent cleaning and catering IT outsourcing under planning in 2005	1999
D	100 per cent printing 100 per cent cleaning and catering There are plans to outsource other functions	2000
E	100 per cent transportation and warehousing management 40 per cent training 100 per cent renting of personal computers 30 per cent maintenance work 100 per cent cleaning and catering There are plans to outsource more activities such as HR, accounting, administration, and manufacturing	1999
F	100 per cent transportation and 90 per cent warehousing 6 per cent IT services 30 per cent training 100 per cent renting of vehicles for company use 100 per cent cleaning and catering There are plans to outsource more activities such as IT, HR, accounting, and administration	1990

as the lack of capable service providers, which pose challenges to companies planning to outsource. To a certain extent, these challenges limit the scope of outsourcing and its pace of development in China. The key findings drawn from the six case studies are summarized as follows:

Drivers of Outsourcing

- Table 9.7 lists the prominent reasons for outsourcing of the six responding companies. Among the identified drivers, some are considered more important than the others with one company (Company B) ranking the most important two. All the companies consider economic factors pivotal in the outsourcing decision process. "Cost reduction" or "cost saving" is the primary reason for outsourcing of all the six companies except Company B which ranks it as the second most important reason. This finding concurs with a wealth of literature, which suggests that most outsourcing deals are driven by a desire to reduce cost (Corbett, 1996; Fan, 2000; Kakabadse and Kakabadse, 2000; Lynch, 2004; Zhu et al., 2001).
- For all the six companies studied, outsourcing enables them to focus on their core competence, to increase their flexibility, and to enable them to access expertise and technology.
- "Capital investment reduction" is also the most prominent reason for outsourcing of Companies C, D, E and F, which expect to reduce capital investment in transportation, warehousing, manufacturing, IT and employees in order to release capital for core business and to improve return on assets. This supports Razzaque and Sheng's (1998) view that outsourcing reduces the need to invest capital in facilities, equipment, IT and manpower. The findings also suggest that for private- and foreign-owned companies, which were established or entered China as a result of the Chinese economic reform, reducing capital investment and cost is an important part of their survival strategy in order to enhance competitiveness and flexibility.
- All six companies choose to outsource their business activities in order to focus on their core competence and increase flexibility. This agrees with the literature, which suggests that organizations should outsource activities for which they do not have a critical strategic need or special capability, and focus their attention on core competence to increase customer value (Jennings, 2002; Lankford and Parsa, 1999).
- "To accelerate re-engineering benefits" is one of the strategic factors that influence the decisions of Companies A and B to outsource while "to facilitate market penetration" is a strategic concern of outsourcing for Companies C, E and F. This finding supports Rothery and Robertson's (1995) and Corbett's (1998) view that re-engineering gives companies the opportunity to consider outsourcing as one of the tools that they can use in the new process to improve company performance and reduce operational costs.
- All six companies consider outsourcing an effort to increase flexibility in the utilization of transportation and warehousing capacity and to reduce

Table 9.7 Drivers of outsourcing considered by the six companies studied

Drivers of outsourcing	Company A (Case 1)	Company B (Case 2)	Company C (Case 3)	Company D (Case 4)	Company E (Case 5)	Company F (Case 6)
Cost reduction	√ (most important)		√ (most important)		√ (most important)	√ (most important)
Cost saving		√ (2nd most important)		√ (most important)		
Capital investment reduction			√ (most important)	√ (most important)	√ (most important)	√ (most important)
To accelerate re-engineering benefits	√	√				
To focus on core competence	√	√	√	√	√	√
To increase flexibility	√	√	√	√	√	√
To facilitate market penetration			√		√	√
Capability of supplier	√	√	√	√	√	√
IT development (Access to expertise/technology)	√	√ (1st most important)	√	√	√	√

Note: Drivers marked with √ are considered prominent reasons for outsourcing by the responding companies.

risks in IT investment. These are consistent with the findings from surveys in the USA and Europe (Claver et al., 2002; Rabinovich et al., 1999). Outsourcing is also used to provide seasonal workforce and to overcome constraints in production capacity. These also agree with previous research findings by Embleton and Wright (1998) and Kakabadse and Kakabadse (2000). The study also reveals that outsourcing has been used to convert a largely fixed cost business to one with variable costs in which expenses can change according to the business climate. This finding is also in agreement with that of McFarlan and Nolan (1995).

- "To facilitate market penetration" is regarded as a strategic reason for outsourcing by Companies C, E and F. Although "to facilitate market penetration" is not principally described as a strategic factor in the literature, this finding is in line with Lynch's (2004) view on global outsourcing – that it can help organizations enter new markets quickly without heavy initial investments and get geographically closer to customers to enhance responsiveness to changing customer needs.

Problems and Obstacles of Outsourcing

- In general, the organizations interviewed are satisfied with the service providers' performance. However, none of them have achieved the desired benefits from outsourcing. All of them have not realized the expected cost reduction in areas of transportation, warehousing, administration and operation. These findings are similar to the results of a survey by PA Consulting Group (1996) that few organizations have achieved high levels of benefits from outsourcing objectives (cited in Fan, 2000). All six companies have encountered some obstacles and problems in the outsourcing process, which are summarized in Table 9.8. These findings support many researchers' views that there are daunting challenges hindering the development of 3PL industry and the demand for outsourcing in China (Hertzell, 2001; Kerr, 2005; Trunick, 2003).
- "Lack of capable service providers" is the major problem of outsourcing identified, which includes inability to provide effective transportation networks, poor transportation tools, old-fashioned warehousing facilities, lack of qualified staff and lack of IT capability. These findings support Mercer's (cited in Kadar and Huang, 2002) conclusion that not many logistics providers in China are considered to be reliable, high-quality providers with the scope and scale to fully meet customers' requirements.
- Another problem cited by the six companies interviewed is "loss of control" over the outsourced activity, which is also one of the most commonly cited inhibitors to outsourcing in the literature (Blumberg, 1998; Lankford and Parsa, 1999; Razzaque and Sheng, 1998).

- "Poor transportation and IT infrastructure" and "local protection regulations" are also regarded as major obstacles to outsourcing, which are not viewed as critical problems in Western developed countries. In addition, "local protection regulations" lead to the increase in logistics cost and damage rate, thus reduce company profit margins. They also limit the choices of companies in selecting their desired suppliers. These findings support the results of several studies (Hertzell, 2001; Kerr, 2005; Trunick, 2003) that poor infrastructure and entrenched regulatory environment are two of the daunting challenges that will hinder the development of 3PL industry in China.
- The six companies studied have no comparison of pre- and post-outsourcing costs in areas like administration, operation and office expenses. This is similar to Fan's (2000) finding from a survey of the British companies that the majority of respondents have no clear post-outsourcing measurement.
- Though widely considered as a major obstacle of outsourcing in the literature, "loss of critical skills" is not evident in this study. One possible explanation is that the six companies interviewed are still outsourcing to only a relatively small degree at this stage and the majority of the outsourced activities are "peripheral".

Table 9.8   Major obstacles and problems of outsourcing encountered by the six companies studied

Major obstacles and problems	Challenges
Lack of capable service providers	Less than expected service quality Failure in realizing expected cost reduction or capital investment reduction Hindrance to further outsourcing of activities
Loss of control	Inconsistent service quality Inefficiency in communication
Poor transportation and IT infrastructure	Higher logistics costs Unreliability in pickup and delivery time Higher rate of loss and damage of goods Poor customer service
Local protection regulations	Higher logistics cost and damage rate Limitation in choices of suppliers
Lack of overall post-outsourcing review	Failure in knowing if the outsourcing process is working as planned Failure in identifying areas of improvements or changes

Comparison between Western developed countries and China

The findings also show that there are similarities and differences between the key outsourcing drivers and obstacles in Western developed countries and China. As shown in Table 9.9, cost reduction, cost saving and capital investment reduction are the main economic reasons for outsourcing both in China and in developed countries. Organizations in China and developed countries alike use outsourcing to achieve certain strategic goals such as to accelerate re-engineering benefits, to focus on core competence, and to increase flexibility. However, facilitating market penetration is also cited as a strategic reason for outsourcing in China but not significantly stressed in the developed countries. This difference is understandable as companies in developing

Table 9.9 Comparison of drivers and obstacles of outsourcing between China and Western developed countries

	China	Western developed countries
Drivers of outsourcing		
Economic factors	Cost reduction	Cost reduction
	Cost saving	Cost saving
	Capital investment reduction	Capital investment reduction
Strategic factors	To accelerate re-engineering	To accelerate re-engineering
	To focus on core competence	To focus on core competence
	To increase flexibility	To increase flexibility
	To facilitate market penetration	
Environmental factors	IT development	IT development
	Capability of supplier	Capability of supplier
		Globalization
Obstacles and problems	Loss of control	Loss of control
	Lack of capable service providers	*Loss of critical skills*
	Poor transportation and IT infrastructure	
	Local protection regulations	
	Lack of overall post-outsourcing review	

Note: Bold items are those identified in China but not in Western developed countries. Italicized items are those found in Western developed countries but not in this study.

countries are generally young and fast-developing, and striving to occupy the maximum market share. The findings also reveal that environment factors, such as IT development and capability of supplier, can influence organizations' decisions to outsource in China, which is similar to the situation in developed countries.

However, the study results indicate that globalization, which is often cited as an environment factor that facilitates the greater use of outsourcing in developed countries, is currently not a major concern of organizations in China when making their outsourcing decisions. This suggests that the focus of the companies in China is still on capitalizing the huge potential consumer market in the mainland. The findings further reveal that organizations in China are facing certain obstacles and problems in the outsourcing process, of which lack of capable service providers, loss of control, poor transportation and IT infrastructure, local protection regulations, and lack of overall post-outsourcing measurement are the major ones. Although the literature indicates that Western developed countries also face many obstacles and problems in outsourcing, loss of control and loss of critical skills are the ones often stressed. This difference suggests that outsourcing in China is still in its infancy, as observed by Trunick (2003).

Conclusion

This chapter has explored the key drivers of outsourcing and the main obstacles or problems faced by organizations in China. The findings indicate that economic, strategic and environmental factors are the main drivers that motivate organizations in China to engage in outsourcing. They are similar to those identified in the Western developed countries. With regard to economic factors, cost reduction, cost saving and capital investment reduction are the main concerns. This accords with the literature reporting the situation in developed countries (Claver et al., 2002; Kakabadse and Kakabadse, 2000; Lynch, 2004; Razzaque and Sheng, 1998).

The findings also show that organizations in China have taken some strategic considerations when making outsourcing decisions. They include the use of outsourcing to accelerate re-engineering benefits, to focus on core competence, and to increase flexibility. This also accords with the findings in the literature reporting the situation in developed countries (Corbett, 1998; Mazziwi, 2002; Quinn and Hilmer, 1994). Meanwhile, facilitating market penetration is also cited as a strategic reason for outsourcing in China but not in developed countries.

The findings further demonstrate that environmental factors such as IT development and the capability of supplier can influence organizations' decisions to outsource in China, which is in agreement with the literature (Kakabadse and Kakabadse, 2005; Lynch, 2004; Razzaque and Sheng, 1998). However, the results indicate that globalization, which is often cited as an environmental factor that facilitates the greater use of outsourcing in developed countries, is not a major concern of organizations in China when making their outsourcing decisions. On the other hand, the capability of the service supplier in terms of service quality, availability of extensive domestic transportation network, financial strength, reputation, reliability, use of latest technology, price, relationship with client, and so on, are regarded as the most important considerations when it comes to the selection of a service provider.

The study also reveals that organizations in China have encountered some obstacles and problems in the outsourcing process, of which lack of capable service providers, loss of control, poor transportation and IT infrastructure, local protection regulations, and lack of overall post-outsourcing measurement are the major ones. Although the literature indicates that Western developed countries also face many obstacles and problems in outsourcing (Al-Qirim, 2003; Blumberg, 1998; Lankford and Parsa, 1999; McIvor and Humphreys, 2000; Razzaque and Sheng, 1998), loss of control and loss of critical skills are often cited as the major ones.

Based on the findings of this study, a framework for making outsourcing decisions in China is proposed in Figure 9.1. The framework suggests that organizations in China should consider both economic and strategic implications when making such decisions. From an economic perspective, companies may need to undertake a total cost analysis to identify and measure all the costs associated with the outsourcing of an activity so as to ensure cost–effectiveness. In addition, outsourcing decisions should also be made from a strategic perspective and be fully integrated into the business planning process to achieve long-term success. A detailed evaluation of IT development and a careful analysis of the supplier's capability may also be required. In order to minimize the risk of failure, companies should also be aware of other potential problems, such as impact on customer service level when deciding to outsource.

With heavy investment in logistics infrastructure and accelerated economic reform, business environment in China has become more and more dynamic. The entry of global logistics providers in the Chinese market will certainly encourage the use of 3PLs. Outsourcing will become one of the most effective business strategies for organizations in China to achieve cost-effective performance and long-term success. To fully investigate the impacts of outsourcing in this fast-changing economic climate, more studies are required to explore the best practices of outsourcing in China. To help determine the validity of the proposed framework proposed in this study, further research is recommended, employing a larger sample across a wider spectrum of industries and companies of different operating scales.

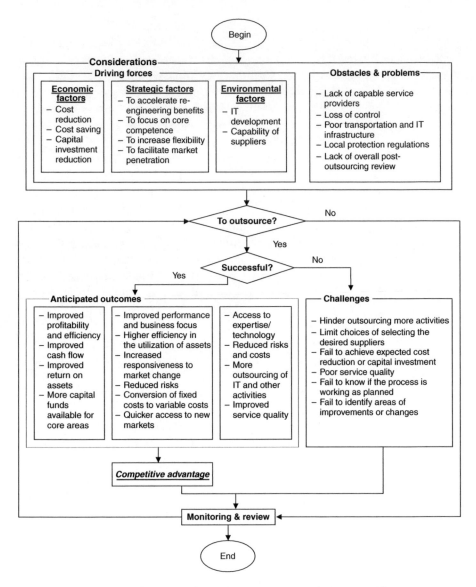

Figure 9.1 A proposed framework for making outsourcing decisions in China

Acknowledgements

The authors would like to thank the six companies and their employees interviewed in this study for providing the detailed information.

References

Agarwal, J. and Wu, T. (2004), "China's entry to WTO: Global marketing issues, impact, and implications for China," *International Marketing Review*, 21(3): 279–300.

Al-Qirim, N.A.Y. (2003), "The strategic outsourcing decision of IT and eCommerce: The case of small businesses in New Zealand," *Journal of Information Technology Cases and Applications*, 5(3): 32–56.

Beaumont, N. and Sohal, A. (2004), "Outsourcing in Australia," *International Journal of Operations and Production Management*, 24(7): 688–700.

Benson, J. and Leronimo, N. (1996), "Outsourcing decisions: evidence from Australia-based enterprises," *International Labour Review*, 135(1): 59–73.

Blumberg, D.F. (1998), "Strategic assessment of outsourcing and downsizing in the service market," *Managing Service Quality*, 8(1): 5–18.

Bolumole, Y.A. (2001), "The supply chain role of third-party logistics providers," *International Journal of Logistics Management*, 12(2): 87–102.

Boyce, J. (2003), *Market Research in Practice*, Townsville: McGraw-Hill.

Brown, A.S. (2005), "The China road," *Mechanical Engineering*, 127(3): 36–40.

Capgemini, Georgia Institute of Technology, SAP, and DHL (2006), "Key findings of overall logistics outsourcing trends." http://3plstudy.com/?p=overall_logistics_outsourcing_trends (accessed 22 May 2006).

Carson, D., Gilmore, A., Perry, C. and Cronhaug, K. (2001), *Qualitative Marketing Research*, London: Sage.

Chen, J.G. and Huang, Q.J. (2005), "Comparison of governance structures of Chinese enterprises with different types of ownership." http://unpan1.un.org/intradoc/groups/public/documents/APCITY/UNPAN003085.pdf (accessed 15 July 2005).

Claver, E., Gonzales, R., Gasco, J. and Llopis, J. (2002), "Information systems outsourcing: reasons, reservations and success factors," *Logistics Information Management*, 15(4): 294–308.

Clott, C.B. (2004), "Perspectives on global outsourcing and the changing nature of work," *Business and Society Review*, 109(2): 153–170.

Corbett, M.F. (1996), "Outsourcing as a strategic tool," *Canadian Business Review*, 23(2): 14–16.

Corbett, M.F. (1998), "Outsourcing: beyond buying services," *Facilities Design & Management*, 17(1): 40–43.

Embleton, P.R. and Wright, P.C. (1998), "A practical guide to successful outsourcing," *Empowerment in Organizations*, 6(3): 94–106.

Fan, Y. (2000), "Strategic outsourcing: Evidence from British companies," *Marketing Intelligence & Planning*, 18(4): 213–219.

Fill, C. and Visser, E. (2000), "The outsourcing dilemma: A composite approach to the make or buy decision," *Management Decision*, 38(1): 43–50.

Forrest, W. (2005), "Analyzing the pros and cons of outsourcing to China," *Purchasing*, 134(2): 17–18.

Gonzalez, R., Gasco, J. and Llopis, J. (2005), "Information systems outsourcing reasons in the largest Spanish firms," *International Journal of Information Management*, 25(2): 117–136.

Hannon, J. (2005), "Outsourcing to China, Orkus Taiwan." www.orkus-asia.com/ ORKUS_Outsourcing_to_China.pdf (accessed 8 April 2006).

Hertzell, S. (2001), "China's evolving logistics landscape." www.mckinsey.com/practices / operationsstrategyeffectiveness / supplychainmanagement / globalnetworks / pdf/China_Logistics.pdf (accessed 9 April 2006).

Jennings, D. (2002), "Strategic sourcing: Benefits, problems and a contextual model," *Management Decision*, 40(1): 26–34.

Kadar, M. and Huang, D. (2002), "The third party logistics market in China, opportunities and challenges," in CLM 2002 Conference, 30 September–2 October (San Francisco, USA, 2002); Mercer Management Consulting, www.mercermc.com/defaultFLASH.asp?section=Perspectives&path=Specialty/transport.htm&tier (accessed 8 April 2006).

Kakabadse, N. and Kakabadse, A. (2000), "Critical review – Outsourcing: A paradigm shift," *The Journal of Management Development*, 19(8): 670–728.

Kakabadse, A. and Kakabadse, N. (2005), "Outsourcing: Current and future trends," *Thunderbird International Business Review*, 47(2): 183–204.

Kerr, J. (2005), "10 keys challenges for the Chinese logistics industry," *Logistics Management*, 44(2): 64–67.

Lankford, W.M. and Parsa, F. (1999), "Outsourcing: A primer," *Management Decision* 37(4): 310–316.

Lieb, R.C. and Bentz, B.A. (2004), "The use of third-party logistics services by large American manufacturers: the 2003 survey," *Transportation Journal*, 43(3): 24–33.

Lonsdale, C. and Cox, A. (2000), "The historical development of outsourcing: the latest fad?" *Industrial Management and Data Systems*, 100(9): 444–450.

Lukas, B.A., Hair, J.F., Bush, R.P. and Ortinau, D.J. (2004), *Marketing Research*, Townsville: McGraw-Hill.

Lynch, C.F. (2004), "Why outsource?" *Supply Chain Management Review*, 8(7): 44–49.

Matteo, M.D. (2003), "Sourcing in China," *The China Business Review*, 30(5): 30–33.

Mazziwi, E. (2002), "Transformational outsourcing," *Business Strategy Review*, 13(3): 39–43.

McFarlan, F.W. and Nolan, R.L. (1995), "How to manage an IT outsourcing alliance," *Sloan Management Review*, 36(2): 9–23.

McIvor, R. (2003), "Outsourcing: insights from the telecommunications industry," *Supply Chain Management*, 8(4): 380–394.

McIvor, R.T. and Humphreys, P.K. (2000), "A case-based reasoning approach to the make or buy decision," *Integrated Manufacturing Systems*, 11(5): 295–310.

PA Consulting Group (1996), *Riding the Wave of Channel Substitution*, London: PACG.

Palvia, P.C. (1995), "A dialectic view of information systems outsourcing: Pros and cons," *Information & Management*, 29(5): 265–275.

Prahalad, C.K. and Hamel, G. (1990), "The core competence of the corporation," *Harvard Business Review*, 68(3): 79–91.

Quinn, J.B. and Hilmer, F.G. (1994), "Strategic outsourcing," *Sloan Management Review*, 35(4): 43–55.

Rabinovich, E., Windle, R., Dresner, M. and Corsi, T. (1999), "Outsourcing of integrated logistics functions – an examination of industry practices," *International Journal of Physical Distribution & Logistics Management*, 29(6): 353–373.

Razzaque, M.A. and Sheng, C.C. (1998), "Outsourcing of logistics functions: a literature survey," *International Journal of Physical Distribution & Logistics Management*, 28(2): 89–107.

Richardson, H.L. (1990), "Explore outsourcing," *Transportation & Distribution*, 31(7): 16–20.

Rothery, B. and Robertson, I. (1995), *The Truth about Outsourcing*, Aldershot: Gower Publishing Limited.

Saunders, M., Lewis, P. and Thornhill, A. (2003), *Research Methods for Business Students*, 3rd ed., Upper Saddle River: Prentice Hall.

The Institute of World Economics and Politics (2005), "Comparison of governance structures of Chinese enterprises with different types of ownership." www.iwep.org.cn/wec/english/articles/2001_06/6chenjiagui.htm (accessed 6 July 2006).

Trunick, P.A. (1989), "Outsourcing: a single source for many talents," *Transportation & Distribution*, 30(7): 20–23.

Trunick, P.A. (2003), "Logistics links are critical in China," *Transportation & Distribution*, 44(8): 50–53.

Weerakkody, V., Curries, W.L. and Ekanayahe, Y. (2003), "Re-engineering business processes through application service providers, *Business Process Management Journal*, 9(6): 776–794.

Welson, R. (1996), "It's hard to buck the outsourcing tide," *PC Week*, 15 July: 1.

Yin, R.K. (2003), *Case Study Research – Design and Methods*, 3rd edn, Thousand Oaks: Sage.

Zhu, Z.W., Hsu,.K. and Lillie, J. (2001), "Outsourcing – A strategic move: The process and the ingredients for success," *Management Decision*, 39(5): 373–378.

Zikmund, W.G. (2003), *Essentials of Marketing Research*, 2nd edn, London: Thomson.

10
Barriers and Enablers when Transferring R&D Practices from the West to China

Joachim A. Timlon and Niklas Åkerman

Introduction

Globalization and the increasing demand on technological development cause many multi-national corporations (MNCs) in rapidly changing industries that are dependent on the technological development to seek new technologies and secure more market-driven R&D. Increasingly, R&D is becoming more internationalized. For instance, in the pharmaceutical industry almost 40 per cent of R&D is undertaken in countries other than the MNC's home country (UNCTAD, 2005). In relation to other organizational functions, it is the last activity to be internationalized (Lewin and Peeters, 2006).

There has been a rapid increase of foreign multinational activities and investments in China since the beginning of the twenty-first century (Hu and Jefferson, 2009; Li et al., 2007; Miesing et al., 2007; Walsh and Zhu, 2007; Xie and White, 2006; Zhu and Li, 2007). Furthermore, the value added by Chinese industry has increased. During the period 2000–2005 the value added in Chinese industry increased by almost 200 per cent (www.most.gov.cn, 2007). In 2003, the value-adding elements essentially revolved around production activities, such as for mass production, whereas in 2006 it also included R&D activities such as design, prototyping and pilot production (Dedrik and Kraemer, 2006; von Zedtwitz, 2004).

China has become the most attractive location to which MNCs transfer much of their R&D activities. According to a survey made by UNCTAD, China will be the highest ranking country of interest for R&D locations during 2005–2009. By the end of 2005 there were 750 foreign-company owned R&D units present in China of which more than 400 were established after 2004 (jp.fujitsu.com, 2007). Substantial R&D investments have already been made in China and more will be made in the future. Estimations based on the 29 most R&D spending MNCs indicate future R&D investments in the coming years of about 2 billion US dollars.

The major driver for R&D transfer to China is to accomplish competitive advantages. However, the methods for accomplishing these competitive advantages are changing. Global integration and local adaptation still is a strategic dilemma for MNCs (Bartlett and Goshal, 1998), which is highly relevant for the internationalization of R&D activities. Traditionally it is argued that competitive advantages are accomplished based on the ability to globally integrate R&D activities and transfer knowledge to geographically dispersed units. However, the source of competitive advantage seems to change from exploiting what is already known and captured in companies' product portfolios to exploring new knowledge for new products based on the specific market conditions in China (Xie and White, 2006).

Altenburg et al. (2006) argue that major reasons for the increasing interest in transferring R&D activities to China are the importance of keeping R&D in close proximity to high-potential lead markets. Farris (2007) argues that innovations are not only created abroad and transferred to China, but there is an increase in innovations originating from China that are transferred between Chinese businesses. This is reflected in the number of patents filed by MNCs in China, which has increased at a rate of 22 per cent annually since the amendment in the patent law in 1992 (Hu and Jefferson, 2009). Von Zedtwitz and Gassman (2002) highlight the proximity to other corporate activities and local customers, together with tapping into international sources of technology and expertise. Gassman and Han (2004) point to the importance of input-oriented factors, such as getting access to personnel, knowledge and innovation, and performance-oriented factors, such as market-specific development and business-ecological factors, such as government policies, persistent growth and peer pressure. Gammeltoft (2005) makes a distinction between six types of motivations for R&D internationalization:

  (i) market-driven, i.e. expanding the use of a company's assets on several markets;
 (ii) product-driven, relating to supporting local manufacturing;
(iii) technology-driven, which is about tapping into foreign knowledge and technology;
 (iv) innovation-driven to generate new assets;
  (v) cost-driven, primarily related to the exploitation of differences in factor costs;
 (vi) policy-drivers concerning requirements or incentives in national regulatory systems.

As MNCs perform both strategic and tactical R&D in their Chinese units, China is no longer "a simple case just for show" (Sun et al., 2006). It seems that R&D activities in China still have huge potential for providing MNCs with a competitive advantage but instead of simply transferring knowledge developed in West, the issue has become more challenging and more complex.

Barriers and enablers when transferring R&D practices

Many have studied the problem of transferring organizational activities between units (e.g. Kostova, 1999; Lewin and Peeters, 2006; Miesing et al., 2007; Minbaeva et al., 2003). The problem of transferring R&D activities in particular has been addressed by Cummings and Teng (2003) highlighting the importance of similar knowledge bases and interaction between the units. Szulanski (1996, 2000) adds to the understanding of intra-organizational knowledge transfers by studying the internal "stickiness", relating to the difficulty of transferring knowledge within an organization, which inhibits successful transfer of organizational practices throughout the transfer process. Szulanski describes the sources of stickiness as being rooted in the ambiguity of production factors and how they interact to create value, an inability to exploit knowledge with an outside origin and, problems related to the relationship between the sender and the receiver of the knowledge transferred. The organizational learning of how to transfer knowledge is an act of understanding, or learning to learn, because in order to make knowledge transfer processes smoother the organization has to learn how to manage stickiness.

Kostova (1999) argues that the perceived difficulty in transferring a practice depends on the different context. She identifies three main factors that can impede the success of transfer: social context, organizational context and relational context. Social context relates to differences between the sending and the receiving country, where different cultures might cause a misfit in transferring practices in the new context. The organizational context relates to difficulties caused by different organizational cultures because they might influence the organizational atmosphere for learning and change. In the relational context, insufficient trust between employees in the sending and the receiving unit can cause difficulties influencing the transfer. Trust also influences the identification with and commitment to the parent company. Thus, contextual differences imply that transferred organizational practices may not fit or may not be accepted in the receiving unit's cultural context. For instance, management practices used in a Western context may not fit in an Asian context and vice versa, owing to culturally different views about decision-making.

Szulanski (1999) suggests that in order to overcome the internal stickiness of knowledge transfer, it might be fruitful "to devote scarce resources and managerial attention to develop the learning capacities of organizational units, foster close relationships between organizational units, and systematically understand and communicate practices" (1996: 37). The suggestion is to build on the notion of "absorptive capacity" as initially coined by Cohen and Levinthal (1989) and defined as a firm's ability to identify, assimilate and exploit knowledge from the environment where R&D plays a vital role in the acquisition of new knowledge from different external environments. The findings seem to consolidate earlier findings about the role of R&D, for instance, in organizational learning literature (e.g. Kim, 1993). Cohen and Levinthal (1990) extended their research to individual's cognitive structures and problem solving with the aim of developing organizational learning processes underlying absorptive capacity, which was redefined as "the ability to recognize the value of new information, assimilate it, and apply it to commercial ends" (1990: 128). In other words, learning capability to assimilate knowledge and problem-solving skills to create new knowledge were requirements for absorptive capacity. In the context of R&D, absorptive capacity would then involve a set of closely related abilities to evaluate the technological and commercial potential in a particular domain, assimilate it and apply it to commercial ends, thereby enabling a firm to exploit new extramural knowledge as well as to predict more accurately the nature of future technological advances (Cohen and Levinthal, 1994). Consequently they argued that absorptive capacity would enable firms to more accurately forecast technological trends and to take advantage of emerging opportunities before their rivals could.

However, although the literature recognizes that learning capacity has a technological and economical potential that can be realized in different domains and contexts, it says relatively little about how a learning capacity is developed. It seems as if the development occurs through organizational learning processes, in which recognition and understanding of valued information, as well as feedback processes, play an important role. However, recognition, understanding and providing feedback are unique human characteristics. With few exceptions (e.g. Argote and Ingram, 2000; Minbaeva et al., 2003) the literature lacks an integrative approach on knowledge transfer that balances a human and an organizational perspective. Although organizational practices are founded on individual knowledge, too little attention is devoted to cognitive structures. Furthermore, although it is recognized that learning capacity could be seen as a dyad-level construct, the principles of learning in dyadic intra-organizational relationships are still at a rudimentary state, as denoted by other authors (e.g. Minbaeva et al., 2003). Thus, there is a need to develop a better understanding of R&D transfer between two intra-corporate units in different contexts as well as developing an understanding of the prerequisites of a dyadic intra-organizational relationship. The overall aim of this chapter is to add to the existing literature on transferring R&D practices in different contexts with regard to the development of learning capacities. More specifically, our aim is to explore how learning capacities are developed to transfer R&D practices that overcome intra-organizational barriers and internal stickiness in a Chinese context.

Successful transfer of R&D practices

In this chapter, we build on the notion of strategic organizational practices as introduced by Kostova (1999), which she defines as those practices that have strategic importance for the company because they provide a distinct source of competitive advantage. An organizational practice is a kind of organizational routine, that is, a predictable pattern of activities made up of a sequence of coordinated activities performed by individuals, which can be viewed as a principle for organizing the way individuals cooperate and become more integrated in order to effectively perform certain activities (Kogut and Zander, 1992; Nelson and Winter, 1982; Timlon, 1997).

Fundamentally, an organizational practice is based on "a set of (un)written rules of how a certain organizational function should be conducted and an accompanying set of cognitive elements" by which these rules are described and made sense of (Kostova, 1999: 310). The rules of a practice reflect a set of underlying values and beliefs. These kind of organizational practices are therefore "infused with value", in that they may acquire meaning for organizational members that is symbolic and normative in nature, and goes beyond technical efficiency. They, therefore, tend to be more complex and broad in scope, and more "people" rather than "technology" focused because these characteristics are likely to make a practice less imitable and more critical for the competitive edge of the company. The "value-impregnated" nature of strategic organizational practices means that the success of R&D transfer is determined by the transferability of meaning and value in addition to the transferability of knowledge.

The accompanying set of cognitive elements reflecting the underlying values and beliefs of an organizational routine or practice can be labelled "meaning structure". A principle or rule describes a kind of causal relationship between how a certain resource is used to perform a certain action. Dixon (1994) argues that sense making is "a function of seeing relationships in the data, such as what is larger or smaller, what is similar to something else, what belongs to the same category, what causes produce what effect, and what is affected, what comes first, second, third in a sequence" (1994: 14). In other words, concepts do not exist in isolation but are connected into what she labels meaning structures for organizing and interpreting data. These causal relations can be defined as a set of assumptions that an individual has about other people, their personalities and behaviour, and can be used to specify the content and take account of the connectedness between cognition and social situation.

In this chapter, the term meaning structure is used rather than the term knowledge to represent and manifest not only the understanding that organizational members have reached but also how and why it was reached. The main reason for using this term "meaning structure", and not "knowledge", is that the former is more encompassing as it includes:

- how the understanding of organizational members is related to that of other organizational members;
- the logic by which the understanding was reached and the data that support it;
- the explicit/tacit assumptions behind the understanding.

Meaning structures are also different from what is normally referred to as information. Information can be defined as organized data in a certain formation, such as charts, graphs, speech, written statements, and so on. Data can, then, be treated as sub-sets of information. Organizational members can through their human sensory receptors perceive information, or more specifically a subset of the information (i.e. data). They can reorganize the perceived data, classify and interpret it so that it makes sense. This means that information can reside in many different places in an organization whereas meaning structures can only reside in the heads of organizational members.

Developing a learning capacity

Morgan (1986: 87) discusses the development of learning capacities in terms of self-questioning abilities and of being '... able to detect and correct errors in operating norms and thus influence the standards that guide their detailed operation'. In his reasoning, single and double-loop learning processes are highlighted. Whereas single-loop learning is related to detecting and adjusting errors in a predefined set of operating routines, double-loop learning, or learning how to learn, relates to questioning the actual routines themselves. Single-loop learning is a process of comparing information from the environment with the standardized operating routines that are used. This comparison then leads to undertaking appropriate action within the given routines. Double-loop learning, on the other hand, not only includes the same steps as single-lop learning but it also incorporates a 'second look', a reflection about the norms and questioning their appropriateness in the situation. Hence, single-loop learning is optimization within a given set of routines whereas double-loop learning questions the routines themselves.

However, the process of developing a learning capacity has some barriers and Morgan (1986) gives a number of examples. Although both single and double-loop learning processes can be related to learning capacities, the use of elaborate single-loop learning systems may actually restrict the development of double-loop learning. If there is a focus on rewarding elements in the single-loop learning system, such as achieving short-term goals, the double-loop learning capacity development is inhibited. Furthermore, the learning process can be hampered when organizational members are not allowed to think for themselves since reflection is needed in order to be able to question institutionalized practices, that is, practices that are 'taken for granted'. Making space for individual thinking, as a consequence, seems essential when developing double-loop learning. At the same time, different individual perceptions of the overall situation could influence the process. Organizational members who do not have an overview might risk sub-optimization since their focus is limited to what they can grasp. As a result, the optimization of one small organizational feature could lead to negative effects on the organization as a whole. Furthermore, in situations when organizational members are encouraged and inspired to maintain their current position in the organizational structure they tend to focus on single-loop learning (Morgan, 1986). Consequently, the questioning of predefined norms gets repressed, since questioning organizational practices would be to go against the system. Instead, focus will be on optimization within the scope of their given organizational position. Thus, group or department thinking hampers the learning to learn process. Furthermore, group thinking can make it more difficult for outsiders to access the norms and values shared by the group members. Consequently, if they are not accessible, the norms and values are difficult to challenge.

Uncertainty avoidance could also be seen as a barrier affecting the ability of learning to learn. When there is intolerance to uncertainty there is often a tendency to oversimplify situations. Problems are only handled if there is a solution at hand that has the potential to solve the problem (Morgan, 1986). In short, the learning to learn process could be described as the ability to remain open to change. In order to counteract the potential barriers in this process Morgan (1986: 91) states five main enablers:

- An atmosphere for openness and reflectivity with an acceptance for legitimate errors improves the learning process.
- Exploring different possible viewpoints and solutions makes it possible to better cope with a multifaceted and changing environment.
- Avoiding predetermined goal setting reduces the risk of putting the learning process in a single-loop learning framework that could constrain the

learning process; instead, a bottom-up perspective on management encourages double-loop learning.

- Designing double-loop learning organizational structures and organizational processes facilitates the above-mentioned features.
- In order achieve double-loop learning, the organizational members' ability to question the appropriateness of the norms is a central aspect. This relates to the ability to challenge the underlying assumptions controlling the operation at hand.

However, these processes do not take place within the organization without any influence from the external environment. The context does not only influence the success of knowledge transfer (e.g. Kostova, 1999) but also influences the development of the absorptive capacity (Cohen and Levinthal, 1990). Focusing on the external dimension of the diversity of knowledge sources, Phene et al (2006) argue that a firm's ability to exploit valuable knowledge from different contexts depends not only on its R&D capabilities but also on the external context in which the knowledge is located; knowledge from different geographical and technological contexts may hamper the firm's absorptive capacity.

More recently, the notion of absorptive capacity has been re-examined and redefined, giving the underlying resources and organizational processes as well as the specific context in which it occurs more emphasis. Zahra and George (2002) argue that absorptive capacity is a set of knowledge-based capabilities embedded in routines and processes for acquiring, assimilating, transforming and exploiting knowledge. Furthermore, they claim that absorptive capacity reflects a dynamic capability as it involves the ability to reconfigure the firm's resource base in the face of changing market conditions, more specifically two sub-sets of potential absorptive capacity – capabilities to acquire and assimilate knowledge, and realized absorptive capacity – capabilities to transform and exploit knowledge. Todorova and Durisin (2007) add to the notion that absorptive capacity is central to a firm's dynamic capability. The dynamic aspect of absorptive capacity is captured through feedback loops. Feedback as well as feed-forward loops describe the process of organizational learning between individual, group and organizational knowledge (Crossan and Berdrow, 2003; Crossan et al., 1999).

Furthermore, in order to be able to identify and exploit new information, some basic skills are needed of which language is one (Cohen and Levinthal, 1990). The influence of language on cognitive structures is further emphasized by institutional theory holding that language has an influence activating cognitive mechanisms and, in turn, triggers action (Agevall, 2005). Not only do present basic skills influence the development of absorptive capacity, but rather, the company can actively invest in developing absorptive capacities by sending personnel to advanced technical training.

Confucian worldview as a core influence of the Chinese context

The traditional culture in the Chinese context is impregnated by Confucianism, which has evolved in China over more than two thousand years. Confucianism permeates the whole society, the learning style as well. There seem to be six dimensions in which the values from the Confucian traditions have an impact on learning (Yang et al., 2006: 347):

- Harmony is the society's ultimate goal.
- The perceived value of the collective is more important than individual interests.
- The priority of activities is "doing, thinking and being".
- Sympathy and self-control is the basis of moral.
- Confucianism promotes traditional social hierarchy and the priority of time is emphasizing the past.
- A harmonized society is more important than the right and growth of individuals.

Confucian values influence the way Chinese people learn, that is, their learning styles, and it also influences the traditional Chinese learning system. The learning practices in China, as opposed to Western cultures, emphasize that 'knowledge arises in a linear way' where memorizing precedes understanding, reflection and questioning. The Chinese exam system is focused on memorizing and truth finding whereas Western systems are based on the notion that memorization does not enhance learning. Consequently, the cultural heritage in China is that authorities are believed to be the sources of knowledge, who impart knowledge through their all-including wisdom. This also influences the Chinese learning styles, which are based on a 'concrete-sequential cognitive style' resulting in a preference that follows the authoritarian teacher to the letter by memorization. The Chinese learners are, as a consequence, reluctant to face uncertainty and prediction, preferring to adopt a more systematic approach at a slower pace. In contrast, the Western approach of 'intuitive-random' learning styles promotes 'seeking the big picture' in a more spontaneous and flexible way. Yang et al. (2006) conclude that processes of organizational development may be hindered by the collective orientation of the Chinese culture as well as by the goal to establish harmony and the prevailing power distance.

To counteract the Chinese cultural, from a Western perspective, inhibitors of organizational development Yang et al. (2006) propose a number of enablers:

- listening.
- giving and receiving feedback.
- counselling.
- dealing with emotions.
- fostering support from superiors and relationships to promote disagreements.
- encouraging conversations.
- providing rewards for employee participation.

Methodology

The primary aim of this study is to capture the organizing and performing of R&D activities that are transferred from the West to China. Case studies provide opportunities to study social phenomena in their specific context (Yin, 1984) and a case study is, hence, suitable for investigating the transfer of R&D practices. They are also particularly useful in answering how questions and they are particularistic, descriptive and heuristic in nature (Merriam, 1998). In this study a case approach makes it possible to study the transfer of R&D practices without setting predefined boundaries that could be limiting and exclude important perspectives.

Cognitive structures can be used to analyse subjective data and to clarify individual and collective cognition about an organization and how the organization functions (Eden, 1992). Cognitive structures can, furthermore, be used to facilitate studies about problem solving in relation to organizational change, and thus, although situation-dependent, provide an analytical value for business research. Since cognitive structures are linked to the specific social context, it is important to specify which cognitive structure is being studied and in which context. In this study cognitive structures related to the way R&D activities are organized and performed in the Chinese context are in focus.

The collection of empirical evidence started with interviews in Denmark in early 2007, and continued with follow-up interviews in autumn 2008. During summer of 2009 the database of empirical findings was extended by interviews in China. The interviewees were chosen either because of their participation in the transfer process or their position as a scientist in China. Therefore, the interviewees have personal experience of the transfer, or implementation, of the knowledge brought from the Danish to the Chinese unit.

Interviews can be used to strengthen a case study not only by providing access to information about the problem studied but also by giving insights into more dimensions of the problem (Yin, 2003). Hence, interviews seem to be the rational choice when studying cognitive structures. Semi-structured interviews in a conversational manner were used in order to access the interviewees' own perspectives and understanding of the transfer process.

Two interviews where performed with Danish previously expatriated scientists and one with the Danish transfer manager in 2007 with a follow-up one in the autumn of 2008. During the summer of 2009 four interviews were carried out with Chinese scientists working at the Chinese R&D unit, one interview with a departmental director and one interview with the managing director in the Chinese R&D unit. The interviews with the Danes were carried out in English and the interviews with Chinese were conducted in Chinese and then translated into English. All interviews were recorded in order to create a case study database. In this way, all data was preserved for analysis.

The case of R&D transfer to China at Pharmaceutics

In 2001, the Danish pharmaceutical company Pharmaceutics established an R&D centre within the field of protein research in Beijing. The major drivers related to the market and to the facilitation of access to global talents. Three main reasons stated were: supporting business conducted in China; creating a cost-effective biotechnology centre; and identifying R&D collaboration partners in China.

However, the management at Pharmaceutics did not expect a cost benefit from transferring R&D activities to China, at least not in terms of costs for middle and upper management. Although the cost of physical resources and for human resources, such as technicians, was lower in China, it did not include R&D managers. Furthermore, the management saw a big potential in working with Chinese universities, although they were aware that no relevant contributions to the research conducted at Pharmaceutics had been done so far. Nonetheless, the intention was to tap into research and development conducted outside Denmark in order to get access to international talent and, benefiting from this internal research pipeline, making the R&D activities of Pharmaceutics global. Previous experiences from collaborating with international research centres in different countries were positive in terms of improved performance in these markets.

Early stages of the transfer

There was a strong intention from the Pharmaceutics managers to create a R&D centre of technological excellence in China within the field of protein research, even though this research was simultaneously being conducted in Copenhagen, Denmark. It was the requirement, however, that the research in the Chinese unit should be conducted in the same manner as in the Danish unit. One department director in the Chinese unit emphasized the learning aspect:

> When we established the R&D centre in China, the plan was to bring the advanced Danish technologies, management skills, and expertise to China to establish the Danish way of doing things in China. So at the beginning we were mainly learning. (Interview, 26 May 2009)

In the early stages of the transfer, the Danish researchers were not convinced that transferring R&D to China was a good idea. Foremost, they were concerned about the competence of Chinese researchers. Their scepticism was based on a conviction that the research being transferred to China could be performed faster and more easily in Denmark because the Danish researchers had a technological advantage. Consequently, a lot of effort was made to find and recruit talents with the proper qualifications. It turned out that this was a significant challenge essentially due to the lower level of education among the Chinese, compared to the Danes, and the lack of researcher experience. This hampered the transfer process. Owing to the lack of experience it took longer for the Chinese to perform R&D activities. In addition, the Danes were too often impatient and did not want to wait for the Chinese to catch up.

The research conducted at the Pharmaceutics R&D centre in China was related to identifying, purifying and analysing protein. When doing research, the process started with E-coli or bacteria from which protein was extracted by separating proteins with different characteristics. By using the proteins' different natures the scientists were aiming to reach specific purified target proteins. In the purification process different kinds of research-related problems naturally occur owing to the complexity of the work. These research-related problems could be approached in a sequential or a parallel manner, trying out one or several solutions simultaneously. Initially, in the early stages of the transfer of Pharmaceutics research activities to China, the Chinese scientists mainly approached problems in a sequential order by trying one solution after another. This was expressed by one previously expatriated Danish scientist as:

> There are some pretty clear differences in how you approach a research task. If you have one experiment where you want to test something, in Denmark you try out five strategies at the same time, and then my feeling is, that

my Chinese colleagues have an approach where they finish one by one instead of taking the broad attack on the problem. (Interview, 15 March 2007)

A similar statement was made in relation to the Chinese educational system when one Chinese scientist held that academic research in China is more sequential than research being done in industrial contexts. Unlike the sequential organization of research in academia, in industry the projects have to be run in parallel. Furthermore, the Danish expatriate stated that unless the Chinese researchers found the proper solution to the problem at an early stage, the Danish parallel approach was regarded as more efficient. The higher efficiency gained by adopting a parallel problem-solving approach was acknowledged by one Chinese scientist adding that:

You can minimize unpredictability if you do parallel experiments. (Interview, 12 June 2009)

By using parallel experiments several solutions could be tested and evaluated at the same time. However, using a parallel problem-solving routine might lead to changes in job tasks. Being ready for change caused some challenges to several Chinese, as explained by one scientist:

When you work with R&D as a researcher, there are a lot of unpredictable elements so the most pivotal character as a good researcher is to be ready for change. One has to change the strategies frequently according to the research results and make new plans, which is quite challenging. (Interview, 12 May 2009)

There was some reluctance among Chinese scientists to take an individual initiative in finding solutions to research-related problems. This was considered by the Danish expatriate to be due to the particular management style used in China with its high respect for authority. This respect was acknowledged from the Chinese part by the department director stating that:

Probably the whole of Asia, not only China, does not challenge the authority that much. I think that is observable and we are aware of that. (Interview, 26 May 2009)

The cultural differences were further emphasized by one Chinese scientist talking about expatriated Danish researchers saying that:

They are quite innovative, usually rich in creative ideas and very active. Sometimes their ideas are wilder. We are raised in an educational system which has only one answer to the question. We lack their way of thinking. (Chinese scientist, interview, 21 May 2009)

As individuals, Chinese scientists were regarded as equally innovative as anyone. But it was said by a departmental director that the cultural aspects had an inhibiting effect. This was further emphasized by one Danish expatriate suggesting that the stringent educational system in China was restricting individual initiative, especially compared to Danish education where criticizing and questioning is more accepted. There was, however, an additional aspect influencing the willingness to take initiatives. The corporate culture with strict project management in Pharmaceutics inhibited initiatives by quickly killing ideas that were not aligned with corporate goals.

From Pharmaceutics's international operations preceding the transfer process, the Danes had learned that substantial communication problems could arise from language difficulties. This was experienced in the R&D transfer process to China as well. Language posed a significant barrier that influenced communication as well as collaboration between Danish expatriates and Chinese scientists. The Chinese workers employed often had insufficient English language skills and the Danish expatriates were not sufficiently familiar with the Chinese language. When communicating in English, the Chinese workers preferred written language over verbal as they had greater control over what was written compared to what was spoken. As a consequence of language deficiency, the Chinese recruits did not always fully understand the routines and principles used within Pharmaceutics R&D.

Later stages of the transfer process

In order to reduce the reluctance of the Danish employees to share knowledge with their Chinese counterparts, the sceptics were asked to be involved in the R&D transfer process, a strategy that proved successful. The involvement consisted of going to China to train new researchers and conducting networking activities, as well as enabling better communication between the Chinese and the Danish units. These expatriates became key persons in the integration of the Chinese R&D unit with the global R&D organization. Open-mindedness, in terms of cultural differences, increased the positive aspects of networking and made the Chinese workers more likely to approach a Danish expatriate. The importance of being open to others was emphasized by Danes as well as by Chinese employees:

It helps if you have good humour and an open approach. If you are not really open it is really hard to get anything done because then the Chinese might be a little afraid to approach you as well. (Danish expatriate, interview, 15 March 2007)

You have to consider all the aspects when you communicate and collaborate with them. The most important thing is that we ought to be humble and frank to eliminate misunderstandings due to cultural differences. (Chinese scientist, interview, 27 May 2009)

The transfer process manager and the Chinese scientists travelled between Denmark and China. The primary reason for travelling was so that personnel from the different units could get to know each other on a personal level, which led to a clear advantage in terms of keeping the Chinese workers up to date with the development of key technologies. By making friends in different parts of the organization communication became easier through increased understanding and trust, which provided a solid base for collaboration. It was especially important to keep the Chinese unit well informed in order to prevent them from feeling alienated from the rest of the organization. The main focus for the trips was usually on activities that were more social than educational. Leisure time activities were arranged both when Chinese were in Denmark and when Danish expatriates were in China. Some managers felt, however, that the visits in Denmark could have been even more efficient because most of the time the Chinese lived together in the same flat and socialized primarily with each other. Had they, instead, been accommodated with their Danish counterparts the cultural exchange and the personal relationships could have been further enhanced. Furthermore, only persons that wished to go abroad as expatriates were sent; because monetary incentives to motivate expatriation were ineffective. On a personal level the opportunity to go to China or Denmark was motivated by the valuable increase in experience in international management and the development of a personal international network.

One additional lesson learnt from transferring R&D to a geographically distant place was always to keep a few expatriates on site. This could preferably be done in a permanent rotational worker-exchange system to access the education and experience it provided. Five years after the establishment of the unit, it was considered an equal partner by the Danes. This significantly increased information exchange. One key to making this possible was to establish contacts and networks between the two units, which were further enhanced by having expatriate scientists in the R&D unit for longer periods.

When research-related problems were approached during the early parts of the transfer process they were, as stated by a Danish expatriate, mostly handled in a sequential manner. However, more recently, the approach adopted to solve problems seems to be more related to the problem at hand. Although the research was still sometimes performed in a sequential order it was indicated that the problem itself determines how it should be solved:

It depends on the problem itself, sometimes you need to wait until one test is ready to test another, and sometimes you can have several tests at the same time. I would say that the nature of the problem decides the approach. (Chinese scientist, interview, 23 June 2009)

In the early stages of the transfer, the Chinese researchers found the change in job tasks difficult, and it was stated by Chinese scientists that changes and new plans were quite challenging. Also, this had to change according to management. In order to cope with this, knowledge-sharing activities were held once a week facilitated by Danish and Chinese expatriates, and in order to increase the Chinese workers' confidence the tasks undertaken in the initial phases of the transfer were fairly easy and of a level that management knew that the scientists could handle. The complexity was then increased over time to give the workers an increasing degree of confidence. However, it was said by the transfer manager that increasing complexity sometimes meant that the projects took longer time than expected. Eventually, the research conducted in China was no less challenging than that conducted in Denmark and the labs were essentially identical. There has been a move towards a higher degree of research being done by individual scientists or by scientists in teams without specific orders to do so, and management is encouraging scientists to experiment with their own ideas. Although not very common, apart from the mandatory ideation, scientists were encouraged to do things without direct orders or explicit manager involvement.

If one has time he or she is encouraged to do things without being told. But one has to communicate properly with his or her boss to check out the feasibility and applicability. Then the scientist can go ahead. (Chief scientist, interview, 23 June 2009)

There was some reluctance towards sharing new explorations. The management decided to adopt a strategy focused on appreciation and support, which together with internal prize competitions were proved effective in coping with these difficulties.

At the early stages of the transfer, management considered the Chinese researchers at the R&D unit to be passive, that is, not taking enough individual initiative. The high degree of respect for authorities among the Chinese employees was considered to be beneficial when it came to accomplishing routine tasks that had to be done urgently, but it did not promote creativity and innovativeness. Management in Denmark wanted this mindset to change. The goal was for Chinese researchers to learn to take individual initiatives and to view mistakes as a natural way of solving R&D-related problems, without fear of losing face or causing the managers to do so. Strategies were employed to accomplish this. In order to change this behaviour the Chinese workers were sometimes ordered to take the initiative. The Chinese R&D scientists had mandatory idea proposals. This resulted in initiatives being taken but not consistently. In order to make a more consistent change:

> You have to break down this respect for authority a bit, I think. The same goes for finding new solutions to problems. You need to have a more liberal working climate. (Danish expatriate, interview, 15 March 2007)

However, it was expressed by several Chinese scientists that even after a few years of knowledge transfer the freedom for innovative thinking was still rather limited. Novel ideas had to be agreed by other scientists and if an idea was not supported by the manager it was not allowed to be explored further. Although managers were still on top of the research being conducted, there had been some change. The working climate and the inhibiting respect for authorities had been changed, as held by one Chinese scientist:

> Yes, we question our boss during work. It is a very open atmosphere. (Interview, 23 June 2009)

The weekly departmental meetings held at the Chinese R&D unit did not only promote sharing of knowledge, they were also held in English to provide a natural way for Chinese scientists to improve on their language skills, in particular spoken English. In addition, the Chinese had the opportunity to take one hour of English courses every week and the company also provided language courses for Westerners expatriated to China. In order to further enhance intra-corporate communication, Pharmaceutics employees were encouraged to take part in exchange programmes. This enabled employees to learn more effectively about each other's culture and to establish closer personal bonds. Furthermore, both the Chinese scientists and the Danish expatriates and managers felt it was important to communicate in an honest way and on the spot, taking immediate action instead of waiting for problematic situations to resolve themselves; and actions taken were aligned with what was communicated, that is, to 'walk the talk'.

This was considered especially important when working in geographically dispersed units. The risk otherwise is that the Chinese R&D unit will feel isolated. Sometimes the Chinese experienced insufficient communication, for example, they were not always informed of changes in the projects. This, according to several informants, could have, at least partly, been resolved by using information and communication technology (ICTs) for increased and simpler information sharing. At the same time, not all information flowed back to the Danish home base. There was a high degree of tacit knowledge making it difficult to codify and document why this information remained in China. Although some of the communication problems could be resolved by using

ICTs the Chinese were also found to be reluctant, for example, to use telephones to contact Denmark when in need for help.

Case analysis

R&D transfer barriers

The barriers in the case of R&D transfer to China at Pharmaceutics can be summarized as follows:

- initial scepticism among the Danish researchers to share their R&D experience and knowledge;
- inefficient way of solving R&D-related problems;
- reluctance to change job tasks;
- reluctance towards taking individual initiatives;
- too much respect for authority;
- fear of making mistakes and losing face, causing passiveness;
- insufficient language skills.

As a result, the transferring process of R&D routines and practices became slow and sluggish. Performing R&D activities at the Danish unit involved the essential principle of how to solve R&D-related problems, namely that of solving R&D-related problems in parallel. This principle is based on the belief that a kind of 'non-authoritarian self-organization with empowered and skilled researchers who are able to easily change job tasks' is an effective way of organizing and performing R&D activities. This principle was going to be transferred to the Chinese unit because it was regarded as a very effective way of solving R&D-related problems (see Table 10.1).

In contrast, the Chinese recruits were used to solving problems in a sequential way, which they applied to solve R&D-related problems, meaning that subsequent possible solutions were tested only when the first was completed and failed to provide a solution. The capacity of the Chinese recruits to learn

Table 10.1 The Danish principle for organizing and performing R&D activities and accompanying cognitive structure

Danish R&D principle	Accompanying cognitive structures
• Solving R&D problems in a parallel way	• Non-authoritarian relation between managers and researchers • Self-organization with flexible job tasks • Empowered and skilled researchers

Table 10.2 The Chinese principle for organizing and performing R&D activities and accompanying cognitive structure

Chinese R&D principle	Accompanying cognitive structure
• Solving R&D problems in a sequential way	• Authoritarian relation between manager and researcher • Don't lose face • Excel in a specific job task

the new approach of solving R&D-related problems was hampered owing to their existing mental model concerning 'work hierarchy', that is, how work is best divided and performed. The R&D work performed at the Chinese unit was initially order-driven where management gave clear directions about how the research should be conducted, which was not questioned by the Chinese researchers because they had a high degree of respect for authority. Owing to this mindset, the Chinese researchers did not take any individual initiative but awaited orders from management, which management, in their turn, understood as 'passive Chinese researchers'. In addition, the strong 'face culture' in China combined with a belief in being excellent at a specific job task further cemented this behaviour. Also, an 'unforgiving' and rigid project management system, in combination with low degree of experience, insufficient language skills and inpatient Danish R&D researchers hampered the learning capacity from being developed (see Table 10.2).

Thus, major R&D transfer barriers were found both at the sending as well as the receiving R&D unit. At the sending R&D unit in the West, R&D barriers were essentially related to lack of motivation to share experience and knowledge, based on the assumption that 'research and development could be done faster and better in the West'. At the receiving unit in China, R&D transfer barriers were connected to individual cognitive structures that accompanied a certain R&D principle, such as 'solving R&D-related problems in a sequential way'. The individual cognitive structures were, in turn, rooted in the Confucian worldview, which influenced the Chinese' learning style at the Chinese R&D unit. For instance, the 'concrete-sequential' learning style among Chinese researchers resulted in a preference to solve R&D-related problems in a sequential way, following the instructions of a higher-ranked manager. This behaviour was perceived by Western researchers as 'inefficient' and 'passive' and the transferring process was riddled with inertia. Consequently, the Western R&D principle was neither acquired nor assimilated and no new capabilities evolved. In other words, the absorptive capacity of the Chinese unit was not developed. Furthermore, the Confucian values could have kept this R&D transfer barrier institutionalized as the basic values of Confucianism, such as harmony, self-control and hierarchy, did not encourage the Chinese researchers to challenge either their cognitive structures or their ways of organizing and performing R&D activities.

R&D transferring enablers

The enablers in the case of R&D transfer to China at Pharmaceutics can be summarized as:

- expatriates as carriers of knowledge building trust through social networking;
- increasing the difficulty of research tasks stepwise, building self-esteem among the researchers;
- appreciative feedback building self-esteem and improving communication;
- a safe learning climate, leading to more self-organized researchers.

In the case of R&D transfer to China at Pharmaceutics, the expatriates were a significant enabler in overcoming the R&D transfer barriers. By involving Danish researchers in the transfer process the initial scepticism was overcome. The involvement meant going to the Chinese unit on a voluntary basis, as monetary or other financial incentives had little effect. Instead, the primary motivator was the opportunity for a lifetime experience that could be gained from working in an exciting new environment. The aim was to train new recruits and share knowledge through networking, for instance, by updating the Chinese recruits about the recent development of different technologies, teaching them how to solve R&D-related problems, and so on. Being empowered to share their knowledge with the Chinese researchers, the expatriates functioned as a direct link between the home base unit in the West and the satellite unit in China. Networking also provided a social dimension. This involved the establishing of personal relationships, learning about each other, and of cultural differences, building trust between the Danish and the Chinese researchers. Social networking was important in reducing the risk of knowledge transfer being rejected by the receiver. Thus, the Danish expatriates acted as human carriers of knowledge and values to the Chinese unit and the social networking seem to have increased the likelihood of that knowledge and value being embraced by the receiving unit.

The Chinese researchers facing the Western approach on how to organize and perform R&D activities had to cope with a number of potentially new situations. They had to be able to manage constant changes in terms of the direction of their research. In the start-up phase, this caused difficulties for the Chinese recruits. It was a kind of flexibility that they were not accustomed to; rather, they were used to receiving direct orders and then following them to completion. It was also needed to develop the Chinese researchers in terms of self-esteem. By applying a stepwise increase of difficulty to the research projects,

Chinese self-confidence was gradually built up by mastering a progressively more complex situation. The increasing complexity also provided value to the Chinese.

Giving appreciative feedback proved to be a constructive tool to improve communication and performance at a Chinese R&D unit. Apparently, giving the Chinese honest and on-the-spot information and feedback demonstrated appreciation and kept the researchers on track in terms of how they performed. When negative feedback was needed, this was done in private in accordance with Chinese culture because of the potential risk that the researcher might lose face among his or her peers. This was a particular risk if negative feedback was given in public. When the Chinese were given appreciation and information they also gave information back, both in terms of information to the expatriates on site, but also in terms of information and research results back to the Danish home base unit. When they felt appreciated they were more likely to feed forward information to the organization, even if they were not sure about the actual results.

A safe learning climate was needed in order to improve the absorption of the new working principles transferred from the home base unit in Denmark. A safer environment also had a positive influence on Chinese eagerness to test completely new and different things. One key aspect that helped create a safer environment was the acceptance of mistakes and seeing it as a natural part of innovation. By applying a corporate culture where mistakes are a part of success made the Chinese less afraid of testing new things, even if that meant a risk of failure. If they were allowed to make mistakes, this also reduced the risk that they would lose face among their peers. Moreover, the risk of their manager's loss of face was also reduced at the same time.

To make it possible to reach innovative research results, the reluctance of Chinese researchers to take individual initiative needed to be challenged. By slowly breaking down or reducing the traditional respect for authority, and questioning what they perceived as incorrect, orders increased. With greater courage to question authority, the likelihood of individual initiative also increased. When their perceived need for direct orders declined the Chinese researchers became more self-organizing in contrast with the order-driven principle that prevailed in the early stages of the transfer.

Discussion and conclusions

Our theoretical point of departure was that the internal stickiness of knowledge transfer might be overcome by developing learning capacities of organizational units based on a close relationship between them and the systematic understanding and communication of such organizational practices (Szulanski,

1999). The theoretical framework was then based on organizational practices that are accompanied by a set of rules for describing and making sense of them (Kostova, 1999) that we labelled as cognitive structures (Dixon, 1994). We used this term rather than the term knowledge to represent and manifest not only the understanding that organizational members have reached, but also how and why it was reached. Successful R&D transfer was then defined as the institutionalization not only of the organizational practices transferred but also of those cognitive structures underlying these practices. The overall aim of this chapter was to add to the existing literature on intra-organizational transfer of organizational practices with regard to the development of learning capacities between organizational units of a MNC by taking into consideration the underlying cognitive structures that accompany organizational practices, and the influence of different contexts. More specifically, our aim was to explore how learning capacities are developed to transfer R&D practices that overcome intra-organizational barriers and internal stickiness of a MNC in a Chinese context.

Despite the stickiness of the organizational practices being transferred, our study shows that R&D principles can be transferred from a Western unit to a Chinese R&D unit within the MNC. This is manifested in that the principle for organizing and performing R&D activities in the West, and the accompanying cognitive structures, becomes institutionalized in the Chinese R&D unit. For instance, the Danish R&D principle of solving R&D-related problems in a parallel way was eventually used at the Chinese R&D unit and the underlying cognitive structures, such as the non-authoritarian relationship between manager and researcher, were reconceptualized as Chinese researchers started to challenge their higher-ranked managers on work-related issues.

Our study shows that both employees' ability and motivation facilitate the transfer from one unit to another within the MNC (cf. Minbaeva et al., 2003). In a Chinese context this may occur as expatriates from the sending unit in the West carry the preferred way of organizing and performing R&D activities to the receiving Chinese R&D unit. Their involvement and participation may be beneficial in two ways. First, participation in the R&D transfer can increase their motivation to share their experience. This is aligned to Morgan's (1986) argument that the participation of cultural differences can increase organizational development. However, in contrast to Yang et al. (2006) who argues in favour of providing rewards for employee participation, we found that the opportunity for valuable international experience and developing a personal network are sufficient motivators for expatriates to participate in the transfer from the West to China. Second, if expatriates are able to perform the R&D practice to be transferred they create a link between the Western and the Chinese R&D units. However, a vital prerequisite for the inter-organizational link to be established, and for the receiving Chinese R&D unit to start assimilating the new R&D practice, is the establishment of trust and personal relationships, which may occur through social networking. Although personal networks are popular universally, in China they have unique and distinct features, such as a long-term perspective and the exchange of favours for organizational purposes, normally referred to as *guanxi* (Gu et al., 2008).

Assimilation of a new R&D principle seems to be facilitated if it is combined with a stepwise increase in the difficulty of the research task related to the R&D principle being transferred. A new R&D principle, such as solving R&D-related problems in a parallel way, may be contrary to the existing principle and cognitive structure on how to organize and perform R&D activities and therefore perceived as too complex. Consequently, it may evoke the fear of making mistakes. In a Chinese context this means the risk of losing face, being "the major expression of the shame culture" in China (Jansson et al., 2007), which may cause Chinese researchers to be hesitant and cautious. This behaviour may be perceived as "passive" and showing "lack of individual initiatives" by the Western unit. A stepwise approach can then build self-confidence among the researchers at the receiving unit, enabling them to master a progressively more complex situation.

Coaching and counselling, giving and receiving feedback, listening and encouraging conversations are important enablers in developing a learning capacity because the result is a work climate that facilitates questioning and reduces authority respect (Morgan, 1986; Yang, et al., 2006). Our study supports the argument that appreciative feedback can be used to build self-confidence and improve conversation at a Chinese R&D unit. Considering the Chinese "face" culture, negative feedback is not given in public. Furthermore, a key value that may facilitate the creation of a work climate that encourages learning is "the acceptance of mistakes" and regarding mistakes as "a natural part of the way of organizing and performing R&D activities". This may make the Chinese researchers less afraid to test new ways of solving R&D-related problems. The "safe" learning climate may also encourage the local researchers to question the existing R&D principle at their own unit, that is, to solve R&D-related problems in sequence as well as questioning authority. This may, in turn, increase the likelihood of more self-organized researchers, that is, researchers thinking more individually and taking more individual initiatives, rather than passively waiting for orders given by authorities as the processes of organizational development may be hindered by the collective orientation in the Chinese culture as well as by the goal to establish harmony and the prevailing power distance (Yang et al, 2006). However, the change of corporate culture requires support from local management (Morgan, 1986; Yang et al., 2006). Thus, we conclude that support from superiors is another important enabler to develop a learning capacity in a Chinese context.

The key enabler to develop the learning capacity at a Chinese R&D unit seems to be the questioning ability because it may change the underlying cognitive structures accompanying the existing R&D practice. A questioning ability, such as the ability to question an existing R&D principle, is a kind of knowledge-based capability (cf. Zahra and George, 2002) embedded in the organizational unit's routines and processes for acquiring, assimilating and transforming a R&D practice. Another knowledge-based capability that seems to be required for developing a learning capacity is the ability to give and receive feedback. Crossan and Berdrow (2003) refer to this as feedback loops, feed-forward and feedback processes. In a Chinese context, feed-forward learning is a process that involves the learning that is fed forward from the sending unit in the West (represented by the expatriates), to individual R&D researchers at the receiving R&D unit in China. Feedback learning, on the other hand, is a process for learning that is embedded in the Chinese R&D unit and how it affects learning at group and organizational level at that unit. An institutionalized feed-forward learning process enables the exploitation of existing organizational capabilities, such as Western R&D practice, whereas the institutionalized feedback learning process enables exploration of what has been learned at the receiving Chinese R&D unit, such as that solving R&D-related problems in a parallel way is more efficient than in a sequential way.

The above suggests that the ability to question and to use feedback loops may result in the reconceptualization of cognitive structures that underlie a R&D practice. Our study suggests that the Chinese researchers changed their cognitive structures regarding the existing R&D principle. This may occur despite the fact that the way Chinese people learn (i.e. their learning styles), is based on Confucian values that emphasize that 'knowledge arises in a linear way' where 'memorizing precedes understanding, reflection and questioning' and that 'authorities are believed to be the sources of knowledge'. Developing a learning capacity is therefore a dynamic process that involves the ability to reinterpret the environment and assimilate this new understanding into new procedures, or rather: to institutionalize the new cognitive structures in the procedures of the organizational unit, such as solving R&D problems in a parallel way based on a non-authoritarian relation between managers and researchers, self-organization with flexible job tasks and empowered, skilled researchers. When a learning capacity has been developed, it instead becomes a learning capability that includes a learning to learn process (cf. Morgan, 1986) that enables the organization to absorb and exploit new organizational practices. Thus, we conclude that in order to develop an absorptive capacity at the receiving R&D unit in China, a learning-to-learn capability is required.

Managing the R&D transfer process from the West to China is indeed a complex task. As our study showed, fundamentally this task seems to revolve around creating a work environment that stimulates learning on different levels in the organization so that knowledge-based capabilities, such as the ability to question and to use feedback loops, become institutionalized at the R&D unit in China. The managerial challenge for developing such a work climate in a Chinese context is to deal with the Confucian heritage regarding how authorities are perceived and expected to act. Managers should, therefore, not fall into the trap of adopting an authoritarian leadership style, giving the impression that they are the source of all knowledge. Managers should also understand that the traditional Chinese learning style has a preference for following an authoritarian leader to the letter. As a consequence, Chinese employees may not welcome uncertainty, preferring a systematic approach at a slower pace in contrast to the Western approach of 'intuitive-random' learning styles that promote seeking 'the big picture' in a more spontaneous and flexible way (Yang et al. 2006). Instead, managers should adopt a more 'egalitarian' learning style that encourages a non-authoritarian relationship between managers and researchers, a high level of self-organized researchers with flexible job tasks who are empowered and skilled in performing R&D activities. Managers should, therefore, engage in coaching and counselling, giving and receiving feedback, listening and encouraging conversations because the result is a work climate that facilitates questioning, reduces unquestioning respect for authority and builds self-confidence among the employees.

Our research purpose was rather to learn from a particular situation, namely how learning capacities are developed to transfer R&D practices, which overcome the intra-organizational barriers and internal stickiness of a MNC in a Chinese context. In other words, we sought to study whether our theoretical framework is suitable in this kind of situation. However, although our study takes different contexts into consideration when transferring R&D practices from the West to China, it is limited to the organizational context of the pharmaceutical industry in that we used a Danish company to represent 'the Western way' of organizing and performing R&D activities and that the relational context in terms of *guanxi* was not studied in depth. Future research would most likely benefit from studying a different organizational context in China, provided that they are open for the establishment of foreign subsidiaries, as well as a different social context to represent the West. Possibly a multi-context case study with different social, organizational and relational context could shed more light on the challenges and complexity of transferring R&D practices from the West to China.

References

Agevall, L. (2005), "Institutioner och institutionaliseringsprocesser," *Välfärdens organisering och demokratin – en analys av New Public Management*, 60,. Växjö: Växjö Universitet, Acta Wexionensia.

Altenburg, T., Schmitz, H. and Stamm, A. (2006), "Building knowledge-based competitive advantages in China and India: Lessons and consequences for other developing countries," Paper presented at the Global Development Network Annual Conference.

Barney, J. (1991), "Firm resources and sustained competitive advantage," *Journal of Management*, 17(1): 99.

Bartlett, C. A. and Goshal, S. (1998), *Managing Across Borders – The Transnational Solution* (2nd ed.). Boston: Harvard Business School Pres.

Cohen, W. M. and Levinthal, D. A. (1989), "Innovation and learning: The two faces of R & D," *The Economic Journal*, 99(397): 569–596.

Cohen, W. M. and Levinthal, D. A. (1990), "Absorptive capacity: A new perspective on learning and innovation," *Administrative Science Quarterly*, 35(1): 128–152.

Cohen, W. M. and Levinthal, D. A. (1994), "Fortune favors the prepared firm," *Management Science*, 40(2): 227–251.

Crossan, M. M. and Berdrow, I. (2003), "Organizational learning and strategic renewal," *Strategic Management Journal*, 24(11): 1087–1105.

Crossan, M. M., Lane, H. W. and White, R. E. (1999), "An organizational learning framework: From intuition to institution," *Academy of Management Review*, 24(3): 522–537.

Dedrik, J. and Kraemer, K. L. (2006), "Is production pulling knowledge work to China? A study of the notebook PC industry," *Computer Magazine*, July.

Eden, C. (1992), "On the nature of cognitive maps," *Journal of Management Studies*, 29(3): 261–265.

Farris, G. F. (2007), "Research on innovation management and technology transfer in China," *The Journal of Technology Transfer*, 32(1): 123–126.

Gammeltoft, P. (2005), "Internationalization of R&D – Trends, drivers and managerial challenges," Paper presented at the DRUID 10th Anniversary Summer Conference 2005 on Dynamics of Industry and Innovation: Organizations, Networks and Systems.

Gassmann, O. and Han, Z. (2004), "Motivations and barriers of foreign R&D activities in China," *R & D Management*, 34(4): 423-437.

Grant, R. M. (2008), *Contemporary Strategy Analysis* (Sixth ed.). Malden: Blackwell Publishing.

Gu, K. K., Hung, K. and Tse, D. K. (2008), "When Does Guanxi Matter? Issues of Capitalization and Its Dark Sides," *Journal of Marketing*, 72 (July): 12–28.

Hofstede, G. (1984), "The cultural relativity of the quality of life concept," *Academy of Management Review*, 9(3): 389–398.

Hu, A. G. and Jefferson, G. H. (2009), "A great wall of patents: What is behind China's recent patent explosion?" *Journal of Development Economics*, 90(1): 57–68.

Jansson, H., Johansson, M. and Ramström, J. (2007), "Institutions and business networks: A comparative analysis of the Chinese, Russian, and West European markets," *Industrial Marketing Management*, 36: 955–967.

Kogut, B. and Zander, U. (1992), "Knowledge of the firm, combinative capabilities, and the replication of technology," *Organization Science*, 3(3): 383–397.

Kostova, T. (1999), "Transnational transfer of strategic organizational practices: A contextual perspective," *Academy of Management Review*, 24(2): 308–324.

Lewin, A. Y. and Peeters, C. (2006), "Offshoring work: Business hype or the onset of fundamental transformation?" *Long Range Planning*, 39(3): 221–239.

Li, L., Barner-Rasmussen, W. and Bjorkman, I. (2007), "What difference does the location make: A social capital perspective on transfer of knowledge from multinational corporation subsidiaries located in China and Finland," *Asia Pacific Business Review*, 13(2): 233–250.

Lyles, M. A. and Salk, J. E. (1996), "Knowledge acquisition from foreign parents in international joint ventures: An empirical," *Journal of International Business Studies*, 27(5): 877–904.

Merriam, S. B. (1998), *Qualitative Research and Case Study Application in Education*, San Francisco: Jossey-Bass.

Miesing, P., Kriger, M. P. and Slough, N. (2007), "Towards a model of effective knowledge transfer within transnationals: The case of Chinese foreign invested enterprises," *The Journal of Technology Transfer*, 32(1): 109–122.

Minbaeva, D., Pedersen, T., Björkman, I., Fey, C. F. and Park, H. J. (2003), "MNC knowledge transfer, subsidiary absorptive capacity, and HRM," *Journal of International Business Studies*, 34(6): 586–599.

Morgan, G. (1986), *Images of Organization*. Newbury Park: SAGE Publications, Inc.

Nelson, R. R. and Winter, S. G. (1982), *An Evolutionary Theory of Economic Change*. Cambridge, Mass.: Harvard University Press.

Phene, A., Fladmoe-Lindquist, K. and Marsh, L. (2006), "Breakthrough innovations in the U.S. biotechnology industry: the effects of technological space and geographic origin," *Strategic Management Journal*, 27(4): 369–388.

Selznick, P. (1957), *Leadership in Administration*, New York: Harper and Row.

Sun, Y., Du, D. and Huang, L. (2006), "Foreign R&D in Developing Countries: Empirical Evidence from Shanghai, China," *China Review*, 6(1): 67–91.

Szulanski, G. (1996), "Exploring internal stickiness: Impediments to the transfer of best practice within the Firm," *Strategic Management Journal*, 17: 27–43.

Szulanski, G. (2000), "The process of knowledge transfer: A diachronic analysis of stickiness," *Organizational Behavior and Human Decision Processes*, 82(1): 9–27.

Timlon, J. (1997), *Collective Learning in Business Relationships – A Way to Enhance the Capacity to Reach Common Objectives that Create Mutual Value*. Göteborg: Gothenburg School of Economics and Commercial Law, Department of Business Administration.

Todorova, G. and Durisin, B. (2007), "Absorptive capacity: Valuing a reconceptualization," *Academy of Management Review*, 32(3): 774–786.

UNCTAD (2005). *World Investment Report: Transnational Corporations and the Internationalization of R&D*. Geneva: United Nations.

Walsh, J. and Zhu, Y. (2007), "Local complexities and global uncertainties: A study of foreign ownership and human resource management in China," *International Journal of Human Resource Management*, 18(2): 249–267.

Wernerfelt, B. (1984), "A resource-based view of the firm," *Strategic Management Journal*, 5(2): 171–180.

von Zedtwitz, M. (2004), "Managing foreign R&D laboratories in China," *R & D Management*, 34(4): 439–452.

von Zedtwitz, M. and Gassmann, O. (2002), "Market versus technology drive in R&D internationalization: four different patterns of managing research and development," *Research Policy*, 31(4): 569–588.

Xie, W. and White, S. (2006), "From imitation to creation: The critical yet uncertain transition for Chinese firms," *Journal of Technology Management in China*, 1: 229–242.

Yang, B., Zheng, W. and Li, M. (2006), "Confucian view of learning and implications for developing human resources," *Advances in Developing Human Resources*, 8(3): 346–354.

Yin, R.K. (1984), *Case Study Design and Methods*, Beverly Hills, CA: Sage.

Yin, R. K. (2003), *Case Study Research: Design and methods*, Thousand Oaks: Sage Publications.

Zahra, S. A. and George, G. (2002), "Absorptive capacity: A review, reconceptualization, and extension," *Academy of Management Review*, 27(2): 185–203.

Zhu, P. and Li, L. (2007), "Direct effect of ownership and technology import: Firm level evidence from large and medium-enterprises in Shanghai," *Frontiers of Economics in China*, 2: 74–91.

Index

Note: Locators in **bold** refers to tables and figures.

Japan
  compound annual growth rate, 64
  culture, 190
    as offshore market, 26–7, 39, 59; for
      call centre services, 72; during
      nascent period of China's
      software services' growth, 39–40
Japanese-Chinese outsourcing, 8
  and cultural blending, 190–1
  and goal setting, 189–90
  information sharing and trust, 187
  inter-firm adaptation and trust, 188–9
  mediated business model, 111–13, 115
  positive impact of trust on vendor
    performance, 191–2
Jarvenpaa, S., 2, 3, 6, 109–135, 190,
    192
Jefferson, G. H., 236, 237
Jennings, D., 217, 218, 219, 225
Ji, Q., 18
Jinan, designated city, 78
John, G., 146, 150, 151
Jones, W., 92, 97
Joskow, P. L., 147
JT-Hyron, 45
Ju, D., 113

Kadar, M., 221, 227
KaiXin001, 179
Kaiser, K., 110, 111, 114, 130
Kakabadse, A., 217, 218, 219, 225, 227,
    230–231
Kakabadse, N., 217, 218, 219, 225, 227,
    230–231
Kankanhalli, A., 168
Kaplan, R., 175
Kellner, M. I., 114
KendleWits, 73
Kennedy, G., 113, 135 n1
Kerr, J., 221, 227, 228
key performance indicators (KPIs), 179
Kim, Y. G., 194
Kirsch, L. J., 186, 189, 190
Klein, P. G., 139
Klein, R. W., 191
Klepper, R., 97
Klepper, S., 47
Klepper's generic three-stage industry
    maturity model, 48

KM, *see* knowledge management (KM)
KMS, *see* knowledge management system
    (KMS)
knowledge management (KM), 165
  lack of indigenous theory, 167
  see also knowledge sharing, balanced
    scorecard (BSC)
knowledge management strategy, 176
knowledge management system (KMS),
    173
knowledge process outsourcing (KPO), 60,
    82, 89–90
knowledge sharing in Eastwei and
    SoftFocus, research study
  balanced scorecard (BSC), knowledge
    strategy using, 175, **176–7**, 178
  canonical action research (CAR)
    method, 169–70; collaboration,
    169–70; iteration, 169–70; rigour,
    169–70
knowledge sharing, balanced scorecard
    (BSC), 175, **176–7**
  guanxi, 167–8, 171
  'in-group', 168, 171
  instant messaging (IM), 169, 171,
    179–80
  leadership style; transactional, 168,
    173–4; transformational, 168, 173–4
  literature review, 167–9
  measuring impact of, 174
  quality of, 178
  quantity of, 178; 'revenue per
    consultant', 178
  see also knowledge management (KM)
knowledge systems perspective 111
Kogut, B., 240
Koh, C., 110, 184
Konsynski, B. R., 187
Korea, as offshore market, 26, 59
  for call centre services, 72
Kostova, T., 238, 240, 243, 257
Kotlarsky, J., 32
KPIs, *see* key performance indicators (KPIs)
KPO, *see* knowledge process outsourcing
    (KPO)
Kracmcr, K. L., 236
Kraut, R. E., 169
Krishna, S., 190
Krishnan, M. S., 114